Edgar Cayce's
Tales of
EGYPT

**1. Goddess Seshat and Hermes-Thoth recording
names and events on the Tree of Life**

Edgar Cayce's
Tales of
EGYPT

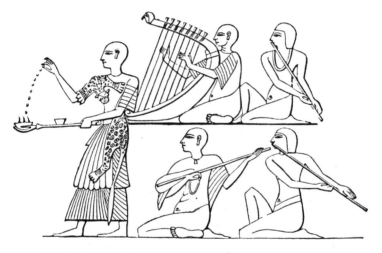

Priests offering incense and music in celebration of the Nile

John Van Auken

A.R.E. Press • Virginia Beach • Virginia

A.R.E. Press
215 67th Street
Virginia Beach, VA 23451-2061

ISBN 13: 978-0-87604-623-4

Cover design by Richard Boyle

CONTENTS

Acknowledgment

The research required to write this book
could not have been accomplished without
the excellent assistance of Alison Ray—
who brought to this incarnation much of what
she learned in her ancient Egyptian lifetime.
Ann Clapp and her long-time Egypt Study Group
also contributed much to this work.

**Scribe with inkstand on table and
pen behind his ear**

INTRODUCTION

Edgar Cayce gave over fourteen thousand readings. They were termed "readings" because it was believed that he was reading minds, reading the Akashic records or The Book of Life, reading the so-called collective unconsciousness, and even reading God's all-knowing mind, which he referred to as the Universal Consciousness. Of these more than fourteen thousand readings, 581 contained content about ancient Egypt. Much of this content came in the form of past-life readings for souls seeking to know what karmic influences were affecting this present incarnation. From Cayce's perspective, reincarnation was a natural process of soul life and soul growth. Not only were souls living today that had had incarnations during ancient times, but these same souls had had sojourns in heavenly realms in-between their earthly incarnations.

In order to give one of these readings, he needed to make a transition from his normal state of consciousness into a sleep-like state (this was one of the reasons for his nickname "The Sleeping Prophet"), and then guide his deeper consciousness to a condition in which he could convey information and respond to questions. The guiding stage of his process required the assistance of a conductor, usually his wife, but occasionally others. The conductors would give him a strong, hypnotic-like suggestion when they noticed his breathing getting deeper and his eye beginning rapid-eye-movement (the REM state), an indicator that he was close to the dream state. The suggestion given changed over the years as he and his little band of helpers learned more about the process and the nature of soul life. The following are two examples (GC is Gertrude Cayce, his wife). Personal names were replaced with file numbers to provide privacy while allowing the readings to be published:

GC: You will have before you the entity, [2441], born July 23, 1905 in Kane, Penna. The entity now seeks a Mental and Spiritual Reading, with information, advice, and guidance as to making practical her spiritual, mental, and material–physical abilities. You will then answer the questions she submits, as I ask them.

GC: You will give the relation of this entity [808] and the universe, and the universal forces; giving the conditions which are as personalities, latent and exhibited in the present life; also the former appearances in the earth plane, giving time, place and the name, and that in each life which built or retarded the development for the entity; giving the abilities of the present entity, that to which it may attain, and how. You will answer the questions, as I ask them.

These suggestions were usually followed by a quiet pause, then the "sleeping" Cayce would respond, and his stenographer Gladys Davis Turner would take it all down in shorthand, later typing it up and storing a copy in the organization's files. The collection of readings is now available on CD–ROM with text–search software, allowing anyone to search the whole of the Cayce work.

The Edgar Cayce readings were in the biblical language of the King James Bible, using "thees" and "thous" and the like. They were also in a linguistic structure that forced a reader to slow down and follow carefully the wording and order of topics being conveyed. In some cases in this book I have edited a Cayce reading for clarity and focus on the point being considered. However, when we do recite a reading, slow down and read it carefully. Despite the difficulty in reading these, there are times when it is worth reading Cayce's original storytelling of people, places, and events.

Here is a brief overview of the conventions used in this book. These stories are composed of various parts of multiple readings. These particular reading numbers are found in the Appendix which contains the key readings for each chapter. Occasionally, there are reading numbers found in the text, which appear after exact quotes from the specific reading cited. In addition, I have blended ancient Egyptian myths and legends with Cayce's stories to make for a more interesting book. In order to avoid confusion, these various sources are separated by three em–dashes: ———. The text is a balanced interplay between the Egyptian legends and the Cayce readings.

The headquarters of the organization that grew up around Cayce and his work is located on five acres in Virginia Beach, Virginia. It is the Association for Research and Enlightenment, better known as the A.R.E. Along with this organization developed the Edgar Cayce Foundation (ECF), Atlantic University (AU), and the Cayce–Reilly School of Massotherapy (massage and hydrotherapies). There is also a camp in the Blue Ridge Mountains of Virginia. Conferences, seminars, retreats, and workshops are conducted at the A.R.E. and throughout an international network of local teams. The A.R.E. has a large web site at EdgarCayce.org. The Association also conducts tours each year to various sacred sites around the world. The address of the headquarters is A.R.E., 215 67th Street, Virginia Beach, VA 23451 USA, and its phone number is 757–428–3588. There is also a toll–free number 800–333–4499.

According to Cayce's own readings, the work of Edgar Cayce and those souls associated with him began in ancient Egypt. This book is about those times and the spiritual–mental dynamics that were set in motion so long ago and continue to influence souls today.

1

A RAY OF SUNLIGHT ON EARTH

I n ancient times a mega-flood, an eruption of a super-volcano, a
succession of powerful earthquakes, and a shower of fiery meteor-
ites brought an end to the mythological lands of Lemuria (Mu) in
the Pacific Ocean and Atlantis in the Atlantic. According to Cayce's visions, remnants of these prehistoric peoples migrated to safe lands and
played a role in the rise of new civilizations, including the extraordinary people of ancient Egypt.

———

Egyptian legends tell of receding floodwaters and the descent of the
"Heron from Heaven"—it was called the *Bennu* bird, the phoenix of Egyptian lore (see illustration 2). According to this legend, the Bennu bird
was the *soul* of the sun god Ra (likely pronounced *ray*, occasionally
spelled Re). The soul of Ra in the form of the Heron from Heaven landed
on the primordial *Ben-ben* mound that rose from the inundation of the
chaos occurring in the latter period of the First Creation. Upon landing,
the Bennu cried out: "I am the Bennu bird, the Heart-Soul of Ra, the
Guide of the Gods to the Duat." The Duat is the underworld in Egyptian
teachings, the land of the night—corresponding to the subconscious
realms of our minds, lying just beneath daily consciousness behind a
veil that separates our earthly awareness from our soulful, heavenly
consciousness. The Bennu's cry marked the beginning of the Second
Creation.

The drying Ben-ben mound upon which the Bennu settled was in
the ancient land of *On*, a place known today as Heliopolis, "City of the
Sun," near modern-day Cairo. In this manner the light of heaven came
to Earth; thus Egypt was born from the ashes of the First Creation.

This tale may be compared to the biblical first creation of Adam and the lands he and his families knew. Then, when the first creation spread darkness, filling in the hearts and minds with all manner of evil, the Great Flood cleansed away the first creation, as described in Genesis 6. After this cleansing the biblical story tells of a new beginning with Noah and his families—thus began the second creation.

———

Edgar Cayce's visions contain many detailed stories of ancient, prehistoric times filled with dates, events, and named people. His Egyptian narrative begins with a strange tale about a *discarnate* soul looking for just the right opportunity to begin anew during the Second Creation. This soul's mind scanned the recovering planet from beyond the veil of material consciousness, and it saw that migrants from the former lands and peoples of Og were now living on and around Mt. Ararat, where Noah's Ark is thought to have landed. Mt. Ararat is in modern-day Turkey. Og was one of the principle regions of Atlantis, according to Cayce, and the area known today as that of the American plateaus or the north portion of the US state of New Mexico and the surrounding highlands today. These migrants from Atlantis retained the spiritual ideals of the earlier children of the Law of One, as Cayce called them, indicating that they retained the belief that an unseen oneness connects all life. The Maya and other Mesoamerican peoples have a legend of the children of God wrestling with the Lords of the Underworld to win the deadly game between the dark and the light. This remnant group, now in Ararat, were seeking to make a new life and a better world by subduing the vices and confusions of their Atlantean experience while holding on to their virtues and higher wisdom.

The celestial soul observing them through the veil intuitively knew that this Ararat clan would eventually come down out of the great mountain and surrounding lands, enter the region we know as Egypt, and begin the wondrous era of creativity, productivity, and enlightenment we see in surviving Egyptian temples, pyramids, papyruses, and statuary. This was the opportunity that the extraterrestrial soul was seeking. However, knowing that a prophet has little honor in his own tribe, the soul searched beyond the Ararat clan for a way to come to these people from another group.

Cayce's vision described a people in the Far East known as the tribe of Zu, in what would be known today as the high plateaus of the Mongolian lands. These people were also refugees of the destruction of the First Creation, but they were from sunken Lemuria in the Pacific. Strangely, these people, and those in India, had ideals and sacred rituals that would eventually become a part of Egypt's early culture. Among the Zu clan was a daughter of their leader whose body, heart, and mind were perfect for the incarnation of this powerful, celestial soul. Her name was Arda. She was a pure, selfless portal into this world; thus, with love and idealism, the celestial spirit overshadowed the young girl and persuaded her deeper self and the very cells of her body to yield to his coming. Having a more *fourth* dimensional mind and heart, Arda responded, and the spark of the Spirit of Life quickened her three-dimensional womb. Though a virgin, having known no human man, she conceived a new and ideal physical body through which the celestial soul could incarnate into this terrestrial world to fulfill its grand mission.

Arda was exhilarated by the new life within her, yet she was uncertain how her people would receive the news. Hopeful, she explained to them what had happened. Unfortunately, her kinsmen could not share in her belief in a celestial conception. They drove her from the tribe in shame. Her father—confused by his ready-to-believe-anything love for her and yet his rigid hold to the laws of his tribe and the realities of this physical world—stood motionless as she was driven off.

Cayce details how she journeyed westward—not by some thought-out plan but by an inner, intuitive push west. Eventually, she camped near the tribe living on and around Mt. Ararat (biblical Asia Minor, modern-day Turkey, see illustration 3). The Ararats (remnant Atlanteans) had no love for the tribe of Zu (remnant Lemurians), so Arda was not welcomed, only tolerated. However, when her child was born and his beauty was perceived by the people of Ararat, she was tolerated a little better. The child grew in stature and wisdom, revealing a knowing that quickly identified him as a prophet, a seer. In one of the young boy's pronouncements, he prophesied the entrance of this clan into the rich lands of Egypt and that they would build one of the grandest cultures on the planet. King Arart (pronounced *aur-art*), the elderly leader of the tribe, was moved by this prophecy and began to hold the boy in high esteem, giving comfort and support to him and to his mother. She had suffered much for her celestial conception, but now the fruit of her womb rewarded her. From this moment on, Arda was an honored woman; she and her offspring were fully adopted into the Ararat community.

Cayce described how her boy was of unusual coloring; his skin being lighter than his mother's, his hair the color of the sun, and there was a radiant mystique about him. Because of these features, the people named him *Ra-Ta*, meaning something akin to "sunlight upon the land."

Young Ra–Ta's remarkable prophetic abilities naturally made him the priest of the tribe. At the age of twenty–one, he led King Arart and his whole clan down out of the mountain region, across the plains, and into the fertile lands of Egypt (see illustration 3 for a map). Egypt was then called the Black Land (*Kemet, KMT*). This was because of the rich black silt that the Nile had left behind as it receded from its flood stages. According to Cayce's story, some nine hundred souls composed this invading horde. A small number today, but this was that biblical time when the planet had been cleansed of many earlier peoples by a karmic reaction to their evil (again, read Genesis 6). Now the planet was being repopulated for a new start. This was the beginning of the Second Creation.

Naturally, the sight of a horde of northern mountain people marching toward their land of ease and plenty was upsetting to the natives of the Black Land, especially to their upper class who enjoyed a life of luxury and leisure. However, the natives had once been invaders themselves, having entered this rich land from the southern mountains of Nubia. Though they were strong then, they had grown comfortable and satisfied for a very long time. Their newfound land required little labor and provided plenty of recreation and sunshine. Adding to the natives' softness was the laid–back passivity of their leader, King Raai (pronounced *Raa-ee*). He had become old and weary of the demands of rulership and thus, surrendered much of his power to the people, wanting to be left alone with his personal pursuits. Even when petitioned by his people to build up the defenses of the country and create a defense plan against the northern mountain invaders, King Raai simply refused to do so. However, he did call for a meeting with the invading king to discuss terms for peaceful co-existence of the two populations. During a series of these meetings, King Raai became enamored with one of the more beautiful Ararat women, seeking her company and companionship rather than actively participating in detailed meetings about the country and co-rulership. King Arart, seeing this native king's disinterest in power, might, and rulership, concluded that his clan could just march into the heart of the Black Land and take over. And that is just what he did, but not violently. Amazingly, the natives put up little to no resistance. That is until the new landlords set up laws and taxes.

In the telling of this story, Cayce sadly stated that King Raai "gave over the activities of the land for the beauty of a woman." But paradoxically, Cayce found some good in King Raai, noting that he *originally* had "brought to that land the study of the relationships of man to the Creative Energy" and that his disposition against bloodshed and war was admirable. In this current situation, this led him to seek a peaceful solution, even though he got lost in the arms of the beautiful Ararat woman, leaving his people at the mercy of King Arart. Cayce even noted that this disposition of King Raai was not simply submission but was based in his principle of nonviolence and that this disposition "became the basis for the studies of the Prince of Peace." Curiously, Raai's peace principle so affected the invading Ararat people that they established schools in the land to help both tribes better understand one another.

This is not to say that all of the people of Ararat agreed with their king. Many were very upset about this, wanting instead to drive the natives back into the Nubian hills from whence they came. In an effort to temper these feelings, King Arart quickly arranged for special educators to go throughout his tribe explaining the ideal of peaceful co-existence and its benefits to the clan in this land of plenty for everyone. These educators were successful, except for a few pockets of discontent and violence.

There was roughly a three-year settling-in period that followed the initial invasion and terms of peace. During this time it was clear that the natives did *not* seek to establish order, laws, or governmental structure. They did not want to organize the labor force and talent of their people. They enjoyed the bounty of their land and its sunshine and fair weather. Conversely, the northern mountain people were intent on building a rich culture guided by high standards and driven by specific goals. The Ararats wanted to develop the resources of this land: its mountain minerals, gems, and gold, the energy of its great river as well as the power of the people's labor and skill. King Arart began establishing laws, developing an infrastructure, creating schools and training centers, and organizing production teams. But he also used the ever-popular means by which a society builds and sustains itself: he raised *taxes*. Tensions rose between the two very different peoples.

Curiously, among the natives was a scribe-sage who explained to his people the aims of the Ararat rulers, encouraging his people to participate and invest themselves in a united effort. The young scribe-sage traveled around his people's communities explaining the mental and spiritual ideas that drove the invaders to do what they were doing, describing their values and philosophies, and how they wanted cultural and artistic development as well as wealth building. The Ararat people were not a community of leisure and materialism, as the natives were.

News of this native scribe's teachings reached the ear of King Arart and his councilors. They demanded regular briefings on the scribe's teachings, concerned about his potential to become the natives' missing leader, replacing distracted Raai. It quickly became obvious that this scribe-sage was articulate, clever, and growing in power and influence among his people. Thus, in another clever decision, King Arart appointed his young, bright, and energetic son to be *acting* king while Arart stepped into the background, retaining a powerful role on the Inner Council. In a move reminiscent of his father's peaceful coexistence, the newly appointed young king selected the native scribe-sage to become councilor on the Ruling Council, raising him from scribe to high councilor. To further establish the scribe's position in the ruling party, the young king changed the name of the scribe to Aarat (pronounce *ah-rat*), thus making him one of the overseeing Ararats.

With the blending of the two peoples through these wise moves with the influential native scribe–sage, the young king then appointed his father's favorite seer Ra–Ta to the post of High Priest of all the land and peoples.

Some time after these moves, a migrating group of Atlanteans arrived directly from Poseidia, the last vestige of Atlantis to sink. The Inner Council of the Black Land decided to include some of these Atlanteans on the Governing Council. However, a few of these Atlanteans tried briefly to dominate the Council but were quickly moved off into lesser roles while more cooperative Atlanteans were appointed in their place. Now the land had three groups of people cooperating for the good of all. Eventually, others would come, even people from far-away Zu. The old Ararat king, the young king, and their Inner Council accepted leaders from each group that arrived to serve on the Governing Council, making early Egypt a most unusual nation. As the word of this cooperative governance spread around the renewing planet, many tribes sent emissaries to see and report on this strange and rare arrangement.

With the Governing Council established, the culture grew. This was not a huge population of millions as we are used to today. A few thousand people composed the entire community of budding Egypt. In fact, the entire planet's population was very small in comparison with today's. Cayce actually gave the number to be 133 million! This is an amazingly small number given today's nearly seven *billion* population.

————

The Cayce readings tell how there were no families, as we know them today. The people lived in groups. Many of the females of the tribes were housed for the evening in buildings connected with the temples while many of the males were housed in buildings connected with the palaces. The females were the channels of incarnating souls to grow the nation while the males were the muscle to run, build, and defend the society. The living quarters were laid out in tiered layers, like a step pyramid. Each hall had three-to-four-tiered floors. The private sleeping rooms were small, monastic–like cells, 7′ x 9′ with 8′ to 10′ ceilings. All items, such as blankets, rugs, and linens, were handmade. These tiered halls of private rooms were connected to huge chambers in the center of the structure for group gatherings assembled for the purposes of education, exercise, special ceremonies, services, and recreation. There were special halls and chambers for conceiving, birthing, and raising children—these were very active in those times for growing the population was a high priority. There were also special halls and chambers for initiations into the sacred teaching and ceremonies. There were halls for conducting the training to produce skilled workers, artisans, and educators needed to build and sustain this growing society. According to Cayce, the buildings were designed and built to demonstrate the three types of relationships: individuals to individuals, individuals to the creative forces through personal attunement to the divine and cosmic forces, and masses of individuals to the creative forces during group gatherings for attunement. God was an integral part of everyday life, as revealed in the extant carvings, paintings, and writings we have of the ancient Egyptians.

According to Cayce, Ra–Ta's spiritual focus and the king's secular focus allowed for the first intentional and cooperative separation of church and state. Cayce said that each person received one gold piece for a day's work, from the king to the growers of grain. All shared equally. There was a national spirit and purpose among these early people, despite some differences in ideas and purposes.

Ra–Ta oversaw the building of temples while the king oversaw the building of palaces, monuments, dwellings, and storehouses. The young king opened mines in the mountains of Nubia and as far away as Ophir (biblically called Kadesh, today called Persia or Iran). These mines brought huge quantities of gold, silver, iron, lead, zinc, copper, tin, and the like into the coffers and smelting facilities of Egypt. Stonemasons were trained. Quantities of granite, limestone, and sandstone were quarried and prepared for the massive building projects.

The high priest gathered a team around him to manage the services in the temples. His innate celestial awareness helped him find priests and priestesses who could accept the ideas of unseen worlds beyond this physical world and metaphysical concepts of the mind and spirit rather than just the body and matter. He sought those who intuitively sensed the existence of and were willing to use pathways and centers within the physical body to develop their *metaphysical* consciousness and abilities. He sought those who accepted that there were activities that occurred *between* incarnate lives and that this bigger view of *soul* life needed to become a part of one's whole experience rather than only viewing one's existence to be a personal, physical life. He sought those who could accept and would use opportunities for soul activity in the higher realms during sleep cycles, dreaming states, and deep meditations.

Ra-Ta was teaching that this inner life was important and worth knowing and developing. However, most of the natives held more strongly to the material outer life and the enjoyment of it rather than seeking some unseen inner life. The natives of the Black Land were a *materialistic* people. Ra-Ta brought a new teaching, one difficult to comprehend from a strictly worldly perspective. Even so, the people remembered how he had manifested remarkable abilities during his early years in the Black Land and how he had led people on archaeological expeditions that found very ancient artifacts of First Creation peoples. His reputation grew, and many natives not only began to listen to him but also attempted to understand his strange ideas and mystical practices. Adding to this was the support of the high priest by their scribe-sage, who helped the people appreciate the high priest's ideas and methods.

Ra-Ta taught that prior to the evolution of matter, there was an *involution* into matter from out of pure spirit and energy and that there was a deeper part of each person that was spirit, energy, and mind, living beyond and within the body. He gathered a little band of what we would call today archaeologists. He had them uncover archaeological evidence to support his teachings about the lost history that would demonstrate the existence of the children of God, the fallen angels of the Nephilim, and humanlike beings of the First Creation that were the ancestors of the incarnate people in this Second Creation. These archaeological artifacts of spiritual realities caused many to come to him to learn more. Some of them even committed themselves to the rigors of his temple training and initiations.

In the temples, exercises for increasing spiritual awareness and attunement to the universal forces were taught and practiced. Several stages of initiation and enlightenment were established. Aspiring priests and priestesses proceeded to advance through these body–changing, mind–changing courses and tests.

The early phases of training were in a place Cayce called the "Temple of Sacrifice," where cleansings and purifications were the focus, mostly relating to perfecting the body as an ideal temple for the soul and soul's mind. Here the metaphysical channels and centers within the human body were activated and utilized. These channels are known in yoga as the *sushumna, ida,* and *pingala,* and the centers are referred to as chakras and lotuses. Activating these was a goal of temple training. But in some bodies there needed to first be a correction or cleansing because these had become contaminated or dysfunctional through misuse or abuse in earlier incarnations.

The next phases of training were in a place Cayce called the "Temple Beautiful." In this temple spiritual enlightenment and attunement to celestial forces were the focus as well as becoming aware of and enlivening each soul's unique purpose for incarnating and thus, discovering his or her mission or career in this incarnation.

It was believed that the body, when cleansed and trained, could help the soul and mind maintain a connection with the heavenly influences while doing good in the earthly realm. The concept that the human body is designed for both physical and metaphysical experiences was known in these very ancient times as evidenced by a much later text, the *Yoga Sutra* by Patanjali. He wrote down what was previously passed on orally in the ancient temples. His treatise explained that within the human body are pathways and energy centers that may be stimulated in such a manner as to bring about *nonphysical* consciousness. Patanjali (pronounced *pa-tan-ja-lee*) published the secrets of our bodies and showed how to use these to experience altered states of consciousness— something that had, heretofore, been exclusive to the initiates in temple life.

Patanjali explained the most fundamental principle: a unity happens when an entity realizes its oneness with the Source and expanse of life with the Whole. He explained that the "unity happens when there is stilling of the movement of thought. In the light of stillness . . . self is not confused or confined. Then, the seer or the harmonized intelligence—which is ignorantly regarded as the separate experiences of sensations and emotions, and the separate performer of actions—is not split up into one or the other of the states or modifications of the mind." (Samadhi Pada 1, Sutras 1–10)

Thus, according to Patanjali, union occurs when an individual perceives that he or she is not simply an individual, but also *universal* and one with the Whole, the All. This is realized in the deepest stillness when the form–shaping, identity–focused mind is quiet, clear, and alert. Then the inner and the outer are united. In Sanskrit yoga actually means *union*.

In addition to these training phases, Ra–Ta's temples developed life-changing ceremonies on and around altars. The altars were prepared according to inner guidance. They included sacrificial altars and beautification altars. They did not sacrifice animals, birds, beasts, reptiles, grains, or humans on these altars. That came much later after this early connection to God–consciousness was diminished by further immersion into physicality and earthliness. According to Cayce, these earlier altars sacrificed individual's faults and weaknesses, blotting them out with "the fires of the unseen forces" that were set in motion by attunement to the powers of the Spirit.

———

On one of my many trips to Egypt, I experienced "the fires of the unseen forces" while meditating in the seventh chamber of the Seti Temple in Abydos. Here's the experience:

My group and I sat on the cold, hard stone floor in this very special chamber and began to still our minds and bodies for meditation. The guards at the temple were laughing and talking; the echo of their voices was so great inside the temple that it was very difficult to meditate. However, rather than give up or get angry I asked myself, "When was I ever going to get back to this temple?" I told myself that I had to succeed *now*. Then, I tried with all my might to filter out their voices and get into deep meditation. It worked. It worked so well that I not only lost consciousness of them, I completely lost consciousness of the temple and my group, entering into a vivid ancient Egyptian ceremony. It was an initiation ceremony involving water and fire. I found myself standing shoulder–deep in a pool of holy water, naked. I somehow knew it was a purification ritual. As I walked up the stone steps out of this sacred pool, attending priests wrapped a floor–length cape around me. They then anointed my head with oil and combed my hair back. My hair was black and thick with oil. Two of them approached and handed me the two scepters of Egypt, the crook and the flail (see illustration 4). Somehow, I intuitively knew that if I wanted to move, I had to hold them out in front of me; to stop, I had to cross them over my chest. I looked up and beheld a line of ancient Egyptians out in front of me. I tilted the two scepters toward them, causing me to glide across the floor, not walk, glide just an inch above the floor. It was an exhilarating feeling to glide so effortlessly. In front of me were two long rows of priests and gods: a row on my left and another on my right. I glided between them. They nodded their heads and smiled approvingly. At least at first I thought this was approval, but as I nodded back, I realized that it was also a nod of encouragement to continue through the next phase of the initiation. I looked up ahead of them to see what was at the end of the rows. To my amazement and concern, it was the sun, the *real* sun! At the end of this gauntlet of priests and gods, I was to enter the fire of Ra. But this Ra was the *real* sun that would burn me to a crisp. I looked hard into the eyes of the priests and gods, expressing to them with my eyes my deep concern about this part of the initiation. They smiled and nodded with more enthusiasm than before. I knew that all I had to do was cross the scepters and I would stop. But some knowing within me kept the scepters pointed straight toward the fiery sun. As I enter it, I felt the searing heat, but instead of burning me, it cleansed me! The Ra fire was burning away all my sins and weaknesses but not harming the rest of me. So happy was I that I began to draw its heat into me, inhaling it, wanting more of it. It felt wonderful! I wanted it to burn me completely, thoroughly, until I was fully cleansed! Suddenly, someone grabbed my arm and began shaking me saying, "John, wake up; we're going to miss our boat. We have to go. Wake up." I struggled to see through the sun's brilliant light. Two faces were staring back at me; they were our Egyptian guide and my colleague. I asked, "Who are you?" After they both looked at each other, they then turned and ordered me to get up, follow them closely, and not say anything that would alarm the guards and others in our group. I obeyed, gradually realizing that I was supposed to be a part of this tour group, yet half of me was still in the initiation ceremony. Once on the bus to the boat, I fell back into the solar cleansing. Oh, it felt so good to be so clean!

Later, when reading Cayce's discourses on Egypt, I came across this fire altar portion of the ancient Egyptian initiation in the temples of Ra-Ta. I felt both elated to have somehow experienced the initiation first-hand (if that is what I experienced) and a bit spooked to know that the ancient events were so accessible. But then Cayce also taught that all time is one time and nothing is ever lost. It is still there in the deeper levels of consciousness. All one has to do is access it with the right intention.

In another experience while in a deep state of consciousness, I woke in a stone chamber in an ancient Egyptian temple. Upon a stone altar was a person reclining on his back, waiting for a chakra adjustment! I know how weird this sounds, but this is how the scene opened. What's even stranger is the fact that it felt so real that I lost all awareness of anything else. I was in this room, standing next to this altar. I approached the person lying on the altar and reached my hands over his heart area. I was wearing a floor-length cape and a high, cylindrical hat, similar to that worn by Amun-Ra (see illustration 5). Somehow I intuitively knew that the cape was to shield me from any interfering or contaminating influences and that the hat was an antenna-like device which channeled the energies of Venus through me! Yes, the planet! These energies were those of the typical astrological characteristics attributed to Venus: love, art (creativity), and beauty. As these influences flowed through me, they entered into the person's heart chakra. As they did, it was as if dials in his heart chakra were being turned so as to better tune his heart to the frequency coming from the planet of love, art, and beauty.

Perhaps this is why I'm writing this book on Cayce's Egypt. It is as if my soul knows that ancient place and time and has some lingering energies that have to find their way out of me today. My intention in sharing these experiences with you is to give possible examples of what Cayce was conveying about these ancient temples and the activities of the initiates and for us to consider the unseen influences of these experiences that are latent within us even today.

———

Now back to the highlights of Cayce's story of Ra–Ta and the temples (a later chapter on the temples goes into this topic in greater detail).

When these cleansings in the temples were combined with the inner guidance to commit oneself to a specific career of service, one could then make great leaps forward in freedom from earthliness and limited consciousness to become a light to this world. This was done only after the seekers had *chosen* to give themselves to these services. No one was forced into the temples, and once in the temples, no one was forced to progress through the various stages. Each had to *choose* or be "called" from within to participate and endure.

The Temple of Sacrifice may be compared to the combination of one of our best hospitals merged with one of our best health spas and yoga centers. Restructuring and cleansing the body could employ several means: from surgeries to scented baths, from chemistry and potions to massage and body movement (likely similar to Tai Chi) or dance, from painful change through physical therapy to nirvanic transformation that would alter the very cells and hormones of the body.

The Temple Beautiful may be compared to the combination of one of our highly creative and idealistic universities, one of our most loving, monastery–type religious facilities, and one of our prayer and meditation centers.

The Temple of Sacrifice transformed the body and body–mind. The Temple Beautiful transformed participants mentally and spiritually. It combined body, mind, and soul development with service to God, to one another, and to the world. The program was not reclusive or elitist. Whether one was channeled to work in the sacred services of the altars or the daily labors of the granary, both were seen as divinely manifesting his or her ultimate potential to magnify God *in* life rather than escape life to be with God. Godliness in this early training was an *active* service, not a static state. Works were as important as faith and enlightenment.

According to Cayce's readings, the purpose for all of this was: "That there might be a closer relationship of individuals to the Creator, and a better relationship of individuals with one another."

Despite many gains, Ra-Ta struggled with disappointment and discouragement. He was in a constant wrestling match with earthly ideals held by many of the people. Incarnate souls easily slipped into the comforts of living only the material life and gratifying physical appetites and egotistical longings. Some people also sought to control others as subordinates, even slaves, for their own use, which did not fit with Ra-Ta's ideal of one God and one family of the children of God, all equal siblings. Many of these negative ideals and pursuits had caused the end of the First Creation. Ra-Ta and his team wanted to prevent these selfish, earthly energies from contaminating the Second Creation.

At the height of Ra-Ta's influence as the high priest, he was also traveling to other sacred centers around the planet. How? By flying! Amazingly, according to Cayce's readings, there was a time long ago when flight was a natural means of transportation—we'll learn more about this in the chapter on ancient flight. According to Cayce's visions, the entire planet had major spiritual centers with temples and pyramids. In addition to Egypt there were centers in what today would be called Iran (Persia), India, the Gobi (not a desert then), Indochina, China, the Pacific Islands, the Andes, Mexico, the plateaus of New Mexico, and even Scandinavia (the land of Odin and Thor). There was much communication among these spiritual centers, each sharing how best to keep the *celestial* wisdom alive despite souls moving deeper into matter and *terrestrial* existence.

Ra-Ta met with leaders of these other centers—some actually visited the Egyptian temples—some were even initiated. There was no language barrier according to Cayce's readings because this was a time when there was one language among all the people of the planet. The biblical Tower of Babel event had not yet occurred.

It was a busy, dynamic time.

Cayce gave a description of Ra-Ta: "The priest in body . . . was six feet one inch tall, weighing a hundred and eighty-one pounds. He was fair of face, not too much hair on the head [lost much of his youthful, yellow hair by this time] or too much on the face or body. In color nearly white, only sun or air tanned." We know from artifacts that most Egyptian priests had shaved heads though they could and did wear wigs, and they all dressed in spotted leopard skins (see illustration 6a and 6b). Since there are no leopards in the Mayan, Toltec, and Aztec lands, their priests wore jaguar skins.

As powerful and influential as the high priest was in these formative times, he became more powerful and influential after he *stumbled*. Ra-Ta's standing in Egypt took a sudden and unexpected turn for the worse. He allowed himself to break one of his own rules. And even though it was for a seemingly higher purpose, the king and council members did not see it that way. The punishment was severe, perhaps too severe.

Cayce's readings tell the story of the fall of Ra-Ta as a combination of temptation and trickery. Some of his subordinate priests had become jealous of the high priest's power and weary of his demands on them. They plotted a way to bring him down from his lofty pedestal and powerful control over them. Actually, Ra-Ta was more vulnerable than may have been imagined. Much time had passed since those early days of founding Egypt, the old king of the Ararats who loved Ra-Ta had retired, his son was now overseeing the kingdom, and the country was flush with wealth and excitement. Ra-Ta had succeeded and was enjoying his success. It felt to him that he could do anything because he was now above the laws and rules. He was supreme; there was no one above him. This gave him a feeling of absolute freedom and independence. The plot to bring him down couldn't have come at a better time, and the scheme was developed around a practice in the temples that was ripe for misuse.

In these early times, repopulating the earth after the major disasters that ended the First Creation had almost wiped away the entire population of the planet. Baby making was among the highest priorities; there was an active baby-making process going on in sections of the temples. Not only did they need to grow the population, but they also wanted to create the most ideal bodies and thereby draw the most enlightened souls into those bodies. In illustration 7 there is an Egyptian scene showing a woman holding a "ba," a soul from out of heaven's crowded soul communities—revealing how active the birthing activities were. The baby-making operation in the temples carefully selected males and females for their genetic qualities and their spiritual ideals. The high priest had established a long and careful procedure that everyone was to go through before being coupled with one another to copulate and conceive. Among the ideal females in the main temple was one named Is-ris (pronounced *ice-ris*). Her mind and body were as perfect as any in all the land. Additionally, one of her skills was dancing—not sensual dancing but movement to music that would uplift observers' hearts and minds as well as her own. The new young king who had taken over for his father was very fond of Is-ris and her dancing. He also considered her to be among the most ideal birthing partners, capable of producing excellent offspring if mated with the right male—and surely the young pharaoh would be on any short list of ideal mates for Is-ris.

The temple priests knew of the king's admiration for Is-ris so if they could pit the young king against the high priest, the high priest would lose, despite his elite status. This was because there would be no changing of the bloodline of the kings, so the Zu-born high priest would be the one to go.

The conniving priests first threatened Is-ris and her family into cooperating with the seduction of the high priest; then they convinced Ra-Ta that he was the most ideal of all men, and since the purpose was to seek the most ideal offspring, he was the best mate for Is-ris, this most perfect female.

Stumbling over a long-developing sense of his own power as well as the resulting vanity, Ra-Ta did not go through the established procedures for such an important mating and broke his own rule about the number of wives a priest could have. He took Is-ris and conceived a child with her. The fruit of their love was concealed for a time in the temple, but when the king finally heard about it, he was furious. A beautiful and wise flower had been abruptly taken from the kingdom without going through the necessary steps to ensure the highest good, and this by a priest who was already wed. This was a terrible injustice that could not be undone. And though Ra–Ta thought that he was above the rules, the council and the king did not. The king reacted swiftly and severely. Since the child was illegal, the king removed her from the temple and put her under the control of palace authorities and a caretaker. Then the king and his army banished Ra–Ta, Is–ris, and 231 of their supporters from the land of Egypt—*forever!*

Disgraced, confused, and despairing, Ra–Ta and his little band of loyal supporters left Egypt. Initially they entered the lands of Lybia, where the priest drew a lot of attention, gaining converts to his teachings and practices. Subsequently, he and his entourage journeyed to the high mountains of Abyssinia (modern day Ethiopia) and later into the mountains of Nubia (the area today that is Upper Egypt, Aswan, and the Lake Nasser region). Here they set up their community. (See illustration 8 for a map of ancient Egypt.)

Cayce's discourses tell how Is–ris and Ra–Ta did not waste their time in these mountains but set about to make the best of a bad situation. Ra–Ta, sobered by his disastrous mistake, was determine to gain higher consciousness and oneness with the Infinite, Eternal Creator. He and his troop regularly entered deep meditation, making passage through dimensions of higher consciousness. They practiced moving from individualness to universalness, from finiteness to infinite oneness with the cosmos and the universal consciousness. Cayce stated that Ra–Ta "awakened to the Ra within him" and Is–ris "awakened to the Isis with her." Cayce also described how they gained conscious awareness of the cosmos and earth's relationship to the universe and the universal forces. They even received knowledge of the ideal location to build one of the Seven Wonders of the Ancient World, the Great Pyramid of Giza—they even received instructions on how to build it! Of course, they asked the universal consciousness how would this be possible since they were living under a *lifetime* banishment from Giza (Cayce's readings spelled it

Gizeh). They came to understand that their expulsion would not be forever. And sure enough, events were not going well in Egypt during their exile. Two rebellions had shaken the once harmonious nation: one among the natives against the Ararats and another led by the young king's own brother against the kingdom! Furthermore, except for a very few priests (one of whom we will read about later), the temple leaders were not as spiritually aware or as mystically powerful as Ra-Ta. Without Ra-Ta's control, some of the priests were actually using techniques and potions to arouse earthly energies and urges rather than celestial, spiritual ones. Adding fire to these activities, the Atlanteans had imported their sex queen and set her up in one of the major centers where she now conducted orgies and the first of the renown fleshpots of Egypt.

All of these events caused the population to cry for the return of the high priest. Even pharaoh began to believe that he had acted too harshly and was fast becoming convinced that the country needed the high priest to return. The king sent messengers to the little band of exiles in the Nubian mountains asking Ra-Ta and his followers to return—all was forgiven.

2

A Great Atlantean Becomes a Greater Egyptian

A n ancient Egyptian myth tells of a *creative essence* appearing out of the infinite, dark nothingness—willing itself into being. This essence evolved into a creator called *Atum* (also known as *Tem* and *Atem*; illustration 9). This name means the "Complete One." Within the Complete One was his shadow, which was the infinite womb of mother *Iusaaset* (pronounced *e-oo-sa–ah-set*; meaning "mother of the first gods" and "grandmother of the subsequent gods"; illustration 10). The two of them—the self–created Atum and the unseen Iusaaset—conceived *breath* and *moisture.* These two offspring became lost in the infinite, dark nothingness; hence Atum sent his eye, the Eye of Light that penetrates the darkness, to find the primordial children. The Eye of Light was Ra (illustration 71). Upon finding the children, Atum named breathe *life* and moisture *order.* Atum bound them together, and with these two united, he made air (the Egyptian god *Shu*) and mist *(Tefnut).* He then kissed his daughter, mist, and created the first mound (firmament), which as we've learned was the Ben–ben Mound. This mound was also known as *Iunu* (ee-oo-nu). The Ben–ben Mound rose from the vast expanse of the motionless sea of the primordial depths (the goddess *Nun*). The Complete One (Atum) rested on the mound, while life–air (Shu) and order–mist (Tefnut) mated to create earth (the god *Geb*) and sky (the goddess *Nut*, pronounced *noot*, rhymes with *toot*). (See illustrations 9 through 15 for images of these Egyptian gods and goddesses, especially illustration 13.)

Earth (Geb) and sky (Nut) then conceived five more godlings: *Osiris,* god of fertility, resurrection, and judge of the heart of every soul; *Isis,* goddess of magic, motherhood, and "Mother of the Universe"; *Set*, god of chaos, confusion, storms, wind, the desert, and foreign lands; *Nephthys*, "Mistress of the House," "Friend of the Dead," and goddess of divine help and protection; and *Horus the Elder*, god of light, whose left eye was the sun and right eye, the moon. (See illustrations 16 through 18 for images of these Egyptian gods.)

The Complete One (Atum) then prophesies to Osiris that he, Atum, will eventually submerge all of the creation back into the depths of the primordial waters—symbolic of the infinite womb from which creation emerged. Until then, Atum will guide the sun through the night and the darkness of the underworld, and Ra–Atum will bring the sun forth every morning to light the passage through day. (See illustration 19 for the image of Osiris and Ra–Atum.)

Aspects of this myth of life's origin have often been compared with the shadowy waters of the biblical Genesis: "The earth was without form and void, and darkness was upon the face of the deep; and the Spirit of God was moving over the face of the waters. And God said, 'Let there be light'; and there was light." (Genesis 1:2–3)

It helps if we think of these gods and goddesses less as "beings" and more as levels or zones of consciousness and specialized energetics within the whole or the Complete One. They also have their individualized motivations and missions as well as unique characteristics that eventually permeate souls who harmonize with these zones and energetics. Thus, the Egyptians would call like–minded souls "the Daughters of Isis" or "the Sons of Ra," and so on. Ra and Isis represent the consciousness and vibrations that the individual souls expressed or harmonized with.

———

Edgar Cayce's narrative of ancient Egypt includes the story of a soul who became a great Atlantean and then an even greater Egyptian. It is the account of one named *Hept-supht* (pronounced *hep-t–sup-t*, silent "h" and no "ph" *f*-sound), from the city of Alta in the region of Poseidia on the continent of Atlantis. Hept–supht eventually moved to the Giza Plateau. Hept–supht worked closely with the Egyptian high priest Ra–Ta.

The first Cayce readings for Hept–supht were most helpful in getting a sense of life in the ancient world. I have edited these for clarity and readability.

"In Atlantis we find the entity [Hept–supht] during those periods before the final destruction of Atlantis, when there were continually waged what may be termed war or *evangelistic* campaigns."

Cayce would later explained that these were not military wars but political, religious campaigns for people's hearts and minds. He continued:

"This was being waged between the followers of the patriarchs of old; of Alta, of Quoauda and those that led a counter campaign against the sons of Baalilal." This may be another name for Belial in the Bible, (Deuteronomy 13:13); or Beelzebub, which is derived from the god Baal, and is considered "the prince of demons." (Matthew 12:24)

Alta and Quoauda (pronounced *quo-aud-a*) were initially god–like beings who later had cities named after them. In a following paragraph we read that the mythological gods Zeus and Zephyrus traveled with Alta and others. This was the nature of the ancient world from Cayce's and mythology's perspectives—gods and humans intermingled, until the legendary Great Flood wiped most everything away and life started over with just humans—though some humans retained their innate godliness while others became animalistic, both mentally and physically.

"The entity [Hept–supht] was among those that were active in the exchange of associations with those in Poseidia, in the city of Alta. And the priest Ra–Ta journeyed from the land of Egypt to Poseidia that there might be gained more of an understanding of the law of One, or God, that there might be the interpretations and the records of same carried to the Egyptian land. Soon after the priest returned to Egypt, the entity [Hept–supht] journeyed from Atlantis to Egypt."

Several readings talk about how much travel there was in these ancient times, and much of the travel was by air ships! We'll learn more about this is in a later chapter. In the readings about the Egyptian high priest Ra–Ta, it was revealed that he traveled often to various locations around the world, meeting with others to discuss the world situation and how to improve people's lives *spiritually*. On this occasion, he came to Alta and met Hept–supht, who had become unhappy with the political and religious unrest in Atlantis. Hept–supht also had an intuitive feeling that the final destruction of the remaining lands of Atlantis was near, which motivated him to migrate to safer lands.

"Hence, as there continued to be the rebellions and the exodus of the peoples from Atlantis before the final destruction, the entity [Hept–supht]—becoming interested in those activities of the Egyptian priest—got himself embroiled with what was going on in Egypt more than Atlantis."

But before Hept–supht left Alta for Egypt, many changes had taken place in Egypt, many that would call on Hept–supht's skill communicating with people of different views and manners. He arrived in Egypt shortly after two rebellions and after the high priest had returned from banishment and was reestablishing himself.

Cayce told the story this way:

"With the return of the high priest, which came at the same time or days in which the entity Hept–supht established itself [sic] as a native of Egypt, the entity began to work with the high priest, the native co–ruler [Aarat], and the young king [son of Arart, who both banished and reinstated Ra–Ta] to bring order out of the general chaos that existed through these troublesome turmoils and periods; and aided the most in directing those that began to be the heads of the various departments in the establishing of the truths or tenets, or practical application of the laws (as would be termed in the present) pertaining to those things that made for chemistry, building, commerce, labor, economic conditions, then the schools, the educational centers, and the varied activities that would be classified in such experiences in the present day—the *arts*, in the broader sense; as workers in precious stones, silver, gold, and the more delicate metals that required the more intrinsic activity of individuals—and music, and the instruments thereof, the recordings of the varied activities necessary that they might be handed down.

"Hence, of particular interest to the entity is the manner in which a record is kept of the activities of *every* branch of man's mental or spiritual activity. For, the entity then aided in these directly; hence came in contact, in direct touch with all those who headed or aided in mental or physical activity to produce that which would be helpful to the *coming* generations in retaining and maintaining that standard set by those as they had journeyed along the way."

"Hence the entity aided the priest in activity, but he aided the populace the more. And, as we have given, aided much in the records; not only of the period but as to how the varied activities were to be in the land pertaining to the records of that which was to be, as well as that which had been, and the records in that monument or tomb or pyramid yet to be opened [the Hall of Records, more on this in a later chapter]. Records also of those that were transferred from the destruction of the Atlantean land. For, the entity was still in charge of these records when the last of the peoples of Atlantis journeyed to the various quarters of the globe; but Alta, Zeus, Zephyrus, and the recorder of Alta were friends, associates—yea, descendents in the flesh with and of the same as the entity."

This last comment refers to a set of Atlantean records carved on stone tablets that were under the care of Hept-supht. Also, the last comments reveal how spirit-mind gods were manifesting in the "flesh" dimension or 3-D physical world. This was a strange time, one that we today consider to be mythology, but from Cayce's perspective they were real beings, events, and activities. Even Jesus affirmed that we are gods (John 10:34), referring to Psalm 82:6, "You are gods, all of you are sons (and daughters) of the Most High." Long, long ago we were all made in the image of God, and as many ancient cultures record, we were the children of God, godlings within the infinite God. However, as materiality and physicality took an increasingly dominant place in our consciousness and perception, we became almost totally consumed by our physical form and nature, losing the godly as it dropped into deep, unconscious levels of our minds. Cayce prophesied that we will soon regain the awareness we had in prehistoric Atlantis and Lemuria.

The reincarnated soul who had been Hept-supht asked Cayce to give him an idea of how powerful he once was:

"(Q) Give in detail the psychic powers he developed at that time?

"(A) This would almost be impossible. To put such into words would be as impractical as it would be to describe what the multiple of colors as related to vibrations brings, reduced to its eleventh or nth degree."

What a curious comment by Cayce. In one of the Atlantis Series readings (340 series), Cayce stated that high psychic ability was so *natural* to Atlanteans that we today could barely comprehend such an existence! Apparently, Hept–supht had this level of psychic awareness and power. Can we image a condition in which we would know the thoughts of everyone around us, the location of people at great distances from us, the movements of nature, the weather, the trees, the animals—and even influence them with our minds? Cayce continued:

"Yet, as may be seen from that given, *psychic* is so often misconstrued. For, it is of the mental or soul, and was that which was *mostly* employed in the experience by the entity, when it would be compared to the materiality that is necessarily employed in this material age—or in an age when 'Only that I may see, or touch, or feel, or taste, do I comprehend.'"

In several readings Cayce stated that, as difficult as it may be for us to accept, the "unseen forces" are more powerful than the seen. The mind is so much more powerful than we know today. As even Jesus pointed out: "If you had the faith and did not doubt, you could say to this mountain, 'Be taken up and cast into the sea,' and it would done." (Matthew 21:21) Few of us believe that today.

Let's read one more of Hept–supht's readings before analyzing them further. Gladys notes on her steno pad that the suggestion given to Cayce was, "Soul–mind seeking further information on his Egyptian incarnation as Hept–supht and its influence in the present. Questions." After this suggestion, Cayce, in trance, repeated the suggestion and then said, "Hept–supht—Help Keep It Shut," revealing for us the meaning of this strange, ancient name. The reading then proceeded:

"Yes, we have the entity, the soul–mind and the experiences in the earth of [378], as known in the present. [Numbers replaced personal names in the files to provide privacy.]

"Ready for questions.

"(Q) Give spiritual help to develop the psychic powers, which will enable me to become a fitting channel for God's work, now.

"(A) In the application of that which has been the experience of a soul through sojourns in the earth, these should not be taken only for their historical setting."

From Cayce's trance state, past-life information is not just for the historical perspective or to know who we were but for the *wholeness* of our soul and the awakening of our *larger* mind, one that has a broader memory complex than a single incarnation on earth. Our soul also has a bigger mission than our single incarnate life.

"As the entity in the present makes the application, or sets in motion the experiences of self in its contact with those [past-life] influences that may be contacted, so will the growth be; so will there be unfolded to the entity those experiences throughout its own appearances, not as to the histology or the genealogical conditions but that which is much deeper—or that known as individuality. And so does growth come."

Next, Cayce states it clearly: "As we apply, make use of, set past-life knowledge and influence in motion, then more comes to us. As more comes, we grow in our understanding, our *deeper* understanding, not our historical or genealogical knowledge. Or, as we have given as to how a soul becomes conscious, aware, of its contact with the universal-cosmic–God–Creative Forces in its experience; by feeding upon the food, the fruits, the results of spirit, of God, of Life, of Reality: Love, hope, kindness, gentleness, brotherly love, patience. *These* make for the awareness in the soul of its relationship to the creative force that is manifest in self, in the ego, in the I AM of each soul, and of I AM THAT I AM.

"So may the entity, the soul of this entity, become aware—through meditating upon those understandings, those truths that are as examples, as witnesses in the earth and its environs—of that which magnifies the Spirit in the earth of the first manifestation that man calls God and His holy angels.

"(Q) Was the entity the one that, at the completion of the pyramid, clanged the sheet of metal?

"(A) Clanged the sheet of metal [that was the capstone to the Great Pyramid] at the completion of Gizeh, that sealed the records in the tomb yet to be discovered.

"(Q) Please describe incident and ceremony.

"(A) The apex [capstone of the Great Pyramid] that has been long since removed by the sons of Heth [great grandson of Noah through his son Ham and Ham's son Canaan; Heth is considered to be the ancestor of the Hittites, also *Hethites*, see Genesis 10 and 23], the crown or apex [capstone], was of metal; that was to be indestructible, being of copper, brass and gold with other alloys that were prepared by those of the period." In another reading Cayce commented again about Heth, speaking to one of his reincarnated daughters: "The entity then was among the daughters of Heth from whom Abraham purchased the land near Socoh." (Genesis 23, ten miles SW of Hebron)

"And, as this was to be (Gizeh we are speaking of) the place for the initiates and their gaining by personal application, and by the journey or journeys through the various activities—as in the ceremonial actions of those that became initiates, it became very fitting (to those as in Ra, and those of Ra–Ta Ra [a name used after Ra–Ta had "awakened to the Ra within him") that there should be the crowning or placing of this symbol of the record [capstone], and of the initiates' place of activity, by one who represented both the old and the new; one representing then the Sons of the Law in Atlantis, Lemuria, Oz, and Og. So, he that keeps the record, that keeps shut, or Hept–supht, was made or chosen as the one to seal that in the tomb.

"The ceremony was long; the clanging of the apex [metallic capstone] by the gavel that was used in the sounding of the placing. Hence there has arisen from this ceremony many of those things that may be seen in the present; as the call to prayer, the church bell in the present, may be termed a descendant; the sounding of the trumpet as the call to arms, or that as revelry; the sound as of those that make for mourning, in the putting away of the body; the sounding as of ringing in the new year, the sounding as of the coming of the bridegroom; all have their inception from the sound that was made that kept the earth's record of the earth's building, as to that from the change. The old record in Gizeh is from that as recorded from the journey to Pyrenees [the initial migration from sinking Atlantis to higher ground; the Pyrenees are a mountain range between Spain and France]; and to 1998 from the death of the Son of Man as a man." Here Cayce is identifying three key stages in the ascent of the children of God to their rightful place: (1) migrate from the old ways, old lands to higher ground, or higher consciousness, leaving those old ways behind; (2) crucify earthly desire in self so that the real self may come through, and die to possessiveness of selfishness and self-seeking (death of the Son of Man as a man); and (3) the cycle comes around again beginning in 1998 as a new era, a new age begins, and the greater opportunities present themselves again.

"(Q) Give a prayer to awaken the best in me now.

"(A) So let my life now shine unto others that they may know that Thou, O God, would speak and meet those I meet day by day. Create in me a pure heart. Renew a righteous soul within me, O God!"

3

THE MISSION OF
THE SECOND CREATION

According to Cayce's readings of the Akashic record, this early period in ancient Egypt's birth closely followed the dramatic cleansing of the planet by the legendary Great Flood as recorded in Genesis 6. The time following the flood was a time for repopulating the earth with new bodies, and these would be more physical bodies. Originally, the children of God projected themselves into this world as phantoms, as ghosts. In fact, the name Lemur, as in Lemuria, means *ghost*, coming from a Latin word referring to the "spirits" of the dead—but these early souls were immortal, having never tasted death. The Great Flood was the symbolic marker of the end of the first creation and the beginning of the second. In the second creation, now deeper into matter and physicality, the children of God would experience the cycles of this reality, which included day and night, wake and sleep, and life and death. Of course, there really was no death for the immortal godlings, but they came to think there was. The Maya have a legend that tells how the Lords of the Underworld (forces of the lower realms of mind) tricked the immortal children of God into playing a game in which the penalty for losing was death (loss of consciousness). This was symbolized in the Mesoamerican legends by the act of decapitation of the loser's physical body. The godlings were actually spirit-minds temporarily inhabiting the physical body, and the death of the body was not death of the godling. Even so, it had an overwhelming impact on the consciousness of the godlings. In the Garden of Eden's story, the serpent's whisper to Eve was that she would "not surely die" if she ate of the apple—but it was going to be such a profound impact upon her consciousness that she would be as if dead consciously, losing celestial awareness from the overwhelming weight of material consciousness.

Cayce's visions observed that many (not all) of the minds and souls of God's children willfully pushed their way into matter and materiality before it was prepared for them. This was taking them out of the natural oneness of heavenly existence and separating them into individual projections. In Genesis 2:18 God observes that this created a sense of loneliness in them, and it was not good for them. Even worse, since the only physical bodies existing at that time were animal bodies, Cayce and ancient mythology reveal that their spirit–minds became contaminated with animal features, such as feathers, scales, fur, and even major body parts, resulting in mixed–up beings that were half man and half horse (centaurs), half man and half lion (sphinxes), half woman and half fish (sirens and mermaids)! All of these *liminal* beings had to be cleansed of their confused mixture and reoriented to their ideal form and vibration—*mentally* as well as physically. And a human body was needed. Sadly, even when a body for God's children was formed, the minds of many souls were now so polluted with animal imagery and vibrations that when properly incarnated in good human bodies, they manifested remnant animal features, mutating the chromosomes as their mental forces and vibrations influenced cell division and specialization. The complete removal of these pollutants was one of the services of the earliest temples in ancient Egypt, known as the Temple of Sacrifice.

Even so, the primary problem was the separation from oneness into what may be called "manyness." It was a massive individuation progression that broke the collective consciousness of the souls into individual selves. According to Cayce's perspective, *self* and *selfishness* were and remain the cause of evil and destructiveness. When an individual soul is conscious of its oneness with the whole of creation, it naturally expresses goodness and creativity. But when perceiving oneself as separate, the lower mind does not see that harm to others is harm to oneself.

The massive water cleansing of the earth through the Great Flood came as a result of growing selfishness, self–gratification, self–exaltation, tyranny, and cruelty of one group over another, and godlessness in most every heart. Two factional soul groups developed among incarnating souls. Cayce referred to them as the children of the Law of One, who attempted to hold onto the original oneness, versus the Sons of Belial (pronounced *bell-ee-al* or *bell-aisle*), who taught and practiced survival of the fittest: get all you can get for yourself, there is no oneness, the strong should dominate and use the weak, even as slaves. Genesis records that "the Lord regretted making humankind, and it grieved him to his heart." The Lord then exclaimed, "I will destroy humanity whom I have created from the surface of the ground . . . for I am sorry that I have made them." The Lord told Noah, "The end of all flesh has come before me, for the earth is filled with violence through them. Behold, I will destroy them with the earth. I, even I, do bring the flood of waters on this earth, to destroy all flesh having the breath of life from under the sky. Everything that is in the earth will die. But I will establish my covenant with you." In Cayce's readings, this covenant was established with many soul groups around the planet; thus many were saved from the flood cleansing and were the incarnate souls that began the legendary "Second Creation," of which the new nation of Egypt played a most important role.

The Temple of Sacrifice also provided services for reducing selfishness, cravings, and out-of-control sensual urges that had come to possess so many souls in the chaos of the First Creation.

In his deep meditative-like state, Cayce was asked to "have before you the Temple Beautiful in Egypt at about the period 10,500 BC after the return of the high priest Ra-Ta from banishment. You will describe in detail this temple and the services held in it, explaining how an understanding of the work carried on there may be of help to us now in carrying forward our healing study and work [today]." Cayce replied, "many of you here were both in and of the temple service, whether in the purifications in the Temple of Sacrifice or the Temple Beautiful. In the Temple of Sacrifice there were the altars to cleanse the bodies of those things that hindered in body, that were emblematical of the source of the stumbling block. In the Temple Beautiful there were the expressions of the service as an activity to maintain and to purify the bodies for the necessary associations of spiritual understandings in material bodies. Do not, my children, confuse your bodies of today with those attributes of that ancient period, with the conditions existent in the Temple Beautiful." Cayce explained this last comment, saying that bodies in those ancient times were much less dense and not so possessing of the souls that inhabited them as our bodies today. Most of us actually think of ourselves as our bodies, not sensing the independence of the mind and soul inhabiting the physical vehicle.

As we learned in chapter one, the Temple of Sacrifice could best be compared to a combination of a modern-day spa, yoga center, and hospital in which the focus was on improving the physical body, which is the temple of the incarnating soul. The Temple Beautiful could best be compared to a combination of a modern monastery, university, and vocational training center in which the focus was on improving the mind and spirit of an individual and preparing him or her for a service that contributes to the whole of the community and the growth of the souls.

Cayce explained that the physical bodies in the most ancient of times were not as physical as our bodies today and could be absorbed into the nonphysical aspects of a soul-mind while they "traveled" to heavenly realms—then, they could be projected again when they returned to the realm of form and physicality. Even the Hopi have legends of a long-ago time when souls could manifest in this world and then leave at will, moving their bodies back into pure energy or spirit and traveling through the door between this world and the heavens.

So different were our ancient bodies that Cayce also spoke of an additional chakra in our thighs that was particularly earthy. It was this chakra that was being removed surgically in the Temple of Sacrifice to help a soul keep its consciousness and spirit at higher levels of vibration and awareness. We see references to this chakra in the Scriptures. In Genesis 24 and 47 there are scenes in which a person is asked to "put your hand under my thigh." These may be indications of the existence of that ancient chakra.

Cayce's response to the request for information about the ancient Egyptian temples continued:

"There had been gathered from all the nations of the earth that which represented from their environ, their surrounding, the most beautiful gift; that it might be a reminder of those, to those, that purified or gave themselves in service or activity there, of the beauty of service of every land in this preparation of the bodies for their greater service and for their intermingling with those of the earth's environ as well as enabling the servants, the workers, the priestess, the prophetess, those that labored—or joyously gave themselves—to give their activity for others.

"The materials [stone blocks] that composed the outer portions of the temples were of the mountains nigh unto the upper waters of the Nile. The temple was in the form of the pyramid, within which was the globe—which represented to those who served that their service was to the world."

The globe of the world was central to the temple's work as they were training people from all over the world and sending helpers to every corner of the planet. We don't think of the ancient people as globally interconnected, but they were according to Cayce. And they had the means via their flying machines, as described in greater detail in a later chapter.

As far as what was actually going on inside these temples, Cayce explained that on the altars of the temples no life was ever sacrificed, neither human nor animal, not even grains. These sorts of bloody offerings came much later after the original higher consciousness was lost. The offerings on these altars were the initiates' weaknesses, poor habits, fears, and vices. Cayce explained that in the center of the altars a sacred fire was ignited to consume these offerings of the soul's weaknesses. However, before an initiate could step away from the altar ceremony, he or she had to assume a new strength, greater purpose, a new virtue, and a higher consciousness. They could not simply cast off their weaknesses; they had to take up a new level of virtue and strength, and even a mission or work that helped make life better for others.

In the desert between the now famous Step Pyramid in Saqqara and the Great Pyramid in Giza there is a huge, beautifully carved, alabaster altar (see illustration 20). It is inside the rubble of a Ra Temple with an attached pyramid (just as Cayce described). The center of this magnificent altar is a raised circle, around which is a huge square with four arrow–like projections that point to the four cardinal points of the planet (north, east, south, and west) and between these projections are four corners that point to the location of the sun in the four seasons. When the sun is in the northern regions, it is spring and summer [in the northern hemisphere, and Egypt is in this hemisphere]; when the sun is in the southern regions, it is fall and winter in the northern hemisphere. Alabaster is a crystal–like stone that conducts light, so the sacred fire on the center circle of this altar would have dispersed its light throughout the altar. Imagine the scene inside a relatively dark temple, with a glowing altar and a flickering fire and all the initiates and attendants in white linen and golden accessories moving in a ceremonial procession, offering up their vices and assuming stronger virtues. What a scene it must have been.

According to Cayce's readings, there were also regenerative ceremonies and devices that would raise the vibrations of initiates so as to rejuvenate their bodies. Cayce indicated that these were first used in Atlantis and then later became a part of Egyptian temple practice. We may have some evidence of these carved on some surviving temples. Today there remains a strange device, reminiscent of a light bulb, on the walls of the Temple of Hathor at Dendera. (See illustration 21 for images of this device; for details, see illustrations 82a and 82b.) In these carvings we see a full–size Egyptian holding a large bulb with a serpent filament. The bulb is connected to a lotus–like socket with a long cord leading back to a well–known Egyptian symbol, the *djed* (see illustration 22).

The djed symbol actually *predates* the dynastic period of Egypt, reaching back into prehistoric times! It continues to appear throughout the period of the pharaohs. Most scholars agree that it is a symbol of resurrection and is called the "backbone of Osiris" after the god who oversees the weighing of the hearts of all souls attempting to pass from this world to the heavens. If their hearts are heavy, they must return and get lighter ones. If their hearts are light, then they may pass on into the heavens and enjoy the fruit of the Tree of Life and the thirst–quenching Water of Life. The djed is a pillar with four cross bars. Upon this particular djed sits the open–arms symbol of the *ka*, considered by some to be the spirit or life force in its quintessence. Human arms are raised in the position for adoration, but the head between these arms is removed—indicating that it is that *feeling* we have when giving thanks to God, but not the thinking or self-consciousness of the act, just the vibration, just the feeling. It is also known to be the "twin," signifying that we have another part to us that is not seen—our godling self.

Again remembering that the two raised arms are symbolic of the spirit, the whole icon illustrates that the spirit runs down our backbone (the kundalini pathway) to give strength and resurrecting energy throughout our being.

The serpent inside of the bulb has a few meanings in ancient theology. It is the self, self's mind, and self's thoughts in contrast to God's or the Collective's. As such, it is the tempter, as it was depicted in the Garden of Eden; but it is also a symbol of the life force within the body, what yoga and Hinduism term the *kundalini*. In ancient Mesoamerica, Egypt, and Greece, the serpent is often depicted with wings, symbolizing the raising of the life force by the higher mind. Modern medicine retains this meaning in the caduceus (see illustration 23), the symbol of health services. The central shaft of the caduceus is the central nervous system; the double serpents symbolize the autonomic nervous system with its two parts, the sympathetic and parasympathetic. The wings represent the mind, especially with higher life-giving thoughts.

Notice that the Egyptians are putting their heads up against the bulb—some with buffering devices, some directly against the bulb. It appears that they are receiving energy, possibly information, or both from this strange device.

Considering the life-giving symbols associated with the bulb, this may be more of a *life* bulb than a light bulb. We know from Cayce's readings that the Atlanteans rejuvenated their bodies using a crystal-based device.

Here's a Cayce reading on that:

"As to the experience of the entity from that sojourn [in Atlantis], there come the innate abilities to create the higher energies within self . . . to find regenerations in the lower form of electrical vibrations."

The temple-wall picture shows a power cord and filament, giving the impression of something electrical. But it may also have been a light bulb in the sense of "the light" of wisdom, because Cayce's readings also talk about communicating with the universal consciousness through these devices.

Here's one of those readings:

"The entity was in Atlantis, a priestess, and the keeper of the white stone or that through which many of those peoples before the first destructions in Atlantis kept their accord with the universal consciousness, through the speaking to and through those activities."

Are the Egyptians depicted on this wall tuning their bodies to liferejuvenating forces? Are they also tuning their minds to universal consciousness and communicating? The ka-arms sit on top of the djed stone. Is this "the white stone" Cayce was referring to?

Today Cayce has guided us to understand that all these ancient devices are also *within* us. The light bulb and life bulb are within us. The bioelectrical current of the life force is within us. Our bodies and minds are capable of rejuvenation and of knowing the consciousness and energy of the Creator and of communicating with God.

Cayce further described bizarre physical conditions that some ancient people suffered. According to him, the initial mingling of celestial minds with physical animals created thought forms that manifested in one's physical body. This caused some people to have animal appendages. These had to be removed before the soul could progress through the temple process. Here are Cayce's words on this in a lengthy quote:

"The individuals, having cleansed themselves of those appendages that hindered them, came not merely for the symbolic understanding. For these, to be sure, were all symbolized—the faults, the virtues of man, in all his seven stages of development [more on these stages in a later chapter]—in the light or the lamp [could he be referring to the bulbs on the Egypt temple walls?] borne by those who served as the Light Bearers to those who entered for their initiation, or for their preparation to be that as given by the teachers—even Ra-Ta. Laying aside those things that easily beset the sons of men, you as you enter here, put your whole trust in the one God, that you may be all things unto all men, thereby crucifying your own desires that they—your brethren—may know the Lord their God. In the temple activities then, there were first the songs, the music, as we have indicated that *you* sing: Ar–r–r—Ou–u—Ur–r; which makes for the losing of even the association of the body with that save the *vibrations* of which the body was then composed; yea now is, though encased in a much more hardened matter, as to materiality; which made for the vibrating of same with light, that *becomes* color, that becomes tone, that becomes activity. Seek then *in* tone, all of you: Ar–r–r–r–r–*ar*; that you may know how the emanations, that are termed as the colors of the body, make for the expression then given. With the music came then the dance, that enabled those with the disturbing forces and influences to become more erect, upright in body, in thought, in activity.

"Then there was the giving by the Prophetess of the seal of life that was set upon each and every one who passed through these experiences, how or in what field of activity the relationships were of an individual to its fellow man in maintaining material existence; being in the world yet not *of* the world."

This "seal of life" may be associated with a very ancient symbol found beneath the Seti Temple in Abydos, one of the most sacred temples in all of Egypt. On one of the pillars in this ancient underground temple is carved the "flower of life" symbol (see illustration 24). This might possibly have been a portion of the seal of life that Cayce's prophetess set upon each and every one who passed through those ancient temple experiences. Another portion of the seal of life may have been specific to each initiate's field of activity.

"*These* then, made for that as you have in your experiences in the present expressed: First in cleanliness, in purifying of the body, in the washing in blood [a metaphor for self–sacrifice], in water, that you may be purified before yourself first and then before others. The anointing with the incense, making for the raising of that you know as your senses or perception or consciousness of the activities to all the faults, by comparison, as arose among others.

"From those activities you have that first as your service of preparation, of birth, of consecration, of purification, of those things that later become the hospitalization, the care of the ill in body, in mind; the divinations of those tempted from within and those tempted from without. Little study is made in the present of this phase of man's experience.

"The teaching, the preparation, the ministering, the song, the music, the activities that give expression, arise in man's experience from those activities in the Temple Beautiful."

In a strange and curious comment during this reading, Cayce asked a question and answered it:

"You ask, where is this temple now? Disintegrated and in that sphere you may enter, and some have entered, where these are sealed as with the seven seals of the law in that these experiences now become as those of your activities among your fellow man."

What does he mean, "in that sphere you may enter" and "sealed as with the seven seals"? The answer lies in the very source of Cayce's insights, which is a sphere of awareness beyond daily consciousness, and in the seven spiritual centers hidden within our body temple. We may learn to open these seals and raise ourselves to greater levels of life.

As Cayce continues this long reading on the temples, he shifts his focus to our times and our opportunities today, and he gets quite "quickened" with the Spirit!

"Then, in using and in applying and associating same with your activities in that experience, and that manner in which you may use same in the present:

"So attune yourselves that you may harken, not as to an experience only; but rather *live* and *be* the experience in the hearts of those that are seeking to find their way; whether in the troubles of the body, of the mind, or whether they are lost among those turmoils of the cry, 'This way—That way—Here and there.' Be the experience to someone to light their lives, their bodies, their minds to your *living* Lord, your brother, the Christ! For He has promised in His words in your own heart, that keeps the hope, that keeps the fires of your own heart aflame, 'You finding me may know the *joy* of the Lord.'

"As many of you served in the temples, as many experienced those purifications for an active service among their fellow man in an *individual* experience, so may you purify your minds and your bodies, or purify your *bodies* that your *mind* may put *on* Christ, the garments of a living Lord, that you may be not as ones stumbling, as ones fearful of this or that, but *sure* and *certain* in the joys of a risen Lord; that indeed your body in its expressions may be the Temple Beautiful for your *living* Lord.

"He your brother, your Christ, hath given that God is God of the *living* way! He *is* Life! He *is* Love. He *is* Beauty. He *is* Harmony. He *is* Music. He *is* the rhythm of the body in dance that is a service to your God. Though others make slight of your manner of speech, of your body, of your walks, of your ways, hold fast to Him; grudging no one, loving all. For as given, in your preparation, in the indication and the vindication in your service in those ancient temples, *self* is lost in the love of your fellow man through the joy of the Lord in you."

At the end of this reading on the temples, he was asked a series of questions and the answers were quite revealing.

"Q: In which temple was I most active? What were my activities in same?

"A: This depends upon the periods in which this may be considered. In the early portion of the activities of the entity, it was in the Temple of Sacrifice or of purification. In the latter portion, when there had been those cleansings of the feet in your own service there, then the activities were in the Temple Beautiful; as a guard to those as they proceeded from one symbol to another in their journey about the Temple.

"Here it may be well that there be given a concept of what is meant by the journey, or what journey is meant. The globe within the pyramid was in the form of the ova, or the egg in its ovate form. From station to station in the seven phases or seals or stands or places of the activities, they were such as to make each station lead from one to another by ever crossing the one; making the continued web." Here we may have an answer to the flower of life symbol. It appears like a web yet has distinct points.

Continuing with the interesting Q & A from other members of this group receiving this psychic reading:

"Q: What part did I take in services in the Temple Beautiful?

"A: The announcer with the cymbal and horn.

"Q: Please give me the information as to whether or not I was in the Temple Beautiful. If so, please give that service which I rendered.

"A: An observer of those seals wherein the effects of the sojourns in the varied activities were to be seen, or the effects from the planetary sojourn. Hence a *keeper* of seals there. Interest in astrology, astronomy, arises from same.

"Q: Was I in the Temple Beautiful and what part did I take in the services?

"A: In the station where your weakness now appears. Take this home with you and find what you must do!

"Q: Was I also in the temple? What did I do?

"A: The priestess.

"Q: Was I?

"A: In the records of that given for each in the journey *out* of the Temple to material application. Or, to put in the parlance of today, a secretary to the stations.

"Q: I would appreciate as much information concerning the Temple Beautiful as would be of help to me. I have a great inner urge to know more about this Temple and its purpose to man at this time. Does this Temple not have a close connection with Destiny? If so, please give.

"A: As the entity was the prophetess to those, it *would* make the indication to the entity of a definite association or connection with destinies. But Destiny, as you have studied and as you have learned is: 'God hath not willed that any soul should perish but hath with each temptation provided a way of approach.' Hence man with his free will makes for whether the body is *as* the temple of the living God or the Temple Beautiful, with its various stations as represented in the various phases of His experience; as is shown in the body itself in *all* of those urges as arise through emotions, through mind, through association, through purifying, through consecration, through determination, through knowledge, through the attributes that become a portion of same.

"As you have seen in that you have given, may give, that led the many, that opened the way to many, it, the temple, your temple, your body, your mind, your portion of the God–Consciousness may be aroused and awakened to the abilities within self to assist in those becoming aware of the necessity of arousing to the destinies of the body, the mind, the soul.

"Q: May I have a message bearing upon that period of time in the Temple Beautiful that may be helpful to me in this experience?

"A: You in your office ever was as the one that tended, gathered, comforted those as they passed from station or phase or experience. In encouraging, in comforting, know that you in your service now may give that encouraging word, that aid, that comfort, by the touch of your hand, by the sound of your voice, by the *sureness* of your purpose, by the centralizing of your ideals in Him.

"Q: Did I take part in the services in the Temple Beautiful?

"A: In bringing others to their activities there, in aiding those that faltered or made for aggrandizement of self, *after* their initiation. So, within and without, and in the present as you rise at times to those heights sublime in your visions of peace and harmony, you may bring help to the experience of a soul that is scared, fearful, lacking, or disturbed. So have you seen, and so do you see those things that make for the faltering steps, bringing help to the maimed in the experiences of those that have—as it were—taken hold and yet faltered. *Keep* your faith."

So effective were the procedures and processes in these temples that the sex queen of the Atlanteans, spoken of in the first chapter, experienced a complete 180° turnaround from her lustful ways to a higher calling and service in spiritual-mental activities for the betterment of herself and those around her! We can imagine how difficult it would have been for her to subdue the deeply set habit patterns she had built from her earlier sexual activities. Cayce's readings explain that the mystical altar fires used in these ancient Egyptian temples to cleanse earthy energies, patterns, and desires from the soul's body, mind, and heart were very potent. If a soul was truly determined to rid itself of these, then all could be cleansed completely. Cayce said that the previous sex queen found new, uplifting vibrations and consciousness in "operatic airs, the folklore music, and the hymns and psalms." In this present incarnation he encouraged her to get involved in chorus and to write stories and songs. Curiously, when he finished giving this reading for the one-time queen of sex orgies in Egypt—the Egypt in which he was high priest—he awoke feeling terrible, all upset, and didn't regain his equilibrium until the next day! He must have relived the challenges of her ancient energies and activities while giving the reading. In this life, she was not overly sexual but was highly creative, with contracts for motion pictures in Hollywood and operas in New York City. Apparently, she had rechanneled her sexual energy into creative outlets.

4

THE ANCIENT WORLD

When Cayce was asked to describe the earth's surface in these very ancient times, he replied that this would be difficult for us to comprehend given our present conditions, but he then attempted to give some concept of what it was like so very long ago.

He began by explaining that the axis poles of the earth were more in the tropical and semitropical regions. Imagine the present cold polar regions of the planet tilted more toward the sun. The Carpathian Mountains (today on the *western* side of the Black Sea) and the Caucasus Mountains (today on the *eastern* side of the Black Sea, just north of ancient Eden and the two great rivers of the Euphrates and the Tigris) were then warm, semitropical regions. He said that the now cold Ural Mountains in modern-day Russia and the northern regions of Asia were turned into a tropical land. He said that the desert in the Mongolian land was then a fertile region, populated with migrants from once great Mu and Lemuria in the Pacific.

Surprisingly, he said that the Nile River entered into the Atlantic Ocean! And what is now the Sahara Desert was a very fertile and inhabited land. Historical climatology supports this view, explaining how the ancient "Nubia Swell" was blocking the Nile from running to the Mediterranean, forcing it through the Sahara and westward to the ocean. Satellite imagery shows the vestige of a river running across northern Africa to the ocean that may have been this ancient Nile.

In what is America today, Cayce said that "the central portion of this country, or the Mississippi basin, was then all in the ocean; only the plateau was existent, or the regions that are now portions of Nevada, Utah, and Arizona formed the greater part of what we know as the United States." He explained, "The Atlantic seaboard formed the outer portion then, or the lowlands of Atlantis." He said that the Yucatan Peninsula, where Atlantean Iltar first settled with stone records (more on this later), was a temperate zone. He stated that the Andes Mountains and the Pacific coast of South America occupied then a portion of Lemuria. He described how the "oceans were then turned about; they no longer bear their names."

After the prehistoric lands had vanished and the planet had been almost totally cleansed of the First Creation beings and the mayhem they caused, there was a long period, nearly ten thousand years, of very low population on the planet. The remnant groups from the First Creation were scattered across the planet, mostly in the mountains, because of the floodwaters. Lava flows and fissures remained active for some time after the disaster. Then, to repopulate the planet and start anew, a shift in the axis poles of the planet occurred, moving them from the tropical region to nearly where they are today.

This shift caused many changes. Cayce said that when the axis shifted, many of the surviving people migrated southward, coming out of the mountains. He particularly mentioned that the white and yellow races came "more into that portion of Egypt, India, Persia, and Arabia." The white race came out of the Carpathian and Caucasus Mountains (this would have included the Ararat Tribe from Mount Ararat, just south of the Caucasus). And the yellow race came out of the Himalayan of Tibet and the Altai Mountains of present-day Mongolia. The black race in the mountains and highlands of Ethiopia, Sudan, and Nubia came down into Egypt. And Cayce added that Atlantean remnants of the red race which had been living in the Pyrenees Mountains (between Spain and France today) came to Egypt.

In Cayce's ancient tales, the five races were a primordial decision by the entire soul group of all God's children who were descending into matter and were making the long, long journey through the cycles of birth, death, and rebirth in this world. It was determined that a kind of division of labor would help shorten the journey; so the total group was separated into subgroups, each dealing directly with one of the five senses of the human body. Each subgroup was to subdue the possessive nature of their dominant sense; so when all were reunited again, everyone would gain by the successes of each group. Cayce directed us to, "Let these [races] represent the attributes of the physical, or the senses and what forms they take, rather than calling them white, black, yellow, red and green, etc. What do they signify in the *sensing*?" Then he gave this: Sight or vision is the white. Feeling or touch is the red. Taste is the black. Yellow is the "mingling in the hearing." And brown would be the sense of smell or the olfactory sense.

We must keep in mind that, according to Cayce's past-life readings, individual souls may move among the five projected subgroups on the planet—a single soul may experience more than one racial incarnation. Some in Cayce's files experienced only one race in all their incarnations; some experienced several races. But the mission of each subgroup would not change: mastering of that group's dominant sense. The racial subgroups projected simultaneously in five specific locations where every location developed an original "Eve" that produced the ideal physical body for each of the five racial forms. (Actually, each race had many ideal "Eves," because repopulating the planet was a major mission then and they needed many mothers.) The projections were, according to Cayce, the brown in the Andes and the present western shore of South America (this was a portion of Lemuria); the black in Nubia, and thereabouts; the white in the Carpathian and Caucasus Mountains; the yellow in the Gobi (not a desert back then, and these were also remnants of another portion of Lemuria); and the red race in Atlantis and the eastern Americas. These were their original locations, but eventually many migrated to other regions.

These racial subgroups of the children of God should not be confused with Cayce's "root races." His root-races idea dealt with the overall human-body prototypes, or various stages of developing a perfect body for the children of God to use while incarnate. There is no discernible genetic difference among the five races: "DNA studies do not indicate that separate classifiable subspecies (races) exist within modern humans. While different genes for physical traits such as skin and hair color can be identified between individuals, no consistent patterns of genes across the human genome exist to distinguish one race from another." —Human Genome Project, 2004.

Cayce's root races are specifically about various body types used by human souls across the planet and through the ages. Cayce actually predicted that a new root-race body type is evolving and will manifest itself as we move into the next era or new age. This new body will have twelve chakras instead of the seven we currently have. It will be lighter, less dense, and more luminescent or radiant. There will also be radiance around all of us, an aura. These will become more prominent as the new body type becomes the norm.

We need to also keep in mind that Cayce stated that the early body types used by incoming souls were not as physical as our bodies today. He predicted that we will regain some of these characteristics and qualities as we evolve into the next root-race body type.

The Changing Population of Egypt

The population of Egypt today is not composed of the descendants of the ancient Egyptians. The Egypt that Cayce was speaking of is long gone and has been for millennia. Many peoples have invaded and occupied Egypt since those very ancient times of Cayce's tales. Here are some highlights: the Arabs invaded in AD 642 and continue to be the primary population in Egypt today; the Romans invaded in 47 BC but never really became part of the population; the Greeks invaded in 332 BC and did become a significant portion of the population, adopting many Egyptian traditions and religious practices; the Nubian conquest of Egypt occurred in 1000 BC, which may have been the reason that Greek historians reported Egyptians to be "very black" with "woolly hair"; the Hittites invaded in 1590 BC, introducing horses and light-weight, fast chariots to the culture (we often think that the chariots in Egyptian depictions were an Egyptian invention, not so), and the Hyksos invaded in 1750 BC. Cayce's tales are about an Egyptian population dating back to 11,000 BC! The present people of Egypt are not the ancient Egyptians. However, the *souls* of the ancient Egyptians have been and are continuing to reincarnate and may be among any of the populations of today.

The Second Creation Period

Because water is so essential to sustaining life on this planet, the first agricultural centers of the Second Creation were founded in the regions of the four great rivers on this planet: the Tigris and Euphrates Rivers (Mesopotamia), the Indus and Ganges Rivers (India), the Huang He (the Yellow River in China), and the Nile (Egypt). The Amazon is not included because no great civilization developed along it—simply too harsh an environment and the rainforest created marshy soil. Using Cayce's timeline, the period roughly from 22,000 to 12,000 BC was the quiet aftermath of the catastrophic ending of the First Creation. The period beginning in 12,000 to 11,000 BC was the beginning of the Second Creation and the world as we know it today.

The Nile

The Greek historian Herodotus wrote, "Egypt was the gift of the Nile." Three tributaries created this amazing river. The first is the White Nile, a long gentle river flowing from Lake Victoria—a high mountain lake bordered by Kenya, Tanzania, and Uganda. This tributary joins with the shorter but more voluminous and nutrient-richer Blue Nile, springing from Lake Tana in Ethiopia. And in ancient times, a third tributary joined these two, the Yellow Nile flowing from the eastern highlands of Chad. The Yellow Nile is now dry but was once a part of this trinity of rivers creating the ancient Nile.

Each year during the rainy season, the ancient Nile River would overflow its banks and inundate Egypt; as it retreated, it left behind nutrient-rich black silt that made Egypt one of the most fertile lands in recorded history. Today, two dams now control the Nile—there is no flooding and no rich silt fertilizer.

Around this river of life-giving water grew one of the greatest cultures on the planet. The ancient Egyptians called the river *Iteru*, meaning "Great River"; the modern name comes from the Greek *Neilos* (*Nilus* in Latin), transliterated to *Nile*.

The Edfu Text, found in the Horus Temple in Edfu, and the Papyrus of

Hunefer tell the story of a "hill people" who became the first settlers in this region. "We came from the beginning of the Nile where god Hapi dwells at the foothills of the Mountains of the Moon." The Mountains of the Moon are likely those that contain Lake Tana in ancient Abyssinia (modern day Ethiopia), the origin of the Blue Nile. This name may be traced back to a Greek ruler of late Egypt, Ptolemy, and the use of the name "Mountains of *Selene*," the moon goddess of the Greeks.

Cayce's readings confirm the idea that hill people first came down out of the mountains along the Nile into the lower lands of Egypt today from ancient Abyssinia (Ethiopia). He also tells of the ancient lands of Nubia and their role in early Egypt. Nubia means "Land of Gold," and much of the gold in Egypt came from the Nubian mountains. Much of Nubia today is under Lake Nasser, a result of the high dam, but portions remain in southern Egypt and northern Sudan. Upper Egypt is the mountain areas from Kom Ombo to Sudan. Lower Egypt is the delta region opening to the Mediterranean Sea.

Even though the hill people were the first to enter Egypt, many subsequent peoples came to this fertile land. Cayce's discourses tell of waves of different groups coming from all over the planet. Each assimilated into the civilization that was to become the great civilization we study today. According to Cayce's visions, the rulers of the earliest Egyptian periods were quite open to incorporating new people into their ruling council and culture, but this changed over time.

It is not surprising that the ancient Egyptian god of the Nile River was named *Hapi*. Happy were all who lived along this river. Hapi was portrayed as a man with women's breasts and a round, jolly belly. As god of the upper Nile, coming through the highlands and rocky cataracts, Hapi is depicted with lotuses on his head, for they grew best there. As god of the lower Nile, leading to the Mediterranean Sea, Hapi is depicted with papyrus plants on his head, for they grew in the delta of the Nile (see illustration 30). In the upper lands, his feminine counterpart was the high-flying goddess Nekhebet, symbolized by the vulture with open wings—symbolic of that which takes no life (vultures do not eat living creatures) and assimilates death to sustain life. In the lower lands, Hapi's feminine half was the goddess Buto, symbolized by a cobra—symbolic of the kundalini life force (see illustrations 31a and 31b).

Each year the gods that guarded the source of the Nile would release just the right amount of rain to ensure the black silt fertilization but not so much water as to harm the civilization. The winged goddess Ma'at watched over the entire universe to maintain order and balance, including the great river Nile. Fixed, eternal order was her charge, yet the free-willed forces of disorder always challenged her. All Egyptians had to help her maintain balance, harmony, and order to ensure that the cycles continued in a manner that gave life and resisted disorder—resulting in minimum destruction and maximum creation and growth.

The Seasons

Ancient Egypt had three seasons. Each of these seasons had four months. Each month had exactly thirty days—totaling 360 days a year.

A new year began when the star Sirius first became visible above the eastern horizon in a brief moment just before sunrise. Sirius is a first magnitude star on a line coming off of the three stars in the Belt of Orion toward the horizon. This began the first season of *Akhet*, the season of *inundation* when the Nile overran its banks and flooded the land. Akhet would have been the fertilizing season. This season began in early September when the star Sirius rose in ancient times (now Sirius rises in early August because of the precession of the equinoxes). The season ended in early January. The next season was *Proyet* (also *Peret*). This was the season for planting. It ran roughly between early January and early May (in ancient times). The third season was *Shemu* (also *Shomu*). This season ran from early May to early September. This was the harvest time.

Since there are 365 days in a year but only 360 days in the Egyptian calendar, there was a wonderfully imaginative period of five days known as the "Days Out of Time" (*epagomenal* days). There is a fascinating legend regarding these days. It goes something like this: At the beginning of time, the Sky (goddess Nut) was married to the Earth (god Geb). But the Sky fell in love with the Sun (Ra) and copulated with the Light. When

Earth discovered this, he cursed his wife, saying, "You may not give birth in any month of the year." In this way Earth hoped to prevent Sky from bringing forth the children of the Sun, children of the Light. The Sky then copulated with an aspect of the Sun called the "Love and Word" (Thoth–Hermes, the "heart and tongue of Ra"). The Love and Word of the Sun made a bet with the Moon and won, receiving a seventeenth part of the Moon's light. Well, a seventeenth part of the Moon's monthly thirty–day cycle is five days! Now these five days were outside of all of the Moon's months; in this way the Sky was able to bear her children outside of any month, thereby circumventing the Earth's curse. Sky gave birth to five Egyptian gods during these special days, one on each day: Osiris on the first day, and then Horus the Elder (both of these gods were the offspring of her love coupling directly with the Sun), then Set (the offspring of her jealous husband, Earth), then Isis and her sister Nephthys (the offspring of her love coupling with the Love and Word of the Sun).

Every four years the ancient ones added a sixth day, as do we in the month of February.

5

THE TEMPLES

There were many temples, but Edgar Cayce's tales speak mostly of two—the Temple of Sacrifice and the Temple Beautiful. We have already read some highlights of these two, but now we look at them in more detail.

He explained: "There was the establishing of those temples called Temple of Sacrifice and the Temple Beautiful. Those activities might be represented (though quite crudely) in what we have today as surgical hospitals and the higher states of learning. For the fires of nature in disease were stopped, are stopped, by separating of the body from growths, from deformities, from the various characters of activities upon the physical body which warp the mind, putting it in those positions of being submerged or in contingence to relative relationships. Just so were the activities of the Temple Beautiful, in which there were found the expressions in music, in body–development, in the mind-training for the presenting of channels for specific activity. The Temple of Sacrifice was a physical experience, while the Temple Beautiful was rather of the mental—in which there was the spiritualization—not idolizing, but crystallizing of activities or services to a special purpose—or specializing in preparation for given offices of activity."

The First Creation had gotten so out of control that many souls had become entangled in distorted forms of matter and their minds locked in illusions and confusions. Much of the work at the beginning of the Second Creation was focused on cleaning up this mess and establishing an ideal material body for the children of God to incarnate properly. This was both a physical challenge and a mental one.

When asked to "please describe the ceremonies in the Temple by which the human-animal combinations could in a life-time lose a tail, or change a paw to a hand, or an animal body or head to a human," Cayce replied, "Surgery—as we would call it now." The questioner followed up with this: "How much transformation from the animal to the human could be completed in a life-time?" Cayce replied, "Little, save in the offspring—by the change of thought, diet, *and* the operative forces. In the third or fourth generation it was completed."

In a reading for the reincarnation of a key person in the ancient Temple of Sacrifice, Cayce told this marvelously revealing story (it is edited for ease of reading and clarity on the issues):

"We have those experiences as recorded here [ethereal Akashic records] of the entity in the earth's plane during that experience in the activities in the Temple of Sacrifice, in the Temple Beautiful. In giving that as we find here, something of the surroundings becomes necessary as the background, that there may be an individual understanding of the activities of the entity, of how healed and of what, and the application of same in the experiences in the present. During that experience of man's advent into materiality, and to the entity individually, there was the losing of appendages, of attachments arising from the injection of the souls of individuals into animal influences—or partially of animal bodies."

Human mythology records many creatures that have mixed bodies—*centaurs*: half human, half horse; *fauns*: half human, half goat; *mermaids*: half woman, half fish; *gorgon*: half man, half serpent; *sphinx*: half man or woman, half lion; *gryphons*: head and body of a lion, face of a human, and the wings of an eagle; *satyr* and *satyress*: young humans that have horse ears, tails, and legs; *Minotaur*: half human, half bull; *harpies*: body of a human with the legs and wings of a bird; *mantygre*: the body of a tiger and the head of an old man with horns; *manticore*: the body and legs of a lion, the head of a man, and the tail of a scorpion or dragon; *demi-gods*: half god, half human with Heracles and Achilles being examples.

Cayce continued with his reading:

"This entity was among those of the natives that had been among the Sun Worshipers, of the various forms of animal matter as used as a portion of the associations and surroundings. It was born of those that were among the rulers of the land that took unto self the beings that were part human (as we would know today) and part of other beings—or animals, see? Hence the desires that are manifested in individuals' activities gave expression of them in the entity then as *Ipt-Sa*, the name called or indicated, meaning 'that one that would be cleansed.' This to be sure became the name *after* the dedication of self and the losing of those influences that made for the beauty of consorting with individuals or of man in those individual experiences.

"These in the activities of the Temple of Sacrifice were removed first by the mental, the physical dedicating of the self to an individual purpose; that of enabling others, of bringing to others that necessary and the necessity of the purifying of body, the purifying of mind, the purifying of intent, the dedicating of purpose, the dedicating of activity for the pure relationships with activities among those that had dedicated their lives to an activity that would present the body as a channel, a means, a manner, a way of being not only as represented in the Temple Beautiful as a *body*—beautiful but as a service also—of every nature, of every character.

"Hence we find the entity going through the individual activity in that experience, and its purposes being that there might be—as has been indicated for others—the glory of the Lord, that it might be made manifested in the individual's activity in and before others.

"The manners then of cleansing:

"First in the Temple of Sacrifice it became necessary, as indicated, for the signifying of the individual's desire, by its activity of purifying of self through those days of purification—that later became exemplified in many of the forms of religious ceremony of purifying and preparation that there might be put away from the body and from the mind those things that would lead or direct or tend to make for the associations with the old self. Then came the periods of passing through the testings that were set as near as possible to the fires of nature, that there might be the emptying as through those experiences that had made for those very influences that brought about the lower forces in the experience of the body. So with this body, passing through those periods; and then the anointing with the oil, the passing through or raising of the vibratory forces within self, the activities and assistance through the priest and the activities that made for the burning of same as it were upon the alters of nature.

"Hence the entity also from those periods of its activity rose to that position in the Temple Beautiful service, which was that organ or that body or that place of service and activity in which there were the trainings as it were of the individuals, from the desires of the natures of flesh itself, purified by the service and activity, through rote—yet the very influences that raised within the bodies that had been brought for purifying the regeneration by the fires of these, by the fires of purification.

"Hence the aid the entity gave was in classifying, aiding in analyzing the individuals' intent and purpose in their selecting their service in their relationships to their fellow man, after their dedication, after their purification, after their activities of the periods sufficient for qualifying (if we would use such a term in relationship to same) the individual for its service in those chosen fields that were pointed out by the entity. As has been indicated, some were teachers, some were ministers, some were healers, some were those in what are known in the present as the trades, the artisans that made for the preparation of material things for the convenience, for the betterment of the individual surroundings. All of these the entity aided in, assisted in, in the Temple Beautiful, to select as it were, to counsel with those from every walk and every clime, from every activity, that those who came for offering themselves.

"Hence as has been given the entity, there are in the present those abilities for the analyzing of individuals' purposes, individuals' aims, individuals' desires. These the entity may assist best in what in the present parlance may be termed as a psychoanalyzing, using thine own material philosophy, thine own material physiology, thy own material philosophies of life itself for aiding in the psychological and psycho-pathic and psychiatric manners of setting individuals in their proper sphere. Yet as in those experiences in Egypt, so in the present, first there must come the purifying in self, in the ridding of self of the conditions in body, the conditions in the mental attitude, that there may be rid from the system, from the consciousness, that which would hinder the entity from carrying on; preventing the entity from returning again as to the fleshpots of Egypt, to the desires of satisfying or gratifying the natures that are of the earth–earthy, of the flesh–fleshly, that are of the human natures as is termed from the correlation with the animal influences or forces. All hate, all malice, all those things that would make for a detrimental influence, those that would turn aside an eye single or service to an eye single of purpose in becoming aware of the love that the Creative Force bears within the experience for each individual that the will of the Father is that no soul shall perish but that with each temptation, with each trial, with each test, even as ever, in the present there remains the advocate with the Father, that there may be no harm, no impurity, no darkness at all in the soul, in the desire, in the purpose of those that seek to know His face, to those that follow even as afar. They, too, as this entity, may purify themselves.

"Then as in the fires of nature, or in the blood of the Lamb that taketh away the sins of the world. While these come also in the fleshly temptations, they come as trials, yet may they not even as with He, be turned into benedictions, turned into blessings to all that seek to know His face? So then may the entity, known even as Ipt–Sa, that the God of justice, the God of mercy, the God of purity, is ever in that way and manner that if there will be less and less of self, more and more for the glorifying of the Father through the Son, those blessings come that become as the fulfilling of those purposes. For while the purposes in each individual attainment are not self alone, but in the purifying of self does the greater opportunity become for each soul, for each entity to be the greater channel, the greater blessing to others."

After Cayce finished the above reading for the reincarnated Ipt–Sa, she asked him two important questions:

"For what purpose did I enter this appearance?" He answered, "As has been indicated, for the fulfilling of that within self that the soul might find the way, even through the flesh, even though under the bondage of those things that were of self–indulgence and self–gratification, that same might be cleansed even as in the present that patience, long–suffering, may be a portion of the individual experience without thought of error, of strife, of turmoil, of any nature, without longings even for those things that appear just beyond the reach, that gratify only the flesh alone."

She then asked, "How may I better use my present abilities that I may turn these influences into those material concepts for the betterment or soul development of self, as well as for the aid, counsel and strength that may be given to those who seek through these channels?" He replied, "As has been indicated. More and more learn to use every influence within the grasp of the entity's concept, that less and less of self, less and less of self-indulgence, less and less of self-glory, more and more that the glory of the Father through the Son may be made manifest in the experiences of self in its relationships with its fellow man. These the manners, these the ways, as has been indicated."

Here is another soul that experienced the Temple of Sacrifice: "The entity was among those of the group that came into Egypt. With the establishing of the Temple of Sacrifice, the entity set about to use the tenets and truths that had been a part of the experience in Atlantis, of the children of the Law of One. These were used as suggestions in those periods, with the elements and drugs used as sedatives, for activities in the Temple of Sacrifice or for the surgery, in preparing individuals for definite services, by the removal of those things that would cause one to become different-minded because of the relationships to the activities in a pre-existence or pre-period of materiality."

Here follows a long Cayce discourse given to a reincarnated priestess from an ancient Egyptian temple (again, it has been edited for ease of reading and clarity on the issues):

"In the Temple Beautiful there was the music for the ones presenting themselves to be offered upon the altars for the cleansing of that which would prevent them from—what would be termed today—consecrating their lives to church through the baptismal service; though in that baptism it was by the altar first for the removing of those things that made for the carnal influence.

"The entity then was among those who had been led in, or through the first experience of being offered on the altar and being presented by the priestess or the activity of that one in the temple so offering same made for the obeisance, as would be called, in pleading for the aid to assist self. It was robed in the garments of the Temple itself, in what later became the character of Egyptian robes of that particular period, made from the linens of the papyrus and the lotus combined and covered with the combination of the colors—purple and white—used as the robes of those so offering themselves. In such a scene was the meeting made.

"As to the activities produced in the entity itself, there was rather the turn to the material abilities in controlling the animal force such as to present same in the music that aided in the worship or service in the Temple's activities later.

"Were each soul today to get rather the vision that the self in life, or Life itself, is the manifestation of the Spirit of God in the earth, and that its soul, the entity's soul, the companion of that Spirit in the material world, each soul would get rather the vision of its own abilities in the earth, if it will but make the use of, the application of, the manifestations of that spirit that will make for the growth of its own soul, the heritage of each and every soul that enters into the earth's plane.

"As may be rightly gathered from that given concerning this entity, this soul, in its unconscious use of life it gave to man such that has been the aid, the help, the companion throughout the years, the ages since.

"In the conscious use of these same influences, with being directed by those that had found—as it were—the relationship between the Creative influence and the creature and its brother, the creature and its Maker, the entity so applied self as to bring harmony into the *kingdom* over which the entity ruled. Not as ruled by might, rather by love. Hence the instruments used were of the reed or flute, that is known in the present, and made the hearts of many merry; not as of those that would gratify the satisfying of carnal forces, but rather that as awakened within each those abilities for the expressing of—in its physical body—the music of the spirit in its activity in and through the body. So in the present, as the experiences of self that go to make up its abilities to quell within the breast of many a tortured soul or many a tortured body that wars within itself with the spirit that is willing and the flesh is weak with its own desires, that as may be given by the entity in word or by the music will bring something to each of the vision that came to those that were under the entity's supervision or kingdom in that sojourn.

"Before that the entity, we find, was in that land now known as the Egyptian, during those periods when there had been turmoils and strifes in the land not only from the internal rebellions following the banishment of the Priest—in the activities of the moral and religious life—but with the return of the Priest. And with the turmoils and strife that arose from that gathering together of so many of those, even from the Indian, the Arabian, the Atlantean, the Abyssinian lands (Abyssinia is Ethiopia today), the entity—with all of these, as a native in the Egyptian land—brought those things that pertain to body adornments, that deal with the activities of those that prepared for the purifications in the temples of Sacrifice. Hence the entity then was in the name Apt-hen, or—meaning, as would be the interpretation in the present—'Where there is life, there is hope.'

"So, the activities in that experience have brought, do bring, the adherence in the present to those things or vibrations that make for the alterations in the activities of the body—as was given through the tenets of the Priest to whom the entity came as a student—in raising the Creative Energies from within that may find their expressions in the attributes of the physical body, through the *sensing* of same in the emotions that are created in a physical body. For the entity aided the Priest during those periods when the regeneration of the body came to him through the casting aside, as it were, of the years of toil and strife through which the body of Ra-Ta itself had passed; and the entity rejuvenated itself with that body in the experience; rising in the latter portion of the sojourn to those conditions wherein it was given entire *charge of* the activities in the *temples* of Sacrifice, or the temples of initiation—where there were those things carried on in the tombs that were prepared for such during those periods of activity.

"The entity then gained, and in the present those things of every nature or character of the orient have their periods of influence; as also do odors, colorings, vibrations that are created by these influences in the experiences of the *mental* mind.

"Hence, as to the abilities in the present and that to which the entity may attain, and how, in giving the expressions of that the entity may receive through its inner self, owing to its regeneration, owing to its activity in that particular sojourn in Egypt, may be said to be that to which the entity may turn within itself to find that it may give to its fellow man for thought, study, development, in the *application* of same in their own experience.

"Then, whether in song, in writing, in verse, in painting, those things that partake of the *higher vibrations* in expressions are the *fields* of activity for the entity in the present.

"Keep in self that which was given in the holy mount of initiation; that what is constructive and of spiritual import must find expression in aiding others to find themselves and their relationships to the Creative Forces—or God."

This next edited discourse gives us some important insights and also appears to prophesy Cayce's return as a liberator to the world.

"Then began what may be truly termed the first national or nation *spirit* of a peoples; for with the divisions, rather than this causing a dispersing of ideals or a dividing up of interests, it *centralized* the interests; for these were being guided by a ruler or king whose authority was not questioned any more, nor were the advisories of the priest questioned, who was acting in rather the capacity of preparing for this very spirit to manifest itself in the way of the national emblems, the national ideas, that stood for the varied activities of not only individuals or groups, but for the general masses. Hence there began the first preparation for what has later become that called The Great Pyramid, that was to be the presentation of that which had been gained by these peoples through the activities of Ra-Ta, who *now* was known as Ra [in another reading Cayce said he was now called Ra-Ta Ra, in some cases, simply Ra]; for with the entering in of Hermes *with* Ra—who came as one of the peoples from the mount to which these peoples had been banished—and the raising of that one who had been condemned with the priest in banishment to one that was to be without question the queen [Is-ris, Ra-Ta Ra's companion], or the advisor to all of her own peoples, there was brought the idea of the preservation of these, not only for those in the present but for the generations that were to come in the experiences and experiences throughout that period, until the changes were to come again in the earth's position that would make for, as it had in this inundation that brought about Ra–Ta's coming in the experience from the gods in the Caspian and the Caucasian mountains, that had brought this change in the peoples. Hence under the authority of Ra, and Hermes as the guide, or the actual (as would be termed in the present) constructing or construction architect with the priest or Ra giving the directions—and those of Isis [Is–ris' new association with the goddess, thus her name was now Is–ris Isis, in some cases simply Isis] in the form of the advisor for the laying in of those things that would present to those peoples the *advancement* of the portion of man, or woman, to her position in the activities of the human race or human experience, these changed the position or attitude of these particular peoples as to the position that was held by woman in her relations to the developing of the conditions that either were to be national, local, or individual; for not only does this become then that upon which man depends for those advancements or advents into the material activities, but the nourishing of, the maintaining of, that to which its (the man's) ideals are to be turned in their activity when they arise at that period when expressions are to be given to the active forces in the material activities.

"This, then, made for an *endowing* of this body Iso, or Isis, [Is–ris Isis] to the position of the first goddess . . . "

Here Cayce was talking about Is–ris Isis but referring to her child with Ra–Ta, named Iso (pronounced *ice-o*). Somehow this now discarnate child's spirit was still being a part of the mother's flesh. A strange concept, but the women I interviewed about this had no problem with it, telling me that having conceived and carried a body in their wombs and then nursed it for so long, it never felt like the baby's body was not a part of their own body. Somehow, disincarnate Iso's flesh was still a part of her mother' body. As to their spiritual connection, this was so tight that Cayce occasionally called them by names that combined their two names: Isi–so and Iso–Isis.

Let's return to Cayce's reading.

"This, then, made for an *endowing* of this body Iso, or Isis, [Is–ris Isis] to the position of the first goddess [in materiality] that was so crowned, and there was given then that place that was to be sought by others that would gain counsel and advice even from the priest, gained access through that of Isis to the Throne [of God] itself. Not that it rose above the authority of the king, but for that developing necessary for the activities of the woman in those spheres of activity in this particular development.

"Then began the laying out of the pyramid and the building of same, the using of those forces that made for the activity of bringing then from those very mountains where there had been those places of refuge that which had been begun to establish these, not only into that which would remain as the place for receiving that which had been offered in the Temple Beautiful on the various altars of the activities of an individual's innate self, but to be the place of initiation of the initiates that were to act in the capacity of leaders in the various activities through this period. This building, as we find, lasted for a period of what is termed now as one hundred years. It was formed according to that which had been worked out by Ra-Ta in the mount as related to the position of the various stars that acted in the place about which this particular solar system circles in its activity, going towards what? That same name as to which the priest was banished—the constellation of Libra, or to Libya were these people sent. Is it not fitting, then, that these must return? As this priest may develop himself to be in that position, to be in the capacity of a *liberator* of the world in its relationships to individuals in those periods to come; for he must enter again at that period, or in 1998.

"In those changes then brought about in these relationships, those who had acted in the capacity of the go-betweens, or the establishing of the closer relationships with Ra-Ta and those acting in the capacity of the leader, or of the council, and of the king himself—then we find the establishing of the king's household; then we find begins the bodily adornment, and the first preparation for such was of the linens that have not as yet been attained in this particular period, since that as was set by those who established this linen development from the cottons, and the hemp, and the papyrus flowers and lotus flowers of this particular period.

"In and with these became the preparing of the Temple Beautiful for a more perfect place of preservation of those things that were to make known later in the minds of peoples, as the changes came about in the earth, the rise and fall of the nations were to be depicted in this same temple that was to act as an interpreter for that which had been, that which is, and that which is to be, in the material plane."

The following reading is for a fascinating, reincarnated Atlantean who had sought to sojourn in Egypt.

"The entity was among those that set sail for the Egyptian land, but entered rather into the Pyrenees and what is now the Portuguese, French and Spanish land. And there *still* may be seen in the chalk cliffs there in Calais [Galice?] the activities, where the marks of the entity's followers were made, as the attempts were set with those to create a temple activity to the follower of the law of One.

"Then in the name Apex-l [pronounced *apex-el*], the entity lost and gained. Lost during those periods when there were the turmoils and strife that brought about the necessity for the sojourning from the land and the entering into the others. Gained when there was the establishing of the associations with those that had built up the Egyptian land. And, as will be seen from those that may yet be found about Alexandria, Egypt, the entity may be said to have been the first to begin the establishment of the library of knowledge in Alexandria; ten thousand three hundred before the Prince of Peace entered Egypt for His first initiation there [10,300 BC]. For, read you, 'He was crucified also in Egypt.'"

This crucifixion comment is likely a reference to the young Jesus' initiation with the young John the Baptist while they were hiding from Herod in Egypt, prior to their ministry in Palestine. More on this will be covered in the chapter on the Great Initiate.

Here's another interesting discourse from Cayce for an initiate of the temples:

"The entity was among those who were prepared through the activities in the Temple of Sacrifice and through the Temple Beautiful . . . for its activities as a ministry to those in other lands.

"Hence in the present may be seen those influences, those forces in which the entity in its study, in its reading, reads of, desires to read of, is a portion of, those things having to do with peoples of other lands. Also the desire for travel that has been innate in the entity; the ability for depicting that which has been told the entity of other cities, of other places, of other lands. The entity is able to and capable of visualizing same, from those experiences through which the entity passed in that particular land.

"Then the entity was of the *natives* of the land, being among those of the native king's household—the king who was dethroned when Arart was made the ruler in the land. In the name then Ah–pet–et, the entity gained throughout. For in its whole activity there was the preparation and the activity in ministering to the needs of others throughout its sojourn.

"As to the abilities of the entity in the present, then, and that to which it may attain and how:

"Hold fast to that you have set as your ideal throughout your experiences in the earth sojourns. For you have seen the activities in Egypt for the ministry to the fellow man, for the hope of that as might be built in the experience of each individual soul for its relationship to the Creative Forces.

"You have seen and been active in the ministry and interpreting for your fellow man in the 'city in the hills and in the plains' [a region in ancient Persia].

"These you have seen confirmed in that you did learn in the hills [of Judea] when *Jesus* passed by! Keep, then, the faith; knowing that in Him is the light, the way. Those things that you minister in your associations with your fellow man, *temper* them with mercy in judgment as you have seen and heard throughout your experiences in the earth. For your star has not set but *arises* in Him, for the way is clear before you!

"Ready for questions.

"Q: What is my seal or emblem and its interpretation?

"A: As would be the globe with the markings of the land, and the Cross that leads the way, with the light of the dove of peace that was the manner and means of making known to the world His reception as the light of the world through the Cross—as you have known and seen. Your colors, then, would naturally be the blues . . . and the red edging here and there. . . . These are those that make for vibrations in your activities that make for an understanding or a way through which vibrations may arise. Also the odors that would make for the raising of the vibrations would be lavender and orris root [roots of Iris germanica, Iris florentina, and Iris pallida, all used in herbal medicine]. For these were those of your choice in the Temple of Sacrifice. They were also your choice when you did walk with those who carried the spices to the tomb [to anoint the crucified body of Jesus]. As to the flowers, these would be the star of the field—or the pointed star in the field, which is the icon of the Egyptian goddess Seshat." [Cayce is referring to a class of flowers known generally as Starflowers. There are several genera and species of Starflowers; all have the appearance of a star. The *Trientalis borealis* has the unusual feature of being based on sevens: seven leaves, seven petals, and seven sepals—which fits with the sevens in the ancient temples, including the body temple's seven spiritual centers. The *Ornithogalum arabicum* is called the Star-of-Bethlehem. For an image of the goddess Seshat, see illustration 25 and illustration 1 opposite the title page.]

"These are the emblems that mean much to you.

"Also music, rhythm, sound, color; these have their vibrations in you; as the sound not of High C, but those that would change from the flats to the sharps that *make* for the variation between the C and its chord in A.

"Q: In what capacity was I in the Temple Beautiful?

"A: As one initiated there. Not as a dweller there, but as one initiated there for a special service in the *whole* of the Temple Service—or of the regime service.

"Q: What is the best time for me to meditate?

"A: This is as a choice. As comes to self. In the early morning hours, or eight to nine in the evening.

"Q: Whose choice was it that my daughter was in the Temple in the Galilean experience?

"A: Her own!

"Q: For what purpose did I come to the earth plane at this time?

"A: To give greater expression of that gained in those experiences that are crystallized in the present activities.

"Q: Any other advice?

"A: Keep self in that which has been set before you, as your purpose, as your desire. For, as indicated, you may see in this the fulfilling of much you have experienced in your activities through the earth. Let your heart be glad in Him; for He hath given you hope, light, and understanding."

The Inner Temple

Let's now move on to some of the methods used in the ancient temples to advance our spiritual awareness, raise our bodily vibrations, expand our minds, and lift our souls to higher levels of existence. To do so, we must move from the outer temples and enter into the inner temple of our bodies. As the disciple Paul once asked, "Do you not know that your body is a temple of the Holy Spirit, which is *in* you, which you have as a gift from God?" (I Corinthians 6:19, my italics) And as Patanjali wrote in the Yoga Sutras, our body is not simply designed for physical activity; it is also wonderfully designed for metaphysical activity. It has pathways through which the life force travels and may be made to raise life and consciousness. It has seven spiritual centers in the form of spinning wheels of energy and illuminating lotuses of unfolding wisdom. This was known in the ancient temples and was used to shift us from a physical focus to a metaphysical one. Let's explore these.

Cayce spoke about the seven tones and seven colors, and how they correlate to the seven spiritual centers in our bodies. The seven-note scale of Western music is *do-re-mi-fa-so-la-ti*, and corresponds respectively to the charkas: root, navel, solar plexus, heart, throat, crown, and third eye (notice that Cayce instructed us that the crown chakra was the sixth and the third eye was the seventh, because, according to him, the true kundalini pathway is in the shape of a cobra in the *striking* position, revealing that the energy rises up the spine to the base of the brain, then over to the center of the brain and the crown, and then, after uniting with universal energy through the crown, flows over to the frontal lobes of our brain and to our third eye).

The seven-color spectrum is *red-orange-yellow-green-blue-indigo-violet*, and corresponds to the chakras in the same order as the musical notes, from the root to the third eye.

Cayce explained that by chanting *Ar-r-r—Ou-u-u—Ur-r-r* we altered the color and tone of our radiant presence. He stated that each of us emanates an aura and tonal sound. Cayce said that, despite our present encasement, you and I might awaken this ancient "light-bearer" portion of our being by toning "Ar-r-r-r-r-AR."

Let's take a moment and intone these ancient chants while imagining the color and tonal shift in our bodies—from root to brain, from dense to light, from earthly to heavenly. Let's *feel* ourselves—as Cayce said we did back in ancient Egypt—"losing even the association of the body." As we sound this, we lift our soul and mind above the physical body into lighter, higher vibrations and radiant expression. The chant transitions from *a-a-ar-ar* in the lower portions of our body to *r-r-r-r* in the chest and neck, to AR-AR-AR, which is a bit higher pitch and slightly louder, in our head and brain: *Ar-r-r-r-AR, Ar-r-r-r-AR, Ar-r-r-r-AR*. Feel yourself rising, lifting, and becoming more buoyant and expanding beyond the body.

From very ancient times and in many parts of the world, chanting for spiritual, mental, and physical health, well-being, and enlightenment has been practiced. Some believe that certain sounds *transcend* the influences of the material physical world and were the sounds of the original creation. An example would be the classic OM sound. Such sounds are believed to have latent power within them that can be released when sounded with the right intention.

Sound is vibration. Vibrations can be raised or lowered. They can be good or bad vibrations. The human voice is a vibration device. It can make sounds that lift and fill the heart and mind with hope and spiritual ecstasy. The objective of chanting or incanting is to raise the vibrations of the body to lift and carry the heart and mind to higher levels of consciousness and enlightenment.

In Genesis, chapter two, the Lord God breathed the breath of life into us, and we became living souls. In chanting, *moving* the breath of life shifts the life force of the body. The life force within us is sometimes called the élan vital and kundalini. When we use the breath to vibrate our vocal cords with specific sounds, we affect the life force of the body, and since the mind inhabits the body, we affect the mind too. As we change the sound, we move the life force from lower vibrations to higher, from lower areas of our body and mental focus to higher. As the molecules in ice become fluid when heated, and if heating continues, they become vaporous, rising from their former solid state to a cloud-like expansiveness, light, ethereal condition, so good chanting can raise the cool, solid vibes of our predominant physical condition to the warm, vaporous vibes of a cloud-like spirit. In such a state our spirit is freed. It is freed from the weight and bonds of the physical and allowed to expand into higher levels of awareness.

The physical body is uniquely designed for both physical activity and higher mental, spiritual activity. There are three primary sound chambers in the human body: the abdominal chamber in belly area, the cardiopulmonary chamber in the chest, and the cranial chamber in the skull. Sounds can be directed toward these chambers and the resonance of these sounds changes the vibrations of atoms, cells, and organs. These sounds *also* affect the *mind-body* connection, raising consciousness throughout the *nervous* system.

Cayce chanting methods use the voice and breath to vibrate select sounds in these three chambers and the seven spiritual centers to improve health, well-being, and enhance enlightenment.

Chanting is *inner sounding* rather than outer singing. The sound of the voice is directed inward rather than outward, as one does when singing. Directing the sounds to the three major chambers with resonance and in a drowning manner, one can truly affect a change in vibrations and consciousness.

As we've seen, Cayce gave insights into how chanting was used in the ancient Egyptian temples, particularly the Temple Beautiful. He said to use an incantation or chant that "carries self deeper—deeper—to the seeing, feeling, experiencing of that image in the creative forces of love, entering into the Holy of Holies within you. As self feels or experiences the raising of this, see it disseminated through the *inner* eye to that which will bring the greater understanding in meeting every condition in the experience of the body. Then, listen to the music that is made as each center of your own body responds to that new Creative Force."

Cayce's chanting is God-centered, meaning that it seeks to attune the chanter to the Divine Source of Life. He taught that such attunement naturally results in greater health, happiness, well-being, and enlightenment.

Chanting begins by *sounding* in the abdominal belly chamber of the body—the root, navel, and solar plexus chakras. Then the sounding shifts to cardiopulmonary chest chamber—the heart chakra and even into the throat chakra. Finally, the sounding is to move into the skull and head chamber—the frontal lobe of the brain, the third-eye, and crown chakras.

The chants are not just attempting to raise and transform bodily vibrations. Each chant attempts to lift and carry the mind and spirit to higher, more harmonic levels of attunement to the Divine, to that Oneness, within which all life exists. Usually, the first series of chants are devoted to raising the vibrations of the body; then, as the body energizes, the next round of chanting lifts the consciousness or mind from lower areas to higher, even into the Infinite Consciousness of God's mind.

For example, when chanting Cayce's *ar-e-om* chant, the *ar* sounds are directed into the abdominal chamber and the lower chakras—like this: *ar-ar-rrr*. As the sound changes to the *e*, one directs the vibrations of the voice to the upper portion of the abdominal chamber to the solar plexus area in the center of the torso, like this: *eeee*. Then, as we shift to the *o* sounds, we move our minds and vocal vibrations to the heart chakra in the cardiopulmonary chamber and to the throat chakra, where the voice box is, like this: *oooo*. The next stage is a bit different from most classic yoga teachings, which would direct the sounds straight up to the crown of the head. Rather, Cayce instructed us to move the sounding to the base of the brain, then over to the center of the brain, and *ultimately* to the large frontal lobe of the human brain. For example, in the third phase of the chant these sounds would shift gradually from *oooo* in the chest and throat to *uuuu* at the base and center of the brain, and then shift easily into the *mmmm* sound in the frontal lobe. This area affects the master endocrine gland of the human body, the pituitary, with the hypothalamus adjoining it. Hold the *mmmm* sound and feel your body and mind shifting from their normal, everyday condition to a more centered and divinely attuned condition.

Thus the Cayce chant would be: *ar-ar-rrr– eeee–oooo– uuuu–mmmm.* In order to get the full effect of this power incantation, one needs to take a deep breath and save some breath for the last sound, which is the most important sound, because it awakens the highest spiritual centers.

You will need to take a three-level breath. Let me explain: In order to fill your lungs, you need to inhale near your diaphragm by expanding your belly; then inhale further by expanding your chest and then, still further, by lifting your shoulders as you inhale. Now your lungs are full. As you sound the chant, control the release of your breath by controlling your diaphragm—gradually passing the breath through your vocal cords. With practice you'll be able to do a good, long chant.

An often overlooked but a very important part of chanting is the silence that follows the sounding. Don't immediately inhale and chant again. Use the silence between chants to imagine and feel that your body, mind, and soul are rising to higher levels of vibration and consciousness. Ultimately, chanting leads to the deep silence of oneness with the indivisible Source of Life. There you abide silently as you are imbued with health, well-being, and enlightenment.

Cayce said that it is helpful if you find a regular place and time to enjoy the benefits of chanting. It won't require anything fancy or much time. All you need is your voice and good, clear intentions. As the Eastern teaching states, "The right method is one wing of the bird of paradise, the other is the right heart—and the bird does not fly with only one wing."

The Birthing Center

We cannot leave the temples without addressing another of their primary services: creating bodies for incarnating souls to inhabit. After all, it was a time for repopulating the earth and nation building—they needed babies, and lots of them.

Practices in the temples were much stricter than those in centers operated in the palaces. Young mothers began their preparation a year prior to conceiving—actually, they had been training for this service all their young lives, but it began in earnest a year before conception. The aim was to become the most ideal tabernacle for growing the most ideal body-temple for the incarnating souls—and to attract the most ideal soul! What a task! But all the young women and their handlers took this mission very seriously and with joy and celebration of their opportunity to be of important service to the community.

Males, too, were prepared long before conception. Their thoughts, attitudes, vibrations, and motivations were carefully developed to bring them to the moment of conception with the most ideal contribution possible.

Conception was to occur without any sensuality or sexual gratification. This was an important part of the overall sacred process for attracting higher-minded souls, conceiving the most ideal bodies, and growing them into the most ideal men and women for service to the community and the greater good. Cayce explained that when conception occurred without sensual gratification as the motivating influence, then the body conceived did not have that weakness in it.

The selected males and females were brought together in a ceremony that accentuated the gift of life, of beauty, and the joy of service. Linens, lights, candles, music, even dance imbued the union with higher motives and purposes. Once the conception had occurred, the two were separated; the woman would spend the next nine months with other women in the most ideal surroundings possible in an effort to keep her thoughts, vibrations, and emotions idyllic: physically, mentally, and spiritually. The birthing process was also as carefully arranged to provide an ambiance of peace, joy, and the celebration of life. Once born, the child stayed with the mother for a period sufficient to insure that the body was properly growing and then weaned from the mother's milk. There were no family units as we have them today. The children were raised in a collective child-raising portion of the temple with trained overseers and instructors. As a child grew and manifested its innate characteristics and propensities, he or she was guided into the appropriate "schools" or training areas of the temples.

The mothers and fathers also had a specific protocol to follow. Once conception occurred, the woman did not copulate again until a minimum of three months after the birth of the baby. However, if she desired to channel a second baby, then she would not copulate for a minimum of a year after weaning the first baby! In that period of time the temple workers would help her rebuild her body before conceiving and gestating another fetus in her. They would also help her reestablish her higher ideals and vibrations. Cayce once noted that many of the practices in ancient temples would be considered today to be extreme trials and sacrifices.

Later on, a social movement toward love-bonded couples developed, and they, too, were permitted to join in the procedures at the birthing centers and were allowed to raise their offspring in quarters assigned to their nuclear family (not extended family, that came much later). Even love-bonded couples had to follow the temple rules for sexual relations, conception, and gestation and eventually submit their weaned children to the training centers under the oversight of the instructors.

These birthing centers were baby mills, designed to produce as many children as possible in as ideal circumstances as possible. Such was the source of the high level of citizenry in the very early period of ancient Egypt. The training centers were carefully arranged to accentuate the higher creative forces—developing artisans *and* ambassadors, mathematicians *and* laborers, and soldiers *and* caregivers. Much of this was lost as immersion into matter deadened the celestial awareness.

6

An Old Soul Returns

ncient Egyptians believed that the universe was orderly and that life was ultimately just and fair. The goddess Ma'at (pronounced ma-aht) personified this belief. When Ra rose from the hidden depths of the primordial sea (goddess Nun), he immediately gave life to Ma'at, whose name means "Truth." The early gods could not have come into existence until Truth (Ma'at) established order, balance, and harmony. The Egyptians believed that if Truth (Ma'at) had not been conceived, then chaos would have reigned and the primordial sea would have reclaimed the manifested universe into her unseen depths. It was also believed that the goddess Ma'at, like the Lord God in Genesis 2:7, breathed the breath of life into all the godlings and they became living beings.

So delicate is Ma'at's truth and order that her symbol in ancient Egypt was a feather. It was against her feather that every soul's heart was weighed on a scale. If the heart was lighter than her feather, then the soul could proceed to the heavens. If the heart was heavier than her feather, then the heart was thrown to a crocodile-headed god (Ammut) who devoured it, and the soul had to reincarnate and get a new, lighter heart. Thoth, the Keeper of the Records, was the feminine Ma'at's masculine counterpart. It was he who recorded in the Book of Life the results of the weighing of an individual soul's heart. (See illustration 26 for the ancient scene of weighing the heart.)

The Greeks called the force that consciously keeps order in the universe the "logos." Ma'at and Thoth were the Egyptian equivalent of the logos—the yin and yang of Truth. In a fascinating twist on this legend, Edgar Cayce identified Hermes (Thoth) and, by implication, Ma'at as the incarnations of the masculine and feminine principles of *the* Logos. He said that there was never a time when the Logos was not among the incarnate children of God, keeping order and tracking the progress of the children as they grew spiritually. According to Cayce, in Atlantis these two were Amilius and Lilith, in Egypt they were Hermes (Thoth) and Ma'at, and amazingly, in Palestine they were Jesus and his mother Mary. Yes, as strange as it may be, Cayce's readings of the Akashic records imply that the godling–spirit that was the legendary Lilith, the biblical Eve, and the Egyptian goddess Ma'at, was also Mary, the mother of Jesus. The god–spirit that was Jesus was also Amilius in Atlantis (companion to Lilith), biblical Adam (companion to Eve—St. Paul actually calls Jesus the "first Adam and the last Adam," 1 Corinthians 15:45), and Ma'at's masculine complement Hermes-Thoth as well as the son of Mary. Cayce's material says that there was never a time when there was not a Christ and a Christ–mass (Christmas), for God, His son, and all His angelic and godly helpers never left us; we left awareness of God and the heavenly hosts.

———

Like Hept–supht's Atlantean and Egyptian connection, Cayce told the story of another soul who spanned two cultures, those of Og and Egypt. However, before her main incarnations in Og and Egypt, her soul sojourned in the Black Land (Egypt) during the First Creation, tens of thousands of years *before* Ra-Ta and the Ararats. In fact, according to Cayce's tales, human souls began visiting earth some twelve *million* years ago—not in bodies, but rather as spirits and minds. Cayce pointed to a passage in the Bible in the Book of Job, " . . . when the morning stars sang together, and all the Sons of God shouted for joy" (Job 38:7), as referring to these ancient spirits and their early activities in this physical world. The "morning stars" gradually over millions of years pushed their life forces and consciousnesses deeper into matter, eventually to a degree of being *encased* in a dense physical body. But for millions of years they were able to come and go as they pleased, light beings of the entire cosmos.

When in pre–Ra–Ta Egypt, this soul was named Oual (pronounced *o– oo-al*, with a long "o," as in the sound of the letter, and then "oo" as in *boo*, then -al). She was among those that "set up the first of the pyramids that became more and more the monuments of endeavors and accomplishments of man." The pyramids that she and her people built were among the archaeological finds that Ra-Ta's teams excavated during their time in the Black Land. Cayce explained that Oual gained and lost in that very early experience. She gained through efforts to provide edifices to higher ideals and purposes but lost through selfish motives that grew as her acclaim grew and she slipped into self-aggrandizement and self-glorification.

Oual withdrew from that incarnation for a reflective sojourn in the unseen realms of the cosmos, leaving earth far behind. Once renewed and intent on doing a better job this time, she reappeared in the land of Og, which Cayce identified as "the American plateaus, or in north portion of now New Mexico, and such." He said that this land was some of oldest land on earth to remain above water. Wiser and more determined to be a selfless channel of blessings to others, she gave to the people of that area the concepts and strengths of the home and home's influence during one's incarnation. This helped the people gain by the consolidation of the strength that results from being a member of a family and of a tribe which is composed of strong families. However, Cayce explained that she did this not so much in the physical qualities of family life but in the *mental* abilities that result from knowing one is of a family and of a soul group. Remember, early beings were not as immersed in matter as we are today; life was much more mental, even psychic than it is today.

Her name in the Og incarnation was Uzld (pronounced *ooz-eld*). Cayce said that not only did she *contribute* to this world, but she also *learned* more about this world. She and her colleagues learned about metals, the minerals of the earth, and the uses for humanity's benefit while incarnate. Interestingly, Cayce told her that a man to whom she was closely involved in that incarnation was going to enter her present incarnation and that they would make a good married couple.

Her soul eventually withdrew from ancient Og, returning to sojourn in realms beyond earth, to reflect and renew. Then, she reincarnated at the time of the high priest Ra-Ta and the young king that we will learn more about in a later chapter. Amazingly, she was able to play key roles in both camps, for she was born of the household of the king but served in the Temple Beautiful as a close attendant to the high priest. Her name was Iskxe (pronounced *ice-kicks*). In that experience she "gained much in earth's forces, gained much in mental application, and this again brings much in the present experience of the entity," according to Cayce.

When asked to give her one of his soulful life readings, Cayce began by saying that he would give her those elements "concerning the development of the entity through the experiences in the earth's plane, the aid, the comfort, the entity may be to others, the development it may bring to itself in this sojourn." Then he proceeded to answer her many questions about the Egyptian incarnation with the high priest in the Temple Beautiful.

He said that in those various activities through which individuals passed in the temple, the individuals found their relationships: relationships to others and to God. Each individual is to come to know itself to be itself and yet one with the Whole. As a result of her training, trials, and preparation to be an assistant in the temple, she had come to know that the horrible acts or deeds committed by people to themselves and to others are to be judged and addressed as *acts* of horror rather than as of horrible souls. This allowed her to transform souls of evil and darkness into souls of the light and love, because she did not begin by weighing them down with guilt and regret. She and her colleagues had gained the power to make the life, the mind, the heart, *beautiful*—as the Temple Beautiful's name implied. These successes attracted many souls seeking to release the bonds upon their minds and hearts.

Cayce explained to her that this particular period in Egypt became the foundation of that taught by the Master, Jesus Christ. "With this understanding, with this association as may be now understood, can there be, could there be, would there be, one safer, one more secure, than in the teachings of, in the understanding of, in the comprehending of the teachings of the Master?" Cayce asked. The elements within the Master's teachings were put into physical beings in those ancient times in Egypt. And she put them into action and service to others in that experience. If, in this present incarnation, she would "again study to show herself approved unto Him, there would come the comprehension, the understanding, even as He has chosen her, and she has chosen Him."

This idea that the Christian Messianic Spirit was also in ancient Egyptian concepts and practices is not new. Many have noticed that the Egyptians were familiar with such relatively modern Christian concepts as the immortality of the soul, the Last Judgment, the Messiah, resurrection of the dead, Hades, Heaven, the oneness of God, prayer, sacrifices, the Logos, the Sabbath, circumcision, immersion, supper with God, the virgin birth of the Savior (Isis immaculately conceived Horus, who subsequently subdued Satan and redeemed the world of sin and suffering), and so on. There are many correlates between Christian teachings and ancient Egyptian ones.

She then asked Cayce to describe the process Iskxe (ice-kicks) used inside the Temple Beautiful and how she would experience this in her current incarnation. He replied, "Each came with that, as has been termed later by some sects, as their confession, and as these needs were expressed or made known to Iskxe, that as was necessary for their awakening was seen, known, felt by Iskxe. This may best be described as *feelings*, rather than words; for, as was said to many by the entity, as was said by the Master to some that would be healed, 'Go wash in the pool, then present yourself to the priest according to the law you have been taught in.' To another, 'Your sins be forgiven you, take up your bed, go into your own house.' To another, 'No man, Lord.' 'Neither do I condemn you, go and sin no more.' The *needs*, as is necessary for the acts of individuals in the present, to lay down or to put off a burden, may be *felt* by the entity, rather than being put into words; yet with the understanding does the entity know *innately* as to whether such a one is to read such and such prayer, is to wash in water to be clean, is to abstain from meats, or those of drug, or what not. Then, that seen is that as is *felt* as the message necessary for each individual who seeks in His name."

According to Cayce, Iskxe intuitively felt the process needed to cleanse and bring out the best in each initiate in the Temple Beautiful— and today she could awaken again to this ability.

From these high teachings, she and Cayce moved on to the more mundane aspects of her work in the temple. He explained that she did not go with the high priest into banishment but remained in the temple. It was not for her best, because she was so upset over the disgrace that fell upon the temple that she lorded over those who remained. But upon the return of the high priest, Cayce said she was "born anew"! He encouraged her to "keep her heart singing, for in your own heart is born anew those blessings you may be to so many! Keep inviolate those words as He points them out to you, for 'The way you know', the faults you know! Be patient, be kind, be gentle, with those who falter; for *many* lean upon you!"

She wondered aloud with the meditative Cayce if she had possibly been a man that incarnation because her deep feelings about that life were of the quality of a man's life. He replied, "You were a woman, a woman who was the ruler over men, and had many men as husbands!"

She asked Cayce which of the pyramids she was involved with building and where were they located (this would have been as Oual, not Iskxe). He replied that her pyramids were nearer the source of materials necessary to build a pyramid, closer to the hill region than the current pyramids in Giza and Saqqara. The source of the materials for pyramid building came from the limestone quarries that are found from Cairo to Luxor and the granite quarries in the Aswan region. In answering her question, Cayce made some interesting comments about several pyramids that have not yet been discovered, which are between the Sphinx and the Nile River. In one of these pyramids are stored the Atlantean records of prehistoric times. There is more on these records in the chapter on the three caches of prehistoric records.

7

HERMES:
A GOD AMONG HUMANS

One of the many fascinating characters mentioned in Edgar Cayce's psychic story of ancient Egypt is the legendary Hermes, often referred to as Hermes Thrice Majestic or Trismegistus (three times great).

————

There is a creation fable that comes from the wondrous "Isle of Flame" that is the ancient City of Hermes. It's about a young godling born out of a celestial lotus blossom (not a terrestrial one). This ethereal lotus emerged from the primordial darkness: its roots in a seething primal mud, its stem in the primordial water, its leaves and flower opening out to the celestial dew and the rays of the Sun of suns. The child in the lotus was Ra, the light that pierces the darkness. Young Ra began to weep because he knew he had to be expressed in multiplicity for the creation to occur—his one true light passing through a mystical prism revealing the many individual rays that compose the one Ray. The resulting multiplicity would make it difficult for the humans to find their singular life source and the eternal oneness. Out of the one came the many, and the many would have to intuit the existence of the one and the truth of ultimate oneness. Ra's tears created humankind.

It is written in the ancient texts: "You have made from your seed an embryo, and you have instilled this in the lotus by pouring the seminal fluid; you have deposited in the infinite expanse of the motionless sea (the infinite womb of Nun), condensed into a single form, and your inheritor takes his radiant birth in the aspect of a child."

This tale and its imagery began in Hermopolis, the City of Hermes.

Hermes is not an easy character to pinpoint in history, and Cayce focuses only on his activities as a divine builder and teacher in ancient Egypt.

Historically, the name Hermes is more closely associated with the Greek god who correlates to the Roman god Mercury, but not so clearly to an Egyptian god. Cayce appears to be referring to the Egyptian god Thoth, which is another Greek name for the Egyptian god Djehuti or Tehuti.

However, many in antiquity considered Tehuti, Thoth, Hermes, and Mercury to be one and the same being, with some cultural variations in the tales about this entity. Additionally, some identify the name Hermes with the vanishing Enoch of the Bible: "Enoch walked with God, and was no more, for God took him." (Genesis 5:18–24). And it is this connection that causes many to say that Cayce's readings pinpoint Hermes as one of the incarnations of the Logos (the messianic spirit of God among us). Interestingly, the ancient Greeks also associated Enoch with Hermes. And in the medieval manuscript *The Dicts and Sayings of the Philosophers*, ca. AD 1477, we find this passage: "Hermes was borne in Egipte [Egypt], and is as moche to seye [much to say] in Greke [Greek] as Mercury [in Latin], and in Ebrew [Hebrew] as Ennoch [Enoch]." Clearly, antiquity connected Hermes with Enoch. And Cayce's readings do, indeed, identify Enoch as one of the incarnations of the messianic Spirit of God among humanity. However, according to Cayce's readings, there never was a time when the Spirit of God was not helping souls on and around the earth.

For the sake of this tale, we will use the joint name Hermes–Thoth.

Hermes–Thoth is represented as an ibis–headed god (see illustration 27). The ibis bird lives between the deep, unseen realms beneath the sea and the visible surface world of earth. Thus, Hermes–Thoth has the power to live between the two realities—the seen and unseen.

Another point, before we get into this, is that E. A. Wallis Budge, author of *Gods of the Egyptians*, concluded after lengthy study that ancient Egyptians were *monotheistic*, having all the gods and goddesses radiate from the one god–center, Ra. All souls, godling or human, were rays from the one Ra (likely pronounced "ray," sometimes written *Re* to better convey the sound). Furthermore, all the godlings contribute to the composition of the whole that is Ra. In this light, Egyptian lore identifies Hermes–Thoth as "the heart and tongue" of Ra. Hermes–Thoth was also the means by which Ra's will was expressed through the spoken and written word.

Hermes–Thoth is considered to have invented writing and record keeping. He is called the Scribe of Truth, the Scribe of the Underworld, the Scribe of the gods, and Keeper of the Records. He invented magic, mystical arts, science, astronomy, astrology, mathematics, geometry, land surveying, medicine, and more!

In order to fully understand this great Egyptian god–leader, we have to also be aware that all of Egypt's important gods had feminine counterparts, equal in power and responsibility to the masculine portion. This was true in the case of Hermes–Thoth. He actually has two major feminine counterparts, depending on which role one focuses on. As the Keeper of the Records, Hermes' feminine complement is the goddess Seshat (see illustration opposite title page and illustration 25). But, in his role as Scribe of the Truth, his feminine counterpart is Ma'at (see illustration 28).

Goddess Seshat is the founder and guardian of libraries. She is the Divine Scribe, the goddess of Wisdom, the Divine Measurer, Measurer of Temples, helper to mathematicians, architects, and scribes. She recorded the speeches of pharaohs during coronations. She kept track of inventories and military campaigns. In illustration 25 and the illustration opposite the title page, you can see that she is depicted with the staff of time and a scribe's writing instruments, and over her head is a stylized papyrus in the form of a seven–pointed star.

Ma'at is the goddess of truth. Her symbol is the feather, revealing how delicate the truth is. She also represents justice. She was responsible for regulating the stars and seasons and keeping order in the universe. She and Thoth are considered to be the Logos of Plato, the Mind of God incarnate. She and Thoth are seen in the famous Egyptian death scene of the weighing of the heart (illustration 26). Together, they weigh every person's heart upon death. Ma'at's feather of truth is placed on one scale, the soul's heart on the other. Thoth records the weighing in the soul's Book of Life. If the heart is light, then he or she may pass on into the heavens. If heavy, a beast eats it, and the soul must reincarnate and live so as to develop a lighter heart.

Hermes–Thoth also played a significant role in helping Isis to immaculately conceive Horus, who was the messiah of ancient Egypt. One might say that he played the role that Gabriel played with Mary. The story goes that Isis and Osiris represented the higher, wiser, and ideal qualities of godliness. But Osiris had a brother who represented the lower, selfish, and illusory qualities of egocentrism. Osiris was the light of Ra to all who sojourned in the earth plane. Set, Osiris' evil brother (also Seth or Seti, all names for Egypt's Satan, see illustration 17) grew so upset over Osiris' dominance that he captured him and cut him in many pieces so no one could see the whole ideal. Without the ideal, humanity fell under the spell of Set, who accentuated selfishness and self–seeking with no regard for others. All forms of sin and violence spread across the planet. Isis became so distraught over the fall of humanity into the hands Set that she determined in her heart to overthrow him and lift humanity up from darkness to the light again. Many gods and godlings withdraw from this world, but Isis wished to remain half in earth's realm and half in heaven's in order to keep the light on for humanity. When it became obvious that Set was going to blind all to the truth of their heavenly origins and the influences of goodness, she sought to conceive and birth a powerful influence to counter Set. But according to the legend, Set had cut and fed the phallus of her husband Osiris to a fish, and it was gone. How could she become pregnant? She cried to heaven for help. Hermes–Thoth brought the boat of the gods down out of the heavenly realms closer to earth so he could hear Isis' complaint. He listened to her belief that humanity was being abandoned by the heavenly forces and her impassioned call for heavenly help to save humanity. Surprised that a goddess as great Isis was calling for help, Hermes–Thoth stopped all the movement of the heavens and the earth, refusing to allow them to move until Isis saved the world. Isis knew that if the sun and moon did not move, all life on earth would die. She became alarmed. Hermes–Thoth asked her if she had been with the humans so long that she had forgotten her divinity and divine powers.

Reflecting on this, she slipped into the depths of her being and found her oneness with the Creator of all life. Now connected to the Source of Life, she threw her enlightened head back and immaculately conceived Horus, the eye of the Light (illustration 71). Ra had been the original light, pure and innocent. But now evil had been seen, forcing a new eye to open, a more discerning eye. Horus grew and became the powerful force to counter Set.

In the struggle between the dark and the light, Set tore the right eye from Horus, but Horus gave the eye as a wisdom gift to Osiris, whom Isis had restored to his original wholeness (minus his phallus). Osiris needed the discerning eye, as he had become the judge of all souls passing out of this world, seeking to reenter the heavens. Now Osiris could judge true, seeing both evil and good. Horus eventually over-comes Set, subdues his influence among humans, and returns the light of Ra to the world. But now humans have known both good and evil, so they must struggle with their willpower to choose which they will mani-fest in their thoughts and actions, in their minds and hearts.

In the same way that the left eye is pure and the right eye is wise and discerning, Hermes-Thoth is depicted with the sun and the moon on his head, signifying the true light that all souls originally knew and the *reflected* light they came to know in the darkness of self-centeredness and selfishness (illustration 27).

———

Cayce's readings refer to Hermes as an Egyptian god who manifested among humans and, with the help of others, built the Great Pyramid of Giza, the major temples that contained the Hall of the Initiates of the White Brotherhood. This White Brotherhood had nothing to do with gender (in reading 845-1, a woman was identified as a key member of the Brotherhood), race, or a particular religion. It was not originally an Egyptian group but a group of souls in the "higher forces" that influ-ence from unseen realms this world from time to time. However, when necessary, members of the Brotherhood may incarnate to carry the light deeper into humanity's reality.

Ra, Hermes, and Isis were major teachers for a time in ancient Egypt.

Before we leave this story, we need to hear of Hermes' role in one of Cayce's key prophecy reading. According to Cayce, the ancient records were kept from those early times in Atlantis and Egypt and will be revealed as the earth changes its position (shifts it poles) and the "Great Initiate" returns "to that land and other lands" for "the folding up of those prophecies." The Messiah's reentry into earth begins in 1998, coming first in the hearts and minds of those who seek the Light, but ultimately returns with the same body he took with him in Galilee for all to see and hear and know.

"Is He abroad today in the earth? Yes, in those that cry unto Him from every corner; for He, the Father, has not suffered His soul to see corruption; neither has it taken hold on those things that make the soul afraid. For, He is the Son of Light, of God, and is holy before Him. And He comes again in the hearts and souls and minds of those that seek to know His ways."

Much more on this is in the chapter on the Great Initiate.

8

A Pharaoh in 11,000 BC?

The first pharaoh of Egypt, according to Cayce, was the leader of the invading tribe from Mt. Ararat. His name was Arart (pronounced *aur-art*). As we have read, it was he who negotiated the coexistence agreement with the native ruler, King Raai. It was Arart who established the Inner Council and the Governing Council, the latter included members of both peoples. It was Arart who cleverly gave the reins to his son Araaraart (Yes, that's exactly how Cayce said to spell it! It's a strange one and is pronounced *aur-ah—aur-ah—art*), pitting him against the native scribe–sage that was gaining so much influence and attention. According to Cayce, these names will be found in a yet–to–be–discovered chamber off the Sphinx's left hindquarter. In Cayce's vision, these were the first two pharaohs of Egypt, and he dates them long before the accepted archaeological dates for the Pharaonic period.

———

Egyptian legends have the first rulers of Egypt as the first gods, who ruled in this order: Ptah (creation god; see illustration 29), Ra (sun god; illustration 14, 73a and 73b), Shu (air god), Geb (earth god) (see illustrations 11 and 12), Osiris (god of the underworld and the dead; illustration 16 and 19), Set (god of the desert and evil, Satan of ancient Egypt, representing chaos; illustration 17), Horus (god of the sky and conqueror of Set, representing order; illustration 18), Thoth (god of wisdom, arbitrator of quarreling parties, associated with Hermes and Enoch; illustration 27), and Ma'at (goddess of truth, harmony, and justice; illustration 28). Notice how they represent a natural process of creation: first, the spark of life (Ptah), then the light of consciousness (Ra, as in Genesis 1), then the breath of life (Shu, as in Genesis 2), followed by the "place" of manifested life (Geb, earth), then the "place" for all that remained unmanifested, unseen (the underworld), then the rise of chaos (Set), followed by the corralling of chaos into order (Horus), and finally comes understanding and wisdom (Thoth), and that brings truth and harmony (Ma'at).

Archaeologically, the earliest pharaohs would be listed as the god-humans: Menes (Narmer), Hor–Aha, Djer, Djet, Merneith, and so on. All of these would be dated from 3100 to 3000 BC.

———

Edgar Cayce's list of pharaohs begins with dates in 11,000 BC! Interestingly, Cayce appears to be also talking about people who were somewhat god–humans, having retained a heavenly awareness from whence they descended—celestial beings temporally sojourning terrestrially. This idea also exists in Mayan lore where the immortal children of God are trapped in a game that they cannot win, a game in which the penalty for losing is death—an illusion of death, because only their bodies died. But the *thought* of death was so strong that the children did die to a degree. However, Cayce's tales indicate that they were becoming trapped in materiality by their own will to push their way into matter and were thus caught in the evolution of matter. They tricked or tripped up themselves. These celestial beings were gradually becoming *terrestrial* beings that had only a lingering whisper of their divine nature.

As of yet there is little evidence to support Cayce's dates. The recent observation that the Sphinx Pit was eroded by tropical rainwater runoff rather than wind, has pushed the dating of the monument to 9000 BC or older. The Inventory Stela indicates that Khufu may have been *repairing* the Great Pyramid rather than building it, pushing the date for the pyramid further into antiquity. Another recent discovery in a large basin region known as Nabta Playa, located about sixty–two miles west of Abu Simbel near the Egyptian–Sudanese border, has a Stonehenge–like calendar circle of stones dated to 4500 BC. This site reveals advanced skill in building and celestial mapping. But overall there is yet little hard evidence to support Cayce's ancient dates for high culture around 11,000 BC. Even so, this is his story, and it is a fascinating one with amazing details and a story that fits with much of the mythology around the planet, in both eastern and western cultures.

According to Cayce, young Araaraart (aur-ah—aur-ah—art) began his Pharaonic reign in 11,016 BC. Cayce said he "took the position as the leader in his sixteenth year and ruled over these peoples for ninety-eight years. The country, as we find, was brought to a higher state of understanding with the surrounding nations, and there was much of the religious ceremonies practiced in this time." Cayce also said that "the first foundations of the emblematical condition as is set in the Sphinx were begun in this rule, for this, as we see, has remained the mystery of the ages." In this he is indicating that the imagery of Egyptian art and sculptor is emblematic or symbolic of the mysterious aspects of life and consciousness, as in the Sphinx being half animal, half human.

Pharaoh Araaraart is attributed with initiating much of grand architecture of ancient Egypt, including the Sphinx and the Great Pyramid. Cayce also attributes a significantly different motivation to rule: it is seeking "benefits of the masses rather than classes; for we find, though this ruler was worshiped by many, he remained much in that spirit of service to his fellowman." Cayce states that this pharaoh's major accomplishments were "in the sealing of the religious rites and of giving of the laws to be used by these peoples in this great land."

Cayce went on: "One of good stature; of goodly countenance, for we find this entity of the larger peoples as came in from the north during the reign of one preceding this entity." That would have been his father, Arart, who led the Ararat people from Mt. Ararat and the surrounding region into Egypt.

In one reading for this entity, Cayce was asked about his associates in this *present* incarnation and their connection to him in that ancient Egyptian incarnation. The answers were interesting and enlightening to our growing understanding of earliest Egypt and to reincarnation and karma. Here are a few of these:

The first association mentioned was that of Pharaoh Araaraart's rebellious younger brother in ancient Egypt, named Ralij (pronounced *Ra-liege*, as in "my liege"). He led the Ibex Rebellion against King Araaraart and his government. It caused many deaths and much suffering and sorrow, even the breaking up of good families and valuable institutions that had served the country well. In this present incarnation Ralij was haunted by low self-esteem and doubt, to such an extent that he considered suicide. When he came to Cayce and asked, "What can this body do to restore his faith in himself and make the will to live stronger or the desire to carry on?" Cayce guided him to take stock of himself; consider where he was lacking, and then work on improving himself in those areas—not working alone, but with the Creative Energies of the Divine within him. Cayce also told him that he was more interested in people than things, so he should get involved with people. He also encouraged him to study people and learn the many ways to help them. However, Cayce cautioned him to first stop judging others and himself so harshly. Cayce said, "assume responsibilities and live up to those [ideals] in service for others, for in such one may find the answering that makes self one *with* that Whole that *fills* the *all*."

The next association was with the native Egyptian scribe who was raised to the level of co-leader with Araaraart. This native was given the name Aarat (pronounced *ah-rat*), thereby aligning him with the Ararat tribe as well as the native Egyptians. In this modern incarnation, Aarat became one of the most important donors and supporters of Edgar Cayce's work and organization, even to the point of funding the building of the first center in Virginia Beach, Virginia in the late 1920s. In ancient Egypt, the king Araaraart went to the native scribe for instruction in the ways of his native people. Cayce's reading says that Aarat had been "the sage of the cult of the true Euranians," or peoples of the hills—a strange term, one worth exploring.

Cayce's longtime stenographer became concerned that she took down the *wrong* term when she wrote *Euranians*, later believing that it may have been "Uranians," not Euranians. Of course, Uranian was a term for the so-called "third sex" in the Victorian era, meaning a female psyche in a male body, and having much to do with homosexuality and lesbianism. But in Cayce's case it has more to do with the *planet* Uranus and the *hermaphroditic* nature of the heavenly soul, which possesses both the feminine (yin) and the masculine (yang) in its extraterrestrial state. In Cayce's paradigm, souls don't just incarnate in earth, they live in spirit and mind all over the cosmos. And when they initially leave earth life, they are active in this solar system of ours, experiencing *sojourns* in the nonphysical realms of the surrounding planets. The planets we see are more than their three-dimensional image to us. They are fourth, fifth, and higher dimensions of soul activity associated with their classical astrological influence. Souls incarnating from a recent sojourn in one of these higher-dimensional planetary realms were occasionally referred to by Cayce as beings of that planet, thus "Uranians" were those souls who had recently incarnated from nonphysical realms around Uranus. And since they were retaining much of their soul qualities, they may initially appear to be hermaphrodites. Usually, the soul projects only one side of its nature, either the masculine or feminine, and usually into the corresponding physical body for a male or female, but not always. Cayce even tells how the early entities incarnate in the realm of earth were naturally male and female in *one* body (the whole soul in body) and could conceive a new physical body *within* their body to allow members of their soul group to also incarnate. As physicality took stronger control over them, they lost this ability and began to project only one gender and created new bodies in the manner we know today through coition. But it wasn't always so, and Cayce prophesied that it would not always be so, for we are growing toward a time when the whole soul will manifest again in one physical body.

Following this line of thought, Aarat may have been the sage of a hermaphroditic people who incarnated from dimensions of Uranus, thus being a people of innovation, breakthroughs, shifts in perception, and even sudden changes. They certainly experienced many sudden changes—as in the surprising invasion of their land by the Ararats, and then the spontaneous elevation of their scribe-sage to co-ruler of all Egypt, and the subsequent rise of Egypt as the world center for enlightenment and high art! However, the Cayce readings clearly associate incarnating souls from Uranus with the ancient lands of Atlantis, only in the early years of Atlantis from roughly 200,000 to 103,000 BC. After that period, the incarnating souls were using male and female bodies rather than the androgenous bodies of the earlier period.

The next association addressed by Cayce was the builder of the foundations for the new monuments in Egypt. The Great Flood had destroyed or buried the earlier monuments, those that Oual had helped to build. Cayce dated the deluge to around 22,000 BC. In 10,500 BC a member of the Ararat tribe was assigned the task of calculating the geometrical lines and planetary movements to place the Sphinx precisely facing east and the Great Pyramid's entrance facing north. His name in ancient Egypt was Arsrha (pronounced *aur-sar-ha*). In Egypt he oversaw the geographical planning and the selection and management of the stonecutters. He was chosen for this most important assignment because all perceived that the Divine was dwelling in him! Arsrha worked with astronomers, astrologers, and seers and was himself the chief mathematician in developing the locations, personnel, and orientations that would help these monuments convey a meaning that others in the distant future marvel over. Therefore, these monuments had to last for millennia and retain their amazing orientation despite settling and earthquakes. It was a *monumental* task, but Arsrha was the right soul for the job.

Another fascinating character in Cayce's list of associates to the young pharaoh was Rhaha (pronounced *rha-ha*), the high priest of the people during the banishment of Ra–Ta and during the troubles that arose in the holy temples as various factions fought for control or got lost in earthy pursuits. Rhaha was the priest to the young king Araaraart and head of the priesthood of the nation during this tumultuous period. As a result, he became a close soul friend of Pharaoh Araaraart, a friendship that continued to the present incarnation.

Of course, the greatest character in this list of associates was the High Priest Ra–Ta, who was in this present life Edgar Cayce and the father of reincarnated Araaraart. The reincarnated Araaraart was Edgar's eldest son, Hugh Lynn Cayce, who eventually took over his father's organization and led it for many years after the death of Edgar Cayce. In their ancient incarnation in Egypt, Ra–Ta led Araaraart into the Holy of Holies of the temple to experience the Divine Influence directly and thereby to become the divinely anointed pharaoh of all Egypt. In those early times they were colleagues on a great mission, but later, after the priest's stumble over moral codes and practices that had been well established, these two fell out of favor with one another, and as we have read, the pharaoh banished the high priest from Egypt—only to later recant his edict and call for the return and reestablishment of Ra-Ta as high priest of the nation. Even so, the two never recovered their initial admiration for one another.

Next on this list of associates was the woman with whom Ra-Ta made his fatal mistake but also with whom he grew and developed his ultimate spiritual enlightenment. Her name in Egypt was Is-ris. She was the daughter of the Second Priest in the temple and devoted herself to service as a spiritual dancer in the temple and before the pharaoh at ceremonial events. Because of her service, she was held in high favor. Is-ris in this present incarnation was again Ra-Ta's (Edgar Cayce's) spouse, Gertrude, and Hugh Lynn's mother (he went by his first two names, perhaps a carryover from having such a long name in Egypt: Araaraart). Many who worked with the Cayce family in those early years of building the new organization believed that Gertrude was the glue that kept this little band of visionaries together through the good and bad times.

Atlanteans played a big role in the development of Egypt and its amazing culture. They were among those who had close association with the young pharaoh. One of these Atlanteans was Ex-der-enemus, who, in cooperation with Pharaoh Araaraart, developed the first insurance system. The king and this Atlantean worked out a way to give assurances to the people who took on the more dangerous jobs. If anything happened to them, their families would be cared for. Also, citizens who suffered great tragedies, such as fire, flood, or unexpected deaths of their breadwinners, would be *insured* in a manner that would allow them to carry on. This was done by the many contributing small amounts to a fund so that the few who suffered were cared for.

But Ex-der-enemus became known for something much more upsetting to this ancient culture: interracial marriage. In these ancient times in this mythical Egypt, the races were new and young. As we learned in the chapter on the ancient world, originally all the souls that descended from heaven were of one race, one people, and one human family. Even after millions of years of mingling with matter, they were still one hu-

man race with one worldwide language (with only a few minor variations in dialect).

However, when it became apparent that the souls of the children of
God were not going to easily leave this dimension as they had originally thought, a longer-term plan had be arranged—one that dealt with
the forces possessing the children in this dimension. Mayan legends tell
how "the people" entered the "seven caves" for a pow-wow over their
problems in this material world. They came out of the caves in *five*
groups—these were the original five races. According to Cayce's visions,
each race was to take up one of the five senses as its primary task to
master; thus all would enjoy the benefits of the division of labor when
they reunited again—all five senses having been conquered.

In the main sacred temple in Egypt, a young, perfect, white female
named Tar-Ello was born, and Ra-Ta knew he had the ideal mother for
the development and growth of the white race. In fact, Ra-Ta considered her to be the most ideal white female he had ever seen, and as
such, he had segregated her from the others. But Tar-Ello's soul was
disenchanted with the hardships and loneliness of temple life. She
wanted to know the world outside and the many different peoples and
races enjoying Egypt's beauty and vibrance. She secretly sought freedom from the temple rules and regulations, especially the selective, dis-
passionate copulating arrangements that existed in the baby mill.

Her disposition did not escape the watchful eye of the high priest
and his team, but it pained them to see their most ideal white-race Eve
wanting out of temple life. Each of the five races had their original, ideal
Eve. Tar-Ello was to be the true Eve of Caucasians.

Ex-der-enemus' job took him all over the country, even into the
temples to insure those who worked there. To the secluded temple virgin Tar-Ello, his life appeared to be so much more exciting and meaningful than hers. She often sought him out on his visits and listened to
his stories about the people and the activities up and down the river
Nile, even the world. Ex-der-enemus had travel seemingly everywhere
and knew most everyone! Curiously, Ex-der-enemus was almost as
lonely as Tar-Ello. Despite his many acquaintances, he was an Atlantean
without a country. Even though she was always chaperoned, the temple

virgin sought his company every time he came, and each time he had more exciting stories to tell her. Her longing to see what he was seeing, to meet and hear the visitors to Egypt grew to such a pitch that it was obvious to all that she was not going to join Ra-Ta's baby mill. Tar-Ello knew that if she went off with Ex-der-enemus to create a family and home and to live the exciting outer life, she would never be able to come back into the temple as a priestess.

What made Ex-der-enemus dangerous was not his worldly knowledge and tales but his race. Ex-der-enemus was of the red race, as were all Atlanteans according to Cayce. At the highest levels of this society and in many other societies around the planet in these ancient times, breeding across racial lines was taboo. This is not to say that it didn't occur, but not at these levels of the social order.

Her freedom came when the high priest withdrew to the sacred mount and was "borne away" from this incarnate life. Ra-Ta died to this world. Tar-Ello was free to pursue new avenues of life, and she did, leaving temple life and joining with Ex-der-enemus.

Interestingly, both of these souls reincarnated during Cayce's lifetime. And even though he was the reincarnation of the high priest who was so upset with her for leaving temple life and bonding with a man of another race, they all got along wonderfully in this life. In Cayce's present-day organization, the reincarnated Tar-Ello was a devoted healer in the prayer-healing group that formed around Cayce's work. As we might expect, Ex-der-enemus was the top-selling insurance man for one of the largest insurance companies in North America. He said that his success was due to his ability to sit quietly in the morning with all the prospects his company had given him and run his hand over their data card, feeling who truly was interested in insurance and who was not. Then that day he would call on the serious candidates, thereby selling the more policies per visit than any other agent.

As you might expect, these two married again. Their Cayce reading said that they couldn't stay together for very long or apart for very long. It was a hot-and-cold relationship with strong magnetism.

I knew them both in this life. Ex-der-enemus and I talked often. He shared many stories with me. He and Edgar Cayce would go out into the middle of the lake near Edgar's home on the pretense of fishing but would only sit in the boat and smoke—Edgar, cigarettes; Ex–der–enemus, cigars. In the incarnation as Ex–der–enemus he lived 775 years; but it was not so this lifetime, as he passed on in his eighties. I also knew Tar-Ello. In this life she was a gentle, quiet, dignified woman of high ideals and purposes.

Other Atlanteans helped by providing technology, such as cosmic rays, electrical knifes that made surgery bloodless, "chariots driven by gas," and the like. Why we haven't found any of these devices is a mystery, for sure. Some sources indicate that their materials were alien to what we know today, so we don't know what to look for. Others believe their whole society was more fourth dimensional than three, so we'll never find much of anything. Whatever the case, we need to discover something, or we will continue to have nothing but legends and theories.

Finally, we reach the last name on this list of Pharaoh Araaraart's relationships, but a very special soul who, according to Cayce's reading of the Akashic record, served Egypt so well that she lived for six hundred years! Now that's biblical aging. But Cayce reaffirmed his statement, saying: "The entity's experience in the life was that of many, many, *many* years, if it would be counted by the years of today—it being more than six hundred years (600)—yes, season years, that is, the seasons from winter to winter, or spring to spring, or summer to summer." One of her many skills was the ability to read old inscriptions, making her an important asset to all the powerful people in the land, even the natives who learned much about their heritage from her. We shall cover more about her in the next chapter.

Pharaoh Araaraart, son of Mt. Ararat King and Egyptian Pharaoh Arart, co-ruler with the native scribe–sage Aarat, and the secular counterpart to the High Priest Ra–Ta, ruled well. He oversaw an Inner Council of these key people; he successfully managed a Governing Council that included representatives from all the different peoples living in the fertile lands of Egypt; he corrected his mistakes; he kept Egypt united, and he laid the foundations for one of the greatest cultures of humankind. The Cayce readings state that there were over 3000 pharaohs. This is such a fascinating statement because there are only 322 known pharaohs among archaeological findings! Of course, archaeologists consider the first pharaoh to have been in 3000 BC, whereas Cayce is dating the first to 11,000 BC. Araaraart was the second pharaoh in Cayce's list and a good one. I worked under him in this present incarnation when he was president of the Association for Research and Enlightenment, Virginia Beach, Virginia. He was a capable president and an international traveler for the work who made many good business arrangements that established the A.R.E. as a holistic–health, personal–spirituality, and ancient–mysteries organization, open to all, and based on the concepts channeled through Edgar Cayce.

9

SIX-HUNDRED-YEAR-OLD SCRIBE!

ayce opened this reading of the Akashic records by stating, "the interpreting of these records, to be sure, is not from English—neither is it from the Egyptian language of the present day [Arabic], but rather from the language that the entity's people brought into the land—not Sanskrit, not the early Persian; though the peoples came from that land which is now a part of Iran or Carpathia." After all of this Cayce never identified that actual language. It's fascinating that this earthly man from Hopkinsville, Kentucky with an eighth-grade education could access and interpret material of great complexity and timelessness while in a deep, meditative state. It says so much about the untapped abilities within each of us and the potential of meditation, deep meditation.

Aidol (pronounced *ah-ee-doll*) was another of the daughters of Ra-Ta, the high priest of Egypt. She was raised in the temple life and came of age during a time when her father was banished from the temple and the nation. She suffered much stress as the remaining daughter of her disgraced father but applied herself to study, meditation, data gathering, and service to all those who were open to her help—mostly the natives who were seeking to purify themselves in the Temple of Sacrifice.

During the uprising of the natives against the leadership, Aidol was held by the natives as one among the ruling people who could be trusted and appreciated their cause. However, she was able to balance this trust without betraying King Araaraart. And when the king's own brother led a rebellion against him, the Ibex Rebellion, Aidol, though attempting to stay out of politics and the fighting, did not abandon the king and his high intentions. As the rebellions were put down, she rose in pharaoh's favor and enjoyed more service in the palace than she was allowed in the temples of her father. During these times, she became more highly educated than most others in the land. She could read the ancient inscriptions. (Yes, there were ancient inscriptions even in this ancient time!) She knew more than anyone else about the various peoples living in Egypt and even around the world, their history, and ancestry and was sought out for information and data on such. Eventually, she became one of the highest-ranking scribes in all the land; some would say the world. Visitors to Egypt would seek her out for her knowledge.

Then, after suffering so much to reach such a high state and the peace it brought, her whole life was turned upside down again. Her father was returning to Egypt and regaining his leadership of the temples as the highest-ranking priest. According to Cayce's readings, her father and his cohorts *forcibly* took her from the palaces back to the temple to serve as Ra-Ta's personal scribe, interpreter, and assistant. All of her national and international activities came to an abrupt end. Even worse, temple activities were minimal during the seven years it took her father to regenerate his body! But rather than sulk about this or fight against it, she took the opportunity to enter into deeper meditation and the transformative practices of the Temples of Sacrifice and Beauty. As a result, she grew into an enlightened soul with the highest of vibrations and intuitive knowing. She grew closer to the Creative Forces, and they flowed through her. Many in the temples recognized these powerful changes in her, including her father, who changed her name to Isis-a-o (pronounced *Isis-ah-oh*, after the goddess Isis) and anointed her a priestess. Even with this new dignity, he retained her as his personal assistant, still requiring scribe duties of her, as only a father could!

When Ra-Ta had finished his regenerative process and was young again, he came out of the temples and began to work closely with the political and industrial leadership to build the monuments of the Egypt, particularly the Great Pyramid in which would be hidden the pyramid prophecy. (More on the prophecy in a later chapter.) Isis-a-o was by his side throughout this period, covering some one hundred years according to Cayce. Then her father withdrew from earth life into the deeper meditations in the nonphysical dimensions and realms of soul life—in other words, he died. He had been incarnate for roughly five hundred years, and it was time for a change.

Isis–a–o remained in the earth life, helping several generations seeking a better life and a greater awareness. According to Cayce's reading of her record, she lived to be more than six hundred years old! And that is as we count time today! Recall how many early biblical souls incarnated for many hundreds of years. It was the way in ancient times. Cayce's readings state that with the proper assimilation of the nutrients necessary for a body to function well and the proper eliminations of the toxins that build up in a body, there is no reason for a body to die— as long as the mind finds purpose in this dimension! Isis–a–o found purpose and service to her fellow incarnate souls seeking a better understanding of why they exist and what life is all about.

In Cayce's reading of her record, he notes that early on Isis–a–o noticed how people had a prejudice toward various features and qualities, giving special privilege to one group or race over another. She watched how people, consciously or unconsciously, perceived differences and judged by these features. This troubled Isis–a–o, and she worked to maintain the truth that all people were children of the great Ra, the great Light, the Creator—and therefore, equal in the eyes of God and should be treated as such.

Cayce stated: "*Innately* we find in the present experience that such mixtures or such variations as to cause the color or the characteristics of individual groups or nations to be different under various environs, will at times bring shudders as it were—because of the recalling of something through which the entity passed. In the present, the sight of the variation in their *beings*, and the showing of special privilege to a group because of such variations, will arouse emotions because of the experience during that particular sojourn [in ancient Egypt]."

Isis–a–o and her father were of the purer forms of the white race; but she interacted with all the races and nationalities in or visiting Egypt without prejudice. She assisted many of the red, yellow, black, and mixed races to pass through the temple initiations and ceremonies. (There's more on the races in Chapter 10.) She also taught them about their unique ancestry and their special role in the overall soul growth of all peoples. And she had much data to support her guidance. She helped in "the preparations to become either artisans, teachers, ministers, or to fill those offices as would be termed in the present as the leaders or directors of the peoples throughout the period."

In the latter three hundred years of her incarnation, she became an effective guide and counselor to many, and these were the happier years of her life.

As Cayce was finishing her reading, he was inspired to share what Isis-a-o had come to know—each entity finds itself in a three–dimensional phase of existence or experience: the world without, the world within, and the mind that may span or bridge the two realities. Each entity has the body–physical, the body–mental (think of this "body" as thought–and–memory–cluster unique to that soul), and the body–spiritual (think of this as Einstein's energy vs. matter, spirit is the energetic essence of an entity). The mind is able to bridge awareness from the physical to the deeper mental via the subconscious and from the deeper mental to the infinite spiritual essence via the superconscious. The spiritual is the life, the motivative force, as it is active upon those influences and forces that manifest in the physical body through the centers called or known as the radial activity of the sympathetic nerve forces (a portion of the autonomic nervous system). The sympathetic nerve forces are activated from without by stimuli, which join to the forces as from within by the ideals held in the mind and heart of the entity. The mind is the builder, the appreciator, the drawer of conclusions, the chooser— always correlating feelings, thoughts, words, and actions to the ideal held in the deeper spiritual or unseen realm of the entity's being. Therefore, the forces from without meet the forces from within by means of the purposes of the individual in its mental self. When the individual holds to its ideals, the inner forces guide the life, not the outer forces. Rather than allowing circumstances in the outer life to dictate outcomes, set an ideal within and strive to live accordingly. It's comparable to a captain of a ship sailing to a destination against a heavy wind; he does not give up but rather tacks against the wind, keeping his overall course to the desired destination.

These concepts were found throughout the Cayce collection of readings, not just those of Isis-a-o.

Lastly, Isis-a-o was not the longest incarnating soul in Cayce's files. In a reading for a soul that he named "Alyne," he gave this information: "She was in Atlantis where she oft laid aside the physical body to become regenerated. She was among the priestesses of the Law of One, serving in the temples where there was the raising of the light in which the universal forces gave expression and brought for the body and mind the impelling influences. She was not only the priestess but also the physician, doctor for those peoples. The entity lived in Poseidia, in the temple, in the spirit influences of the material activities for some six thousand years—if counted as time now."

She lived for 6000 years! Cayce continues with this:

"With the last of the destructions that were brought about by the sons of Belial through the activities of Beelzebub [literally, "lord of the flies"], the entity journeyed with those people to the Yucatan land, establishing the temple there. But with those inroads from the children of Om and the peoples from the Lemurian land, or Mu, the entity withdrew into itself; taking, as it were, its own flight into the lands of Jupiter."

Activities of Beelzebub and the sons of Belial drove our light-bearing priestess out of Atlantis to the Yucatan Peninsula. Eventually, even the Yucatan became too negative a place for her, so she took flight to the nonphysical realms of Jupiter—Cayce's way of saying she physically died. Of course, in his paradigm there is no death, so her soul simply "took flight."

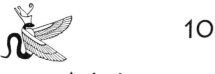

10

A WOMAN GOD-CHILD

Cayce began his next story by telling the enquiring individual that she was a member of a group of souls that incarnated in ancient Egypt with a united purpose to affect dramatic improvements in the lives of souls trapped in materiality. Her Egyptian incarnation began as one of the daughters of the High Priest Ra-Ta. The priest and his staff were running a birthing program in the temples that sought to attract the minds and energies of celestially aware souls into ideal physical body-temples. These bodies were to have as little earthy, materialistic energy as possible, so the mating couples had to be chosen carefully. And all children were wards of the state or the "church," depending whether they were born in the palaces or temples. These children were raised in a carefully controlled environment and trained in the higher ideals and purposes of the state or church. They were kept from the many contaminating influences in the outer world.

There were also many career-training programs, each designed to prepare souls for their ideal career—one that fit their innate talents and motivations. Among the training programs were those for souls who were being deliberately raised and trained to be "light bearers" in the midst of the weaknesses of selfishness and sensual urges that possessed most incarnate souls.

Among these select souls was one named *It-El-Sut.* Cayce explained: "*It* indicates the woman, *El* indicates a child of the divine, and *Sut* is her personal name. Thus she is *Sut, a woman God-child.*"

Sut grew in wisdom, beauty, cleverness, and high interpersonal skills. These qualities, combined with her being the daughter of the high priest of the land, helped her make many important contacts in both the temples and the palaces. She even became a key liaison between the

Atlanteans and the ruling council of Egypt. She actually sponsored the Atlantean leader Ax-Tell and his migrating troupe before the ruling council.

These activities resulted in growing resentments of her among pharaoh's advisors—not so much with pharaoh himself, for the young king desired to build connections with peoples around the world, even remnant Atlanteans. But pharaoh's councilors felt that all of these matters should be going through them, and normally they did. Sut simply had a much more dynamic mind and personality, and she intuitively understood people, even people of alien cultures. And she could be a very persuasive advocate.

However, she had one great passion that began to overwhelm her normal level-headedness and caused her more trouble than all of her noble negotiations. Sut was driven by inner compulsion to abandon the automatic assignment of children to the palace and temple wards. She became an extremist in her advocacy for homes and nuclear families. This was the total opposite position of her powerful father and pharaoh. Both of these leaders believed that the children were better trained and protected from negative influences in the wards. And the ward system had successfully trained and prepared children for activities in special services and vocational guidance, in line with the spiritual, mental, and material ideals held by most all leaders. And despite the appearance of suppressing individualism and self-realization, the ward system had proven that it could discover youngster's innate abilities and latent potential. Even Sut was a product of the ward system and an example of how well it achieved its goals.

But Sut was driven by a deep passion for home life, or at least her imagination of what family life would have been for her and might become for others. She would not let go of this issue, causing her to fall in disfavor with many of the leaders. She resorted to using her beauty, sexual wiles, and charming personality to get support for her cause. Cayce noted in his reading of her Akashic record that in her effort to persuade others of the rightness of this cause, she developed interpersonal skills that became innate traits of her soul throughout all of its following incarnations. He said she even reached a level at which her very presence would persuade people without her even trying. She became an orb of persuasive energy. Even so, he warned her, "Such an influence upon others may be for weal or woe."

Her zeal took her dangerously close to, what Cayce called, that "very thin line between the ridiculous and the sublime." Fortunately, Sut did not cross that line often, and when she did, she knew it and found her way back quickly. She eventually won her cause in ancient Egypt, receiving the power and authority from her father, the high priest, and from the pharaoh to establish homes—but only for those souls who desired such. The ward system would continue for most children. But Sut had opened the minds and hearts of many, and over the following years this trend toward homes and nuclear families overshadowed the ward system. In building families she learned a great deal about what worked and what didn't, eventually making her an excellent marriage and family counselor—on physical, mental, and spiritual issues. Cayce said that she learned relationships between a man and woman have to take into account each one's *ideals* about establishing of homes, their individual physical likes and dislikes, the mental capacities of each, the physical abilities of each as related to a correlating or paralleling of purposes. There *cannot* be congeniality where the ideal and purpose of the sex life is not harmonious and complementary one to another. There *cannot* be a congenial home where the desires of the spiritual are not at least in unison with one another's *spiritual* ideals, because the spiritual *is* the life force flowing through the relationship. If the relationship is only physical and mental, it will not live on through the many transitions and challenges that occur in relationships.

So strong was Sut's desire for homes and so deeply set in her soul, that Cayce stated that even today there was "an aversion within the entity, almost to that point of hate, of seeing, experiencing, or even hearing of broken homes, broken ties, from any cause."

It-El-Sut had, what Cayce called, "divine abilities," adding that "many know that such exist, but it depends upon their *own* awareness or stage of development as to what stress or emphasis they give to same. These become, then, a faculty, a consciousness within the ability of the entity to use in the present."

Once her passion had found its way, It–El–Sut withdrew from incarnate life (died) at the rather young age of one hundred and ninety. Interestingly, her husband in this present life had been her companion in ancient Egypt. Cayce advised her to give him a little breathing room this lifetime, tempering her innate zeal, and he would make a good husband to her and father to their children.

As Cayce ended her reading, he addressed a serious weakness lingering in It–El–Sut's soul: she feared human nature and its weaknesses in her loved ones. He said her fears came from the Egyptian incarnation when her own offspring gave into human appetites and became deadened to the higher purposes and ideals, lost in gratifying emotions and urges. This haunted her soul. All the spiritual growth she had achieved was somehow not carried on to her children. Had she lost the benefits of the ward system by raising them herself? Hadn't she loved them and guided them sufficiently? Her soul carried this fear into the incarnation with Edgar Cayce. Fortunately, Cayce advised her (before she had children) that in this present life, she could be the touchstone of goodness and rightness for her loved ones and keep them on the right path—though a zigzag path it might be. He also told her that she—consciously and unconsciously—can control people, and she should occasionally do so! He did warn her not to do so to her own or their undoing—best keep God's spirit guiding oneself in conversations and counseling.

Reincarnation in Cayce's paradigm was a process by which a soul and soul-mind could learn about itself, about relationships with others, and about the nature of that essence we call "God." The law of karma was a good trainer for the soul, meaning as people use their free will, they experience the effects of same —not as punishment or retribution, but as education and enlightenment. This woman God-child was going to have another opportunity to help her loved ones grow: physically, mentally, and spiritually—and she had all the skills necessary to do so, especially her mindfulness of the potential for getting lost in this world and in one's weaknesses.

11

THE UPS AND DOWNS OF ONE EGYPTIAN'S LIFE

Of course, not all was happiness on the ancient Nile, even in the midst of wealth, beauty, and ease, trouble found its way in people's lives as shown in this next Cayce story from Egypt, the tale of one idealistic Egyptian named Ra-La-Ral—who later reincarnated and worked with Edgar Cayce in this lifetime.

Cayce began this tale by saying: "Yes, we have the entity and the soul-mind, with those experiences in Egypt." He went on to explain that it was the time when there came into the land the peoples who began the establishment of civilization, as we would term today, or the turning toward the one God. At this time the entity was in the name Ra-La-Ral and was the son of the high priest, Ra-Ta. When his father was banished, Ra-La-Ral remained in the temple, loyal to the king, Pharaoh Araaraart, son of the old king who came down out of Mt. Ararat. Such loyalty was rewarded; Ra-La-Ral was raised to act in the capacity of spiritual advisor, who was the most important priest in the temple, and to oversee the building of new temples. However, leaders of the rebellions attempted to sway his loyalties. And though he was only eighteen years of age, Ra-La-Ral remained loyal to Araaraart and cooperated with the pharaoh's plans and activities. Hence, the entity neither joined with those who rose up with the natives in a rebellion against the king nor with those in the king's own household that rebelled.

Loyal Ra-La-Ral was multitalented. In addition to his priestly wisdom, he was also an interpreter for the Atlanteans who continued to trickle in from their lost continent, attempting to join with this new, growing culture in Egypt along the beautiful river.

In his capacity as the spiritual advisor, Ra–La–Ral grew to be one of power, based not only on his talents but also on his own morals, high position, and key associations.

When his father Ra-Ta was banished from the kingdom for violating the temple rules, one of which dealt with the number of wives a priest could have, Ra–La–Ral reacted by taking an oath to have only one wife throughout his entire incarnation and encouraged others to do the same. None did. It was simply not the custom in those times.

Curiously, among the women of the temple, Ra–La–Ral found no mate who suited him and his high ideals. He remained single at a time when marriage and babies were seen as an important part of nation building.

When his father, Ra-Ta, returned to the kingdom from exile, the whole country celebrated. It was a gala occasion. The palaces and temples were alive with celebrants. People from around the countryside turned out to cheer Ra-Ta's return. Despite how well Ra–La–Ral had run the temples and how honorably loyal he had been to pharaoh, he knew his father would rule the temples again. Resigned to this, he received his father and his large entourage (now only 167 people) with open arms and good cheer. And, to his surprise, there was an unexpected gift in this reunion. Cayce told of how Ra–La–Ral experienced a greeting "embrace and a kiss" from one of the new daughters of his father (from a different mother than Ra–La–Ral's) that opened both his heart and the heart of the young princess. The two felt love and a desire for companionship instantly upon physical contact. At that very moment they each knew they were the ones to build one of the first monogamous relationships in a time when such was simply not the norm.

The princess's name was Isibio (pronounced *ice-ibee-o*). She had been born in Nubia, the second daughter of Is-ris and Ra-Ta. Isibio and Ra–La–Ral eventually wed and had two boys and two girls. Later, when the Ibex rebels captured the mind and heart of their son Loi-Pthl (pronounced *loy-pa-tal*), Ra–La–Ral did everything in his power to regain the boy's trust without betraying the king's. But the boy was emotionally lost to the rebellion, which was led by the king's brother Ralij, the Prince of Ibex, who had many supporters. Unfortunately, in putting down the rebellion, the soldiers of the king killed the young boy Loi-Pthl along with others in the rebellious territory of Ibex (Cayce was never clear on exactly where ancient Ibex was but indicated that it was in eastern Egypt near Nubia). These events and the loss of his beloved son broke the spirit of his father Ra–La–Ral and caused him to lose power as he withdrew into despair and inactivity. He retired from the king's service, the priesthood, and temple work. He traveled with his remaining family to Nubia, the birthplace of his wife Isibio.

While she was the spouse of Ra–La–Ral in Egypt, Isibio became one of the temple priestesses. When she returned to Nubia with her broken husband, she set up a temple in the Nubian hills. She established schools and medical centers. Her mind and soul grew through this period of service as she gave to those who came to her seeking guidance and help. She attracted many because she was so fair in appearance and wise in the spiritual and moral influences on each soul's life and the lives of souls as a community. She also knew the secrets of temple initiation and transformation and helped many gain enlightenment. She also gave in song, in music, in daily labors, or in whatever field she chose. Her ability to encourage others in various fields of endeavor added to her influence among the people. Yet, despite all of this good, there were those in Nubia who did not want her and persecuted her for setting herself up as a teacher in Nubia.

Ra–La–Ral and Isibio also had a daughter who became a major emissary to temples around the world! This young, dynamic lady studied and worked with both her grandfather, the high priest Ra-Ta, in the main Egyptian temple and her mother, the high priestess of the temple in Nubia. The daughter's name was Del-lli (pronounced *del-el-lee*). She was a musician in reeds and strings and a worker in fine linens. She had a heavenly voice and used it in song and chanting. Cayce said that if her parents and teachers in this reincarnation during Cayce's time guided her correctly, she might awaken "the song of the inner self" and as a result become a blessing to many.

The reincarnation of Ra–La–Ral asked some interesting questions of Edgar Cayce during this present lifetime. The answers are of much help to us in our soul growth. He asked the trance-state Cayce to explain soul life and growth, and Cayce replied, "As is seen in the unfoldment of a life, a soul, in each experience—that to which it may attain depends upon that which is built in the formative years of its personality [outer self]. It either conforms to the ideals of its individuality [deeper self], or is changed to become something apart—bringing adversities and contention when made separate. When made one with that which is as a continuity of Life and Force as manifests itself in the earth through the influences of the Divine, as through the Son, then do the blessings come; as was said, 'Suffer little children to come unto me, for of such is the kingdom of heaven,' that 'He that offends one of these, my little ones, has offended me indeed.' Keep, then, inviolate the soul's experiences. Thrust not your own dominion, yet teach, train the little one to know, in Him is peace and understanding, in Him is the way for all earth—as in heaven—to know the joy of being alive!"

Recall that in his incarnation in ancient Egypt as Ra–La–Ral he watched a young boy, his son, lose his life because others darkly influenced him during his formative years, and as his father, he was unable to overcome those dark influences to save his son. Now in this incarnation, Cayce's guidance encouraged him to help those in their formative years to build the inner strength and make an inner connection with the Divine in order to avoid being misled.

Ra–La–Ral also asked Cayce to describe the difference between intuitive forces and occult forces and how he may aid in their development? Cayce replied [edited for clarity, my italics], "From experiences of an entity's whole being do the intuitive forces arise, while occult forces are those activities as a whole. Then, intuitive forces are developed more by the *introspective activities of a conscious mind* until it is able to bring to bear such experiences of the entity as they act upon those necessary actions as present themselves in one's daily experience. Individuals—now, this is well for all to learn!—often call this *entering into the silence*. Hence this ability is gained by constant introspection through entering into the silence. And people who practice this individually and in groups are able to bring to the surface the activities of their whole selves, the entity as a whole. Hence they are called sages, lamas, or such. These, when they are made to be what is commonly termed *practical*, yet remaining spiritual in aspect—that is, sticking to the truth!—they become masters.

When they are turned to channels that are to induce influences over individuals because they have that ability to hold an individual, then they are abuse. Hence the entity in its study may make for self, through the study of occult forces, by introspection, or entering into the silence, apply what he gained in his life—see? This is opening a deep subject! It's worthy to be understood! And well that the entity be grounded in—not as mystics or as mysterious individuals—grounded in that termed Christian religion and prayer, with that termed as introspection, meditation, or mysticism, or occult influences brought in. They are one and the same in their essence, but know they are all of one source. Then, be sure they are good—must come from the source of good; and, as the Son came from the Father, they are in Him, and the approach to the source is through Him—and there is no other!"

In this new incarnation, the souls of Ra-Ta, Ra-La-Ral, Isibio, Del-lli, and Loi-Pthl worked again together, but this time they held tightly to that which was ever good, avoiding the ancient problems that still whispered distractingly in their subliminal consciousness. Resolved and released, their souls grew in understanding, enlightenment, and love. In the Cayce files, eighteen people were told that this was their last incarnation; they would not be returning to this world and this life. All that held them here had been released. Now free of the wheel of birth, death, and rebirth, they would have other journeys in the infinite realms beyond physicality and matter.

12

THE REGENERATION OF
THE HIGH PRIEST

The return of the banished high priest Ra-Ta is one of Cayce's many fascinating tales with little gems, not the least of which is the complete and total rejuvenation of the body of the aged priest—allowing him to live actively for another hundred years!

The people, particularly the natives, demanded Ra-Ta's return from banishment. They had grown tired not only of the contention among factional political forces in their once harmonious nation but also of the growing corruption and degradation of their higher ideals and morals. They knew that the high priest had helped create and maintain standards they once enjoyed. Many, including pharaoh, felt that the nation had lost its spiritual way, becoming too materialistic and earthy. As we have learned, two great rebellions had occurred: one in pharaoh's own family when his brother attempted to usurp authority and another among the natives who had become disenchanted with the Ararat leadership and Atlantean influences. Both rebellions were put down, but they had broken the nation's sense of being a united people. As a result, leaders from many institutions, including pharaoh's court and the Governing Council, sent word to the priest that all was forgiven; please return to your duties. Initially, Ra-Ta and his community were not eager to leave the tranquility of the Nubian mountains and return to all the busyness of fast-growing Egypt and its many national and international activities.

Ra-Ta had become more spiritually and mentally powerful than ever before, but his body was now old and feeble. Cayce explained that during his exile the high priest entered more and more into deep meditations whereby he developed closer relationships with the Creative Forces and the god Hermes-Thoth; as a result greater were his abilities to manifest celestial, godly powers—miracles. But Cayce said that the priest's greatest miracle was a radiant peace that touched everyone near him and living around his little band of practitioners. This peace was enjoyed by the peoples in Nubia and was reported back to Egypt by many emissaries. All of Egypt wanted to be near the great priest and enjoy his rare energetics, for peace had left Egypt.

In addition to the miracles and peace, he and his community had built and continued to build a library of knowledge and wisdom. They developed a system of reckoning the location and orientation of the planets and stars as well as the various groups of stars and constellations. They discovered numerous influences that hold in place this particular solar system and planet. They also calculated the longitudes and latitude, the magnetic fields, the poles, and other important factors influencing life on Earth. Hence, in the Nubian land there were, according to Cayce, the first reckonings of those periods and cycles of the sun and its influence upon human life—the solstices, the equinoxes, seasons, the poles, magnetic fields, planetary orbits, solar radiation, sun spots, and so on. Also, while in Nubia, there arose the understanding of planting by the phases of the moon, the effects of the tides, the calling of an animal in certain phases of the moon or seasons of the year, and the combining of elements in the mineral kingdom, vegetable kingdom, and animal kingdom, in various periods. All of these were first conceived through his growing connection to the creative, universal consciousness.

Cayce tells how the very presence of the enlightened priest and his entourage would affect all of Egypt in ways the people never imaged! The Golden Age of Egypt was yet to come, and the return of the high priest was the spark that would light this fire.

During the exile in Nubia, Ra-Ta and his followers had continued the spiritual practices and had grown in their hearts and minds. Their vibrations, their knowledge, and their consciousness were much higher than they had been. Through those years of building Egypt, Ra-Ta and his supporters had slipped from high spirituality and consciousness into personalities and politics, losing some of their original ideals in the emotions and passions of human nature. Now, after these nine years away from those distracting influences, they were stronger mentally and spiritually. The Nubians had come to appreciate the high priest and his ways. According to Cayce, Nubians were a warlike people, and history records that the Egyptians called them the "people of the bow" and Nubia the "land of the bow," because of the quantity and quality of their primary weapon and skill in using it (see illustration 32). Many Nubians supported the priest in the capacity of guards—even acting as his escorts back through Upper Egypt to his temples in Lower Egypt near Heliopolis.

So great was the priest's contribution to the Nubians that memorials to the priest were placed in the mountains of that land. Cayce explained that whole mountains were honeycombed with deep tunnels leading to large chambers in which "perpetual fires are *still* in activity." Ra-Ta's community had lived and worked in and around these mountains for many years. They had built a community. They did not expect to ever come back to Egypt.

News of all of these achievements and activities in Nubia had been making their way to the people and to the leaders of Egypt. It seemed to many that the kingdom had acted in haste in their lifetime banishment of the priest and his followers. And remaining in the Egyptian temples were those, who had retained their higher attunement and purification and desired to bring peace to their friends and their people. They kept attempting to persuade the ruling council and the king that there must be the reestablishment of the high priest in his place in the land for the good of all. The king agreed, as did many on the council.

Ra-Ta's and his community's initial resistance to returning caused some in Egypt to consider ways that they could *compel* the priest and his ministers to return, even soliciting pharaoh to send his army after them! But, according to Cayce's reading of the ethereal Book of Life from which he told this tale, a series of emissaries and careful negotiations resulted in the return of the priest. Ra-Ta was now returning with the full power of a Pharaonic edict.

However, when it was time for the aged high priest to return, many began to fear that he was not physically able to carry on as he had insufficient strength to give to the people that which he had begun in the Egypt.

Cayce's readings asked us to imagine the effect all of this news had upon the peoples who classed themselves as the elect, the chosen, the elite, and yet recognized that there had developed among them envy, selfishness, strife, contention, and those things that are the lusts of the body and had separated them from their initial high ideals and hopes. They recognized this and wanted to correct it, but now their leader, their example and guide appeared near death! Worry spread throughout the community that the priest had become so decrepit that he would not live to guide the people again.

But the old priest had a few surprises left in him. He withdrew into the Temple Beautiful and began a long process of *regenerating* his physical body. How? First, the Cayce readings indicate that he let go of all of life's issues that had *aged* him! Take a moment to think about this deeply: he let go of all that had aged him. He simply let go them, choosing rather to fill himself—body and mind—with the *now*, with the mission before him and a great people.

Then, he began to *recreate* his body in its *elemental* forces for the purpose of carrying on for one last major service to humankind—a mission that Hermes had instilled in him while in exile. This mission was to leave records of the world from that day until when there is the change in the human race that awakens them to their celestial origins. The descent of the children of God into matter and back out into spirit will pass through seven stages, many of which will be darkness as to who they really are and what their ultimate destiny is. (More on this in the chapter on the seven stages.) This message, this record was to be in stone in a monument that no one could overlook or ignore. And that monument was the Great Pyramid. In this edifice, this Wonder of the Ancient World, was recorded a prophecy, a pyramid prophecy that would amaze all who came to know its message. The entire pyramid prophecy will be covered in a later chapter.

With this mission driving him, Ra-Ta began rejuvenation.

The high priest had come to know that the regenerating forces are found in deep meditation, harmonic music, select potions, the right diet, and the reunion of body, mind, and spirit for a high purpose that was good for the community, the nation, and the world. Cayce explained that the motivating influence for his physical rejuvenation must be for "the *whole* of the human race, whether *any* enter physical incarnation as servants, as kings, as ministers, as those that mete penal justice, or those that would become emissaries, or ministers, or those that are of those sources that in material things bespeak of the lore of the attributes of physical relationships. All are to, and for, and of, that that makes for an awakening of those conditions, that make for an awareness of that manifested at that period." The glory and beauty of ancient Egypt and its people and culture must be as a blessing to humanity: physically, mentally, and spiritually. And the record of the souls must be recorded in the Seventh Wonder of the Ancient World, the Great Pyramid, for all to see and know the truth about who we really are, why we incarnate, and what our ultimate destiny is.

Motivated by this mission, Ra–Ta entered deep meditation while a highly skilled and unusually magical musician played rejuvenative music. This musician's name was *Oum-Teck-Pt*. It is so fascinating that his name begins near the sound that symbolizes the beginning, duration, and dissolution of the universe in ancient Hinduism, *Aum* (with an "o" sound). Cayce said that the "oum" portion of his name indicated musi–cality. The "teck," or more likely "tek," portion indicates *voice* (we may also consider this to be *sound*). "Pt" is an abbreviated sounding of Ptah, the god of creation. Thus Oum–Teck–Pt is "one who brings creation (in this case, re–creation) through musical sound."

He was not an Atlantean, not even an Ararat, but born and raised among the natives! Yet he was innately skilled in music, and not just musical music, as we know it, but a very rare form of music. Cayce explained that Oum–Teck–Pt knew how to use music to "arouse the developing forces in a body" to heal it, even transform it. He actually knew musicality of biological life as it grows. Everyone recognized his rare abilities, making him the chief musical choice of the king, the priests, the Council, and the whole community!

However, so sensitive was Oum-Teck-Pt that during the tumultuous times of banishment and rebellions, he had to withdraw from the community and the temples. Cayce tells how he hid in the hills and sand dunes and caverns of the land—even hiding occasionally among the tombs. During this period he watched humanity, observing the musicality of their turmoil but kept himself away from those vibrations. He made instruments and developed tones like vowels that would stimulate the spiritual centers or chakras of the body.

When old Ra-Ta lay before him in the temple seeking rejuvenation, Oum-Teck-Pt knew what to do. He alternated stringed and wind instruments, playing each through the seven-note scale, holding on each while Ra-Ta would tune his seven chakras, those energy vortexes within his body, to the vibrations of the notes—both via the vibrations of the strings and the moving sound of the wind. Over and over, these two worked: tuning, retuning, and fine-tuning his chakras. In turn, they generated rejuvenative hormones and energies through his body and lifted the lotuses of his mind.

In addition to these sessions, Ra-Ta ate to nourish his body rather than please the palate. He cleansed his body of toxins. He developed tonics that aided the body's regeneration. He experienced massages and hydrotherapies that renewed his muscles, tissue, and circulation. He also set aside time to renew his thoughts and purposes. Each of the seven chakras had a mental dynamic, a lotus of understanding to be reawakened. He opened his heart and mind to *life*, shedding the dulling effects of daily cares and struggles. His mind and body became a channel of pure life, energy, and high purpose.

After seven years of this, Ra-Ta came out of the temple a regenerated man—shocking everyone. The word of his regeneration spread around the world. Emissaries from around the world came to see the rejuvenated priest. Word spread that aging was not a certainty. Somehow one could rejuvenate and live as long as one wanted to or needed to. The high priest was now considered a god! His name became Ra-Ta Ra, or simply Ra. The whole of the nation was with him in building the Great Pyramid exactly as he, Hermes, and other enlightened guides directed. The nation came alive again—one people, one mission, no contention, no factions. For the next one hundred years they worked together building the Great Pyramid and recording in its stone the story and prophecy of the children of God and their journey through matter and selfishness.

When it was accomplished, the high priest Ra-Ta Ra went back into his temple and quietly withdrew to the deeper meditations beyond physicality and earth—in other words, he died to this world and these dimensions. The mission he sought to pursue so long ago with his virgin mother of the tribe of Zu, Arda, and the peoples of the tribe of Ararat was completed. Even so, he knew that the souls of the children of God were headed deeper and deeper into matter and individuality, and even his soul would return to new incarnations that were more materialistic and human than godly and enlightened. Even so, he knew someday that all of this would be done and all souls would awaken spiritually to their celestial true selves and their eternal life in cosmos with their Creator and the community of the souls of the universe. But until that wonderful time, earth and the cycles of incarnations were going to be the schoolhouse for soul growth and karmic processing.

13

A Most Important
Female Pharaoh

A n Egyptian legend tells how an unseen consciousness within
the infinite darkness dreamed of the creation in his hidden
heart. From his heart he spoke the sounds of qualities, and
thus the creation appeared in the darkness. This was the heart of *Ptah*
(pronounced *pa-tah*), the "Opener"—in the sense of opening the heart
and then the mouth to sound the names of the manifested creation.
This was so reminiscent of Genesis' naming of the creatures. As the
creation progressed from dream and heart to physical manifestation,
Ptah became the primordial mound of earth upon which physical creation began. The original mound was called *Tatenen*. Ptah–Tatenen is the
"source of food, divine offers, and all good things," and his realms were
the deep regions *beneath* the earth "from which everything emerges,"
including plants, vegetables, and minerals. Everything is the work of
Ptah's heart and speech: gods are born, towns are founded, and order is
maintained. He is also "the ear that hears" the prayers of the people,
especially the prayers of the craftsmen who built the wonders of ancient Egypt.

Pharaoh Hatshepsut (pronounced *hat-shep-soot* or *hot-shep-soot*, meaning "foremost noble lady") was known as the "Beauty of Ptah" (see illustration 29 for an image of Ptah, and illustrations 33 and 34 for images of
Hatshepsut).

————

Another legend tells this wonderful story this way:
Amon–Ra, king of the gods, sat upon his throne and looked upon the

land of Egypt, and he said, "I will create a queen to rule over Ta-mery [Beautiful Land], I will unite the Two Lands [Upper and Lower Egypt] in peace for her, and in her hands I will place the whole world. Egypt and Syria, Nubia and Punt [northern Somalia], the land of the gods, shall be under her sway." And when he had spoken, there was silence among the gods.

While he yet spoke, Thoth entered into his presence: Thoth, the twice-great, the maker of magic, the lord of Khemennu [Hermopolis, the city of Hermes]. He listened to the words of Amon-Ra, king of the gods, and in the silence that followed he spoke:

"O Amon-Ra, Lord of the thrones of the Two Lands, King of the gods, Maker of humans, behold in the Black Land [Egypt] in the palace of the king is a maiden, fair and beautiful is she in all her limbs. Aahmes [ah-ah-mess] is her name [also known as Ahmose], and she is wife to the king of Egypt [Thutmose I]. She alone can be the mother of the great Queen, whom thou wilt create to rule over the Two Lands. She is in the palace of the king. Come, let us go to her."

Now the form of Thoth is the form of an ibis so that he may fly swiftly through the air and none may know him, and as an ibis he went to the palace of the king. But Amon-Ra took upon himself the shape of the king of Egypt. Great was the majesty of Amon-Ra, splendid his adornments. On his neck was the glittering collar of gold and precious stones, on his arms were bracelets of pure gold and electrum, and on his head were two plumes [see illustrations 5, 80a, and 80b]; by the plumes alone could men know the King of the gods. In one hand he carried the scepter of power, in the other the emblem of life [ankh]. Glorious was he as the sun at midday, and the perfumes of the land of Punt were around him.

In the palace of the king of Egypt was Queen Aahmes, and it was night. She lay upon her couch, and sleep was upon her eyelids. Like a jewel was she in her beauty, and the chamber in which she slept was like the setting of the jewel; black bronze and electrum, acacia wood and ebony were the adornments of the palace, and her couch was in the form of a fierce lion.

Through the two Great Doors of the palace went the gods; none saw them, none beheld them. And with them came Neith [goddess of war and hunting], goddess of Sais [a region on the western banks of the Nile], and Selk, the scorpion goddess [commonly known as *Serqet*, a goddess of magic and protection]. On the head of Neith were the shield and crossed arrows; on the head of Selk, a scorpion bearing in each claw the emblem of life [ankhs].

The fragrance of the perfumes of Punt filled the chamber. Queen Aahmes awoke and beheld Amon–Ra, King of the gods, Maker of humans. In majesty and beauty he appeared before her, and her heart was filled with joy. He held towards her the sign of life [ankh], and in her hand he laid the sign of life and the scepter of power. And Neith and Selk lifted the couch on which the queen reposed and held it high in the air so that she might be raised above the ground on which mortal men live while she spoke with the immortal gods.

Then Amon–Ra returned and was enthroned among the gods. And he summoned to his presence Khnum the creator [*ka-newm*], he who fashions the bodies of humans, who dwells beside the rushing waters of the cataract [Aswan, Egypt]. To Khnum he gave command saying, "O Khnum, fashioner of the bodies of humans, fashion for me my daughter, she who shall be the great Queen of Egypt. I will give to her all life and satisfaction, all stability, and all joy of heart forever."

Khnum the creator, the fashioner of the bodies of humans, the dweller by the cataract, made answer to Amon–Ra, "I will form for thee thy daughter, and her form shall be more glorious than the gods, for the greatness of her dignity as King of the South and North."

Then he brought his potter's wheel, took clay, and with his hands fashioned the body of the daughter of Queen Aahmes and the body of her *ka* [spirit, "twin" to her physical body]. The body of the child and the body of the *ka* were alike in their limbs and their faces, and none but the gods could tell them apart. Beautiful were they with the beauty of Amon–Ra, more glorious were they than the gods.

Beside the potter's wheel knelt Hekt, lady of Herur, goddess of birth [Hekt was a goddess in the form of a frog, layer of many, many eggs, thus goddess of birth]. In each hand she held the sign of life, and as the wheel turned and the bodies were fashioned [the physical one and the spiritual one], she held it towards them that life might enter into the lifeless clay.

Then Khnum, the fashioner of the bodies of human, and Hekt, the goddess of birth, came to the palace of the king of Egypt, and with them came Isis, the Great Mother, and her sister Nephthys [keeper of the secret place], Meskhent [goddess of childbirth and the birthing place, also called *Meskhenet*], Ta-urt [protectress of pregnant women and infants], and Bes, the protector of children [and households]. The spirits of Pé and the spirits of Dep [two spirits that created two dwelling places that became one] came with them to greet the daughter of Amon-Ra and of Queen Aahmes.

And when the child appeared, the goddesses rejoiced, and the spirits of Pé and the spirits of Dep chanted praises to her honor, for the daughter of Amon-Ra was to sit upon the throne of Horus of the Living, and rule the Land of Egypt to the glory of the gods. *Hatshepsut* was she called, Chief of Noble Women, divine of Diadems [Crowns], favorite of the goddesses, beloved of Amon-Ra. And to her the gods granted that she should be mistress of all lands within the circuit of the sun and that she should appear as king upon the throne of Horus before the glories of the Great House. And upon her was the favor of Amon-Ra forever.

———

Cayce's Egyptian tales include Hatshepsut, painting her in a most spiritual light and connecting her to Moses' search for God and the Promised Land.

Though the Bible develops the Moses story extensively, there is little physical evidence to support the biblical existence of Moses and the Israelite slaves in Egypt or even of an exodus of Israelites out of Egypt. Most scholars date the biblical exodus to about 1445 BC. Curiously, Edgar Cayce's readings of the Akashic records also point to this time period and connect Moses with one of the greatest female pharaohs in Egyptian history, Pharaoh Hatshepsut, who ruled from 1479 to 1458 BC as "King of Upper and Lower Egypt." She was the third woman to be pharaoh—the others being Merneith, who ruled from 3050 to 3000 BC, and Sobekneferu, who ruled from 1806 to 1802 BC. Egypt did not pass over females when it came to who was heir to the throne; the eldest child of the royal bloodline, whether it be a daughter or a son, inherited the throne and the crown.

Of course there were more famous Egyptian women, such as Queen Nefertiti (wife of Pharaoh Akhenaten, daughter of Pharaoh Ay) and Pharaoh Cleopatra VII (daughter of Pharaoh Ptolemy XII, an unpopular king who was kept in power by Roman general Pompey). Pharaoh Hatshepsut had more power than these two women. Hatshepsut's two-decade rule was the longest among ancient Egyptian women, at a time of the New Kingdom's "golden age." She is said to have amassed enormous wealth that she channeled into building projects, and she launched military campaigns. In every sense of the terms, she was *king* and leader of the armies.

Hatshepsut's father was Thutmose I and her mother, Queen Ahmose [Aahmes]. Hatshepsut was born around 1508 BC and is recorded to have "disappeared," assumed to have died, in 1458 BC. Cayce indicates that she left Egypt, choosing to travel with Moses in a search for the biblical "Promised Land." If the Exodus was around 1445 BC, that would have made her sixty-three years old when she left the throne and journeyed across the Red Sea.

———

A tomb and mummy of her were never found in Egypt, until today, when some believe that they have found her body. In 1903 a mummy was found lying on the ground next to the sarcophagus holding the mummy of Hatshepsut's wet nurse in a tomb in the Valley of the Kings in Luxor. For decades, that mummy was left unidentified and remained in the tomb because it was thought to be insignificant. In 2006 Egyptologists began searching for Hatshepsut's mummy, and the unidentified mummy was their first consideration. At the same time, the *Discovery Channel* gave Egypt $5 million to set up a DNA lab to test mummies. The lab was established in the basement of the Egyptian Museum in Cairo. The unidentified mummy was brought from Luxor to the museum for DNA testing. The lead Egyptologist, Dr. Zahi Hawass, said his first clue that it could be the lost queen was the position of the left hand on her chest—a traditional sign of royalty in ancient Egypt. Experts then made a stunning match. A tooth, which had been found in a relic box displaying Hatshepsut's insignia and containing embalmed organs, fit a gap in the mummy's jaw. DNA testing also has shown similarities between the mummy and the mummy of Hatshepsut's grandmother, which had been identified earlier. The lead Egyptologist told The Associated Press that "we are 100 percent certain" the mummy is that of Hatshepsut. On June 27, 2007, the lead Egyptologist unveiled both mummies—Hatshepsut's and that of her wet nurse, which had initially been investigated as possibly being the famous queen. The strikingly different mummies were displayed inside long glass cases draped with Egyptian flags. Hatshepsut's linen-wrapped mummy was bald and much larger than the slim, child-size mummy of the wet nurse, which had rust-colored locks of hair. The lead Egyptologist said that Hatshepsut's mummy suggested that she was obese, probably suffered from diabetes, had liver cancer, and died in her 50s.

Despite this modern news, the Cayce readings indicate that Hatshepsut and her daughter Sidiptu left Egypt with Moses and the Israelites. If this is true, then the mummy is not Hatshepsut's. And there is some evidence to support this.

Molecular biologist Scott Woodward, director of the Sorenson Molecular Genealogy Foundation in Salt Lake City, Utah, noted: "It's a very difficult process to obtain DNA from a mummy," said Woodward, who has done DNA research on mummies. "To make a claim as to a relationship, you need other individuals from which you have obtained DNA, to make a comparison between the DNA sequences." Such DNA material would typically come from parents or grandparents. With female mummies, the most common type of DNA to look for is the mitochondrial DNA, which reveals maternal lineage, said Woodward, doubting that the research could state 100 percent certainty about the mummy's owner.

Egyptologists also believe that Hatshepsut stole the throne from her young stepson, Thutmose III, who scratched her name from stone records in revenge after her disappearance or death. Thutmose III became known as the "Napoleon of Ancient Egypt" as a result of his many war campaigns. But it is just as likely that the defacements were due to her joining with Israelites in their search for God and the Promised Land beyond Egypt.

———

Hatshepsut's most famous accomplishment is her funerary temple in ancient Thebes, on the west bank of the Nile, across from the city of Luxor today. The colonnaded sandstone temple was built to serve as tribute to her power. Surrounding it are the Valley of Kings and the Valley of the Queens, the burial places of Egypt's royal leaders.

Hatshepsut was one of the most prolific builders among the pharaohs, commissioning hundreds of construction projects throughout both Upper and Lower Egypt. Almost every major museum in the world has a collection of Hatshepsut statuary.

Cayce gave two wonderful readings on Hatshepsut. Here's a portion of one:

"The wisdom of Hatshepsut may be in the entity in the present experience as a *builder* in a mental, a commercial or a material way. The spirit of the mother in that experience, then, may *yet* aid and guide in the present; *beautiful* in body, *beautiful* in mind in the experience, yet turned the world upside down!

"Then, in self find the way to aid; and call again on Ra-Ta and on Hatshepsut. They are as Urim and Thummim, a channel only." The mind is the light; the brain is the device, or channel, through which this light comes—as were Hatshepsut and Ra-Ta.

Whether the mummy is really the physical remnant of Hatshepsut or she died with the Mosaic tribes in their search for God and the Promised Land remains unclear. But, as Cayce's readings indicate, her spirit and power to assist seekers remains ready to help, even today—as a channel, not the Source.

Here's an edited portion of another reading on Hatshepsut:

"The entity then was in that land now known as Egyptian, during the period when the princess Hatshepsut was in power; and the entity's name was Sidiptu, hence a [step] sister of that leader Moses, the law giver of Israel. During the reign of the mother [Hatshepsut], the entity was associated with those peoples later despised on account of the love

(physical) that the mother found in association with a peoples [Israel-
ites, the "chosen people"].

"And the entity was then pledged to one of the leaders of Israel, in
the house of Levi; and being despoiled by an Egyptian, it was *this* one
that the brother Moses slew, hence causing that disruption which
brought—at the latter period of the mother's and the entity's sojourn in
the land—a *new* Pharaoh to the ruling of the peoples; this one coming
then from the mountain or southern land of an almost divided land
over this incident.

"This is of interest, then, in the entity's experience in the present: one
that has had an experience that deals with the universal manifestation
of a spiritual or unseen power is sacred to the entity."

Cayce has pointed us to the time of Hatshepsut as the era of Moses
and the Israelites in Egypt. What follows is a historical story, and it may
be the best fit with the biblical story.

The royal bloodline in ancient Egypt ran through the *women*, not the
men. Hatshepsut was the daughter of Thutmose I and his wife of royal
blood, Ahmose [Aahmes], thus Hatshepsut continued the royal bloodline. She reigned as pharaoh until she disappeared. Some believe that
she ran away to escape capture and death at the hands of Thutmose III
and that he wrestled complete power from her during the Kadesh Re-
volt in 1458 BC, when he took complete control of Egypt's armies.

Thutmose III was *not* a legitimate heir to the throne, because he was
the son of Thutmose II and his *concubine* Iset, who was not of royal
blood. This may be why Cayce called him a "new" pharaoh, not being of
the lineage. Even Hatshepsut wrote that she considered him to be a
bastard child of her deceased husband and not in line for the throne.

But Thutmose III's counselors schemed to have him marry a woman
of royal blood, thus a son by her would be rightful heir to the throne.
This would give Thutmose III a degree of ownership of the throne. He
first married Sat–jah of royal blood, who bore him a son, Amenemhet.
But this son died suddenly in his youth. Could he have been the Bible's
firstborn of pharaoh that died as a result of Moses' Passover curse on
every first-born son that did not have the blood of the lamb upon their
door?

Thutmose III also married Merytre–Hatshepsut, who was *not* a daughter of Hatshepsut but was of royal blood. Merytre–Hatshepsut bore him a son, Amenhotep II, who gave his father sufficient rights to the throne. Curiously, this son and heir, Amenhotep II, also lost his first-born son! He then had a second son, Thutmose IV. Thutmose IV eventually became a pharaoh, but he wrote on the famous Dream Stela that he was not the rightful heir. The Dream Stela stands today between the Sphinx's front legs. Was this because his older brother was the true heir but had died during the Passover curse? Furthermore, records indicate that during the reign of Amenhotep II he was not able to conduct any military operations, as his father had. Could this have been because he had lost much of his army in the biblical Red Sea miracle, in which the sea parted for Israelites but closed upon pharaoh's army, killing them all?

Another supporting fact is the forty–year reign of the pharaoh who, according to the Bible, "knew not Joseph" (Exodus 1:8), but unknowingly adopted the Israelite baby Moses as his own. This pharaoh came to love Moses but used the Israelites as slaves. There is only one pharaoh who could fit such a lengthy reign at this time period, and that is none other than Thutmose III, the Napoleon of Egypt. This would identify Thutmose III as the pharaoh of the Israelite oppression and Amenhotep II as the pharaoh during the Exodus.

Also, if the Israelites began the exodus in 1445 BC, were in the desert for forty years, and then destroyed Jericho as they entered the Promised Land, this would set the time for the destruction of Jericho around 1405 BC. Historical records are very close to this date for the destruction of Jericho, which is dated to 1400 BC (John Garstang, *The Story of Jericho*, 1948, p. 122).

These historical events do seem to fit with the biblical story of Moses and the Exodus. Yet, despite all of this history and the lengthy, detailed Bible story, there is only one small line on one stela in all of Egypt that indicates the existence of the Israelites in Egypt. It is at the bottom of the stela for a more modern pharaoh, Merenptah, who ruled from 1202 to 1199 BC, some two hundred years after the Exodus and the destruction of Jericho. The translation of the hieroglyphics is: "Israel lies fallow; his seed is not" (see illustration 36). Why the historical data is so scarce is a mystery that may never be fully explained.

———

The largest and most precisely carved and inscribed obelisk on the entire planet is Pharaoh Hatshepsut's in the Karnak Temple in Luxor (illustration 35). It is one solid piece of red granite, 97 feet tall, and weighing somewhere between three hundred and seven hundred tons. An inscription at its base indicates that it took seven months to cut and transport the obelisk from its quarry. It is believed that the inscriptions were done at the site where it was erected. Near this massive obelisk stands a smaller obelisk erected by her father Thutmose I (1504 – 1492 BC). It is 75 feet high and weighs between 140 and 160 tons. Hatshepsut raised four obelisks at Karnak, only one of which still stands, the most impressive one.

Hatshepsut's obelisk is a testament to her glory and the skill of her stonemasons. Its inscriptions honor Horus, Ra, Amun, and her father Thutmose I, and also describe the obelisk: *"Worked with fine gold illuminating the two lands like the sun. Never was the like made since the primitive times of the Earth."* The "gold" in this passage is referring to the pyramidal cap, usually plated in electrum, a naturally occurring alloy of gold and silver, with trace amounts of copper and other metals. The "two lands" is the term for Upper and Lower Egypt, considered to be two different lands united under one pharaoh.

Egyptian obelisks were carved from single pieces of stone, usually pink or red granite from the distant quarries in Aswan. How such massive, heavy stones were transported hundreds of miles and then erected without breaking under their weight remains a mystery. Of the hundreds of obelisks that once stood in Egypt, only nine now stand. Many are found today in the central parks and museum concourses of New York, Paris, Rome, Istanbul, and other cities. Hatshepsut's remains the most magnificent and stands where it was first placed.

2. Bennu bird, the phoenix of Ancient Egypt

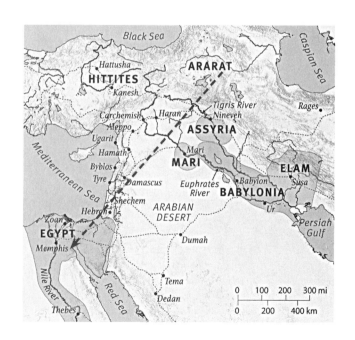

3. Map of Mt. Ararat and the journey to Egypt

4. Osiris holding the crook and flail

5. Amun-Ra (Amon-Ra) and
the antenna-like headdress

6a. Egyptian priest with wig
and leopard skin

6b. Egyptian priest with
shaved head and leopard skin

7. In the mother's arms is a *ba* (a bird's body with a human head), symbol for a soul

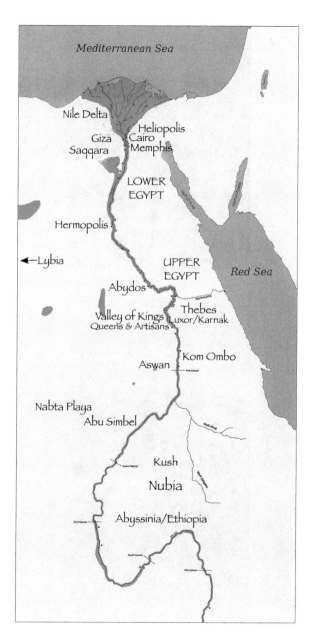

8. Map of Ancient Egypt

9. Atum (Ra-Atum)

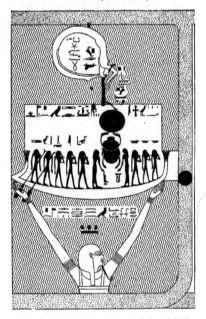

10. Goddess Iusaaset giving birth
from her crown chakra. Nun below
holding the sacred boat on
the primordial sea

11. Gods Geb, Nut, and Shu

12. Detail of Geb, Nut, and Shu

13. Creation montage, depicting the "Creative Forces" as gods

14. Two images of the god Ra

15. Goddess Nun

16. Osiris, Isis, and Nephthys

17. Set and Nubti. Nubti symbolizes
double mindedness

18. God Horus

19. Osiris and Ra-Atum

20. Alabaster altar in Ra Temple

21. Rejuvenative and illuminative bulbs

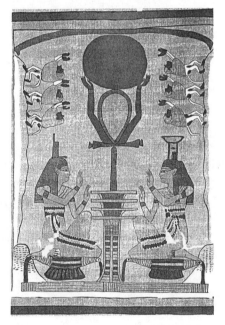

22. The djed, "backbone of Osiris"

23. Caduceus, "staff of Mercury"

24. Flower of life

25. Goddess Seshat

26. The weighing of the heart

27. God Hermes-Thoth

28. Goddess Ma'at

29. God Ptah

30. God Hapi, god of the Nile

31a. Nekhebet and Buto with the all-seeing eye

31b. Nekhebet and Buto on the royal crown

32. Nubian bowmen

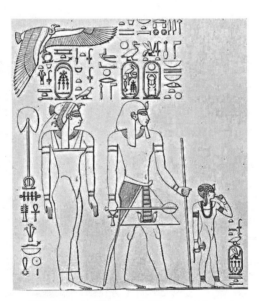

33. Aahmes (Ahmose), Thutmose I, and
young Hatshepsut

34. Pharaoh Hatshepsut

35. Hatshepsut's obelisk

Merenptah Stela

"Israel lies fallow; his seed is not."

36. Israel Stela whole

37. Ezekiel's wheel

38. Raghira's vimana

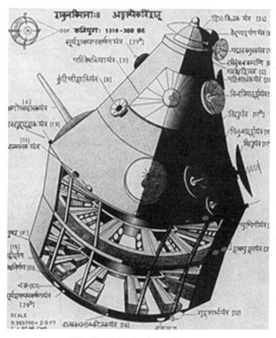

39. Double-decker vimana

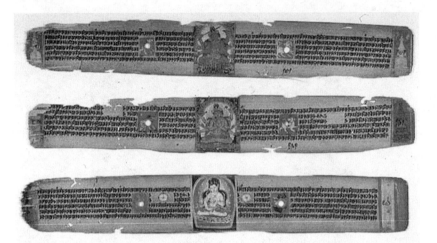

40. Palm leaf manuscript

41. Nasca Plains

42a. Pre-Columbian plane (supposed Zoomorph)

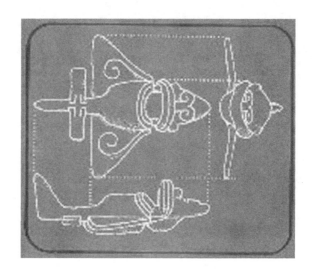

42b. Schematic of pre-Columbian plane

43a. Flying images on beam in Seti I Temple

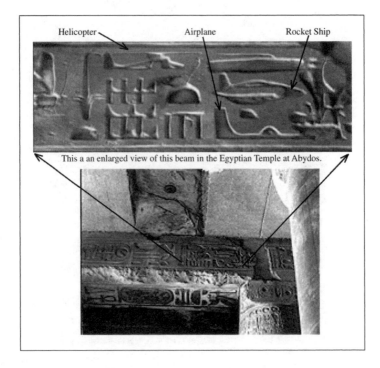

43b. Flying Images on beam in Seti I Temple

44. Wooden bird

ANCIENT TIMES
As Recorded in the Aztec Sun Disk

The Five Suns (Ages)

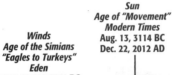

Sun
Age of "Movement"
Modern Times
Aug. 13, 3114 BC
Dec. 22, 2012 AD

Winds
Age of the Simians
"Eagles to Turkeys"
Eden
50,00-22,800-3114 BC

Earth
Age of the Jaguar
Darkness-"Like Wood"
Mu/Lemuria
12-10 Million Years Ago

Fiery Rain
Age of the "Blue Maze" People
Atlantis
210,000-106,000-50,000 BC

Water
Age of the Fish-like People
Mu/Lemuria
12 Million to 50,000 BC

45. Aztec Disk of the Ages

46. Piedras Negras

47. Sphinx Complex

48. Sphinx's Dream Stela

49. Drs. Zahi Hawass and Mark Lehner
drilling under the Sphinx

50. Artist depiction of Mayan Hall of Records

51. The Step Pyramid of Dosjer

52. Hellenikon Pyramid

53. The Giza Plateau Pyramids

54. The eight sides of the Great Pyramid

55. Looking toward the entrance to the
passageway to the Queen's Chamber

56. Inside the passageway to the Queen's Chamber

57. The Pyramid of Kukulcan in Chichen Itza

58. The Coral Castle

59. Looking up inside the Chamber of
the Triple Veil at the "boss mark"
See arrow

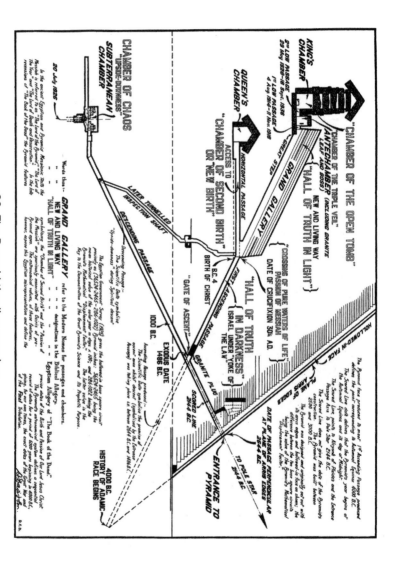

60. The Pyramid timeline overview

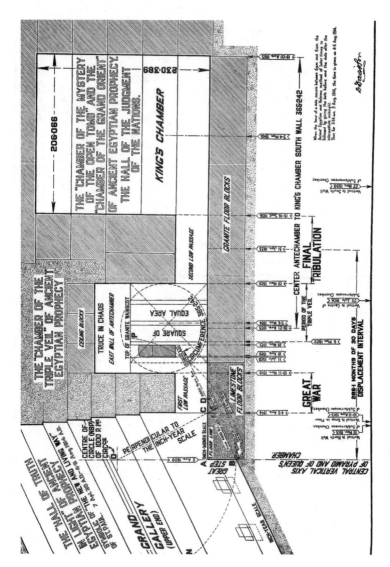

61. The Pyramid timeline "Great Step" and "Chamber of the Triple Veil"

Pyramid Prophecy Timeline

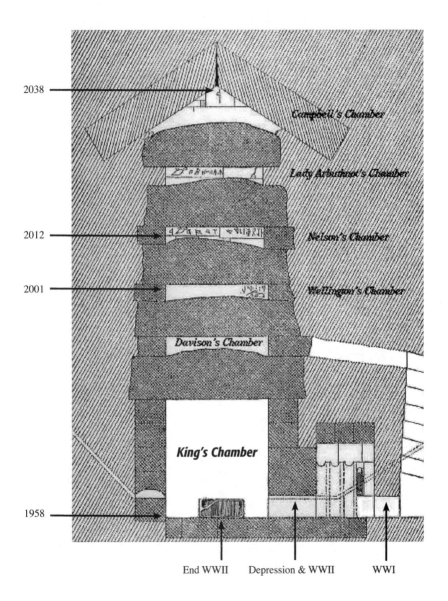

62. The Pyramid timeline "King's Chamber"

63. Nut swallows the sun each evening and births it each morning.

64. The World as the Beetle

65. Birth as the Cockerel (rooster):
Mystical Abraxas

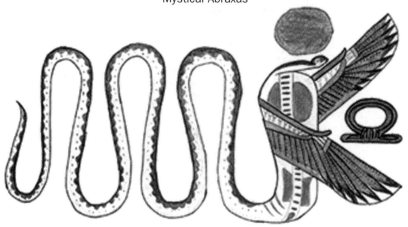

66. Mind as the Serpent

67. Wisdom as the Hawk

68. The Cross and the Crown

69. The Gate, the Door (Heaven's Gate)

70. The Sacred Heart
(artist's depiction)

71. Goddess Sati with the
Eye of Light watching over her

72. Ra as Aton with rays
ending in caring hands

73a. Ra circled by raised cobra with
single point of consciousness

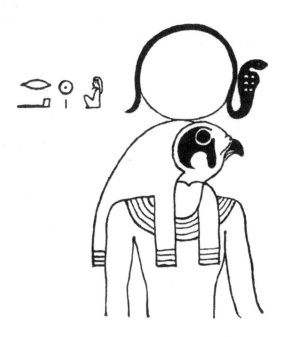

73b. Symbolic depiction of Ra- or
God-Consciousness and glyph

74. Anubis

75a. Sennedjem's Anubis' jackals catch the Scent of Heaven in the lotus

75b. Detail of Anubis' jackals and lotuses

75c. Close-up of Anubis' jackal and lotus

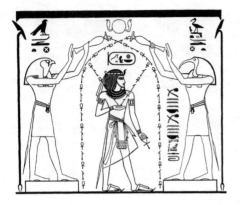

76. Horus and Hermes-Thoth purifying incarnate man with symbols of Life (ankhs) and Guidance (staffs)

77. Winged scarab of resurrection from the dung of life and winged consciousness above the daily awareness

78. Symbols of higher thoughts and raised kundalini and lotuses

79a. Hathor's Glyph: "The mind's place is with the heart."

79b. Hathor's love in the Age of Taurus among the papyrus reeds in the Nile

79c. Love (Hathor) brings forth the life force, higher consciousness, vision, and affection

80a. Amun-Ra (Amon-Ra) and Mut

80b. Amun-Ra, Mut, and Khonsu

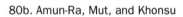

80c. Goddess Mut holding Anubis' staff of guidance

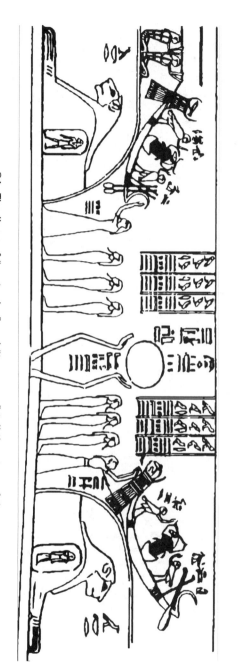

81. The lions of "yesterday" and "tomorrow" tell the story of the entrance into incarnations and the exit out of earth lifetimes.

82a. Egypt bulb on temple wall

Serpent–Kundalini

← Ka–Spirit

Djed–Resurrection

82b. Egypt bulb with detail

83. A section from *The Egyptian Book of the Dead*

14

ANCIENT FLIGHT

I n chapter one we learned that the high priest Ra–Ta traveled around the world by flight, sharing and learning what other temple leaders were doing. It is difficult for us to believe that ancient peoples had the technological know–how for air travel, given our evolutionary view of life—everything old is primitive, we are the apex of evolution. Of course this view overlooks Cayce's statements about an involution out of pure energy that occurred prior to the evolution up through matter.

In one of his readings for a reincarnated Atlantean he told him: "The entity then controlled those activities where communications had been established with other lands, and *the flying boats that moved through air or water* were the means by which the entity carried many of those to the Iberian land, as well as later those groups in the Egyptian land—when there had been the determining that the records should be kept there." (my italics)

Consider one of Edgar Cayce's readings for a soul who flew often in ancient times: "Before that [incarnation] we find the entity was in the Atlantean land, during those periods particularly when there was the exodus from Atlantis owing to those activities which were bringing about the destructive forces. There we find the entity was among those who were not only in what is now known as the Yucatan land, but also the Pyrenees and the Egyptian. For the manners of transportation, the manners of communications through the airships of that period were such as Ezekiel described of a much later date." Cayce associates these Atlantean airships with Ezekiel's vision of flying wheels, living crea- tures, and the spirit, and wherever the spirit would go, the wheels and creatures went. (Ezekiel 1:20-21) Were Ezekiel's envisioned wheels ancient airships? Let's explore this further.

Ezekiel's Flying Wheels

Around 525 BC, the biblical prophet Ezekiel described seeing flaming wheels in the sky, which moved as the spirit within them desired or willed. "The four wheels had rims and they had spokes; and their rims were full of eyes round about. And when the living creatures went, the wheels went beside them; and when the living creatures rose from the earth, the wheels rose. Wherever the spirit would go, they went, and the wheels rose along with them; for the spirit of the living creatures was in the wheels. When those went, these went; and when those stood, these stood; and when those rose from the earth, the wheels rose along with them; for the spirit of the living creatures was in the wheels. Over the heads of the living creatures there was the likeness of a firmament, shining like crystal, spread out above their heads. And under the firmament their wings were stretched out straight, one toward another; and each creature had two wings covering its body. And when they went, I heard the sound of their wings like the sound of many waters, like the thunder of the Almighty, a sound of tumult like the sound of a host; when they stood still, they let down their wings." (Ezekiel 1:18–24) (See illustration 37.)

During Edgar Cayce's deep trances, in which he was capable of connecting with the Akashic records and the universal consciousness, he explained that ancient peoples were indeed, for a time, much more evolved technologically as they possessed the legendary powers so often attributed to the Atlanteans, including flight through air and space. He also explained that they gradually lost this wisdom and ability as they became more earthly and materialistic. This wisdom required one to maintain a oneness, an attunement with the cosmic forces. Cayce indicates that we are in a new era in which the higher awarenesses and powers will be returning. The question of how we use these powers today remains to be seen.

Curiously, Cayce's first description of Atlantean flight was by *psychic* means! According to Cayce, the Atlanteans were initially so at one with the cosmos and cosmic energy that they could "transpose" themselves from one part of the universe to another—body, mind, and soul! They eventually became more confined to the realms in and around earth and developed high-tech machines that harnessed the radiation of the sun and stars through tuning crystals. The harnessed energy could then be used for driving their space, air, and underwater flying machines. Cayce described one type of their flying machines as an electrical impelling device. But as they became increasingly physical to the point that they lost their cosmic consciousness, they began to develop low-tech, nature-compatible physical devices to transport themselves around the planet. These were those pachyderm skins filled with gases that were often depicted in publications in the 1920s and '30s. These lighter-than-air gas machines were simple, clean, and environmentally harmless (though not so friendly to pachyderms).

It's important to keep in mind that Cayce saw all of us as reincarnated souls from those ancient times. Therefore, the wisdom is latent within us and within the *collective* human consciousness. Flight to the stars may come faster than we currently imagine. Once the understanding comes through the veil separating deeper cosmic consciousness from daily earth consciousness, we could be building and flying farther than we ever imaged. When asked if we would ever travel through space at the speed of light, Cayce replied that we'd be traveling at the speed of *thought*—the only speed capable of traversing the distances in space. This may be a return to the psychic travel of the earliest Atlanteans, "transposing" themselves from one end of the universe to the other. Our great breakthrough may not be a new alloy or composite, but a new level of consciousness.

Flight in Ancient India

Some of the most ancient literature on flying vehicles is found in the classic epic poem *Ramayana*—comparable to Homer's *Iliad* and *Odyssey*. In the *Ramayana* flying ships are a natural part of the story, as if they were commonly understood and used by the people. Dating the origin of *Ramayana* is difficult; scholars have speculated that it was created from as early as 6000 BC to as late as 400 BC! Most date the poem to around 1500 BC.

Two types of flying vehicles appear in this Indian classic. The first is called a "Puspaka car." It is described as resembling the sun and belonging to Rama's brother Raghira, who purchased it from the powerful Lord Ravan. It is an aerial car that goes "everywhere one wills it to go." It is said to resemble a bright cloud in the sky. Consider this passage: "King Rama got in, and the excellent car, at the command of Raghira, rose up into the higher atmosphere" (see illustration 38).

The second type of flying vehicle is called *vimana*, one of the most common terms used in ancient Indian texts. A vimana is described in the *Ramayana* as a "double–deck, cylindrical aircraft with portholes and a dome" (illustration 39). It was said to fly at the speed of the wind and had a melodious sound as it flew. In some ancient Indian texts, vimanas were said to have been so numerous in design and style that it would have taken several books to describe them all. There are extant manuscripts that can only be described as flight manuals for controlling various types of vimanas.

In Chapter 31 of *Samarangana Sutradhara* (literally, "Battlefield Commander") written by King Bhoja, an Indian aircraft is described as looking "like a great bird with a durable and well–formed body having mercury heated by fire underneath it. It had two resplendent wings, and is propelled by air. It flies in the atmospheric regions for great distances and carries several people. The inside construction resembles heaven created by Brahma himself." King Bhoja wrote this in the eleventh century AD but claimed his knowledge was based on Hindu manuscripts that were considered to be ancient even in his time. Some of the techniques for manufacturing flying craft described in King Bhoja's book have been in use by British and American aircraft companies since World War I and have been found to be sound aeronautical principles, even though described nearly a thousand years earlier in this old Sanskrit work. King Bhoja writes, "By means of the power latent in the mercury which sets the driving whirlwind in motion, a man sitting inside may travel a great distance in the sky."

So advanced was flight that the ancient Indian literature contains many varied descriptions of aerial acrobatics! For example, in one manual we find these terms and movements: *Dayana* (coming down), *Uddayana* (flying above), *Sundhara* (hitting the target with high speed), *Kanda* (rising suddenly), *Vyanda* (coming down quickly), *Karpostika* (flying still or hovering), *Smasrina mandala vartina* (spiral or circling flight). The ancient Indian sage Bharadwaja explains many types of vimanas (flying crafts), such as *áakuna Sundara, Rukma, Tripura, Vairajika, Garuda,* and several more. He also gives detailed descriptions of different parts and mechanisms in these crafts, two of which are *Suryasaktya-Karsanadarpana* and *Souramani,* which literally mean, respectively: solar mirror and solar cell!

Many of the Indian texts describe terrible battles in the sky using these flying machines. Some describe what may have been the end of this wondrous flying age, the dropping of a terrible bomb: "Gurkha flying in his swift and powerful vimana hurled against the three cities of the Vrishis and Andhakas a single projectile charged with all the power of the Universe [atomic or nuclear?]. An incandescent column of smoke and fire, as brilliant as ten thousand suns, rose in all its splendor. It was the unknown weapon, the Iron Thunderbolt, a gigantic messenger of death which reduced to ashes the entire race of the Vrishnis and Andhakas."

Some Indian flying vehicles were said to be able to "mount up to *Surya mandala,*" meaning the solar region—the planets! And still others could go to the *Naksatra mandala,* which is the stellar region—the galaxy!

One of the palm leaf manuscripts found in India is the *Amsu Bodhini,* which contains very detailed information about the planets. The information is so specific that only someone who actually traveled to the planets or sent flying machines to them could know these details. The information includes the different kinds of light, heat, color, and electromagnetic fields of the various planets, including Earth. And it also contains information about the methods used to construct machines capable of attracting solar rays and separating this energy into its components. It also includes instructions for the manufacture of machines to transport people to other planets! Amazingly, it details unknown alloys that the ancients used to construct flying crafts that cannot be seen by the human eye. (See illustration 40 for an example of a palm leaf manuscript.)

Chaldean and Babylonian Flight

Indian manuscripts are not the only ancient texts to describe the knowledge and use of flight. In the ancient Chaldean work *The Sifrala,* there are over one hundred pages of technical details on building a flying machine! It contains words that are best translated as "graphite rod," "copper coils," "crystal indicator," "vibrating spheres," "stable angles," and the like. *The Hakatha* (Laws of the Babylonians) states: "The privilege of operating a flying machine is great. The knowledge of flight is among the most ancient of our inheritances—a gift from those from on high. We received it from them as a means of saving many lives." Who were these beings from "on high"? Some quickly answer aliens, but the ancient literature, including the Bible and its book of Genesis, would indicate otherwise. Chapter 6 of Genesis clearly describes three types of beings on the Earth in ancient times: humans, Nephilim, and the Sons of God. Edgar Cayce's readings indicate that those were times when many souls were still so attuned to the cosmic forces as to be like gods or aliens to everyday humans.

Mayan and Inca Flying Evidence

The Maya and Incas also contribute to the mystery of ancient flight. The Nasca Plains in Peru, with their magnificent and enormous land drawings that can be seen only from the air, add to the growing evidence that the ancient ones must have had the ability to fly. (See illustration 41.) In the South American mountains there are short "roads" that run directly off of a high mountain precipice! They appear to be takeoff runways for flying machines; what other possible use could these have? In Central and South America, archaeologists have found pre-Columbian models of airplanes! Some attempt to write these off as children's toys, but with all the necessary features of an airplane. (See illustration 42a and 42b.)

Ancient Egyptian Flying Machines

Ancient Egypt also contributes to the mystery of ancient flight. How could such flying machines be carved in the stone of a temple that is at least 3250 years old? The temple is located in what many agree is the most sacred ancient city in Egypt: Abydos. This city was the Mecca or the Jerusalem of the ancient Egyptians. As you can see in illustrations 43a and 43b, the stone contains the glyph of a helicopter, a rocket ship, and an airplane. Above the rocket ship you can see another craft that some believe is a submarine.

Archaeologists say that this particular piece of stone is just a *palimpsest*, meaning: "A manuscript, typically of papyrus or parchment that has been written on more than once, with the earlier writing incompletely erased and often legible." Of course, this palimpsest is not a manuscript and is carved in stone, not papyrus or parchment, and would be the result of some very strange rewriting over incompletely "erased" glyphs in the stone. But this is their answer, and they're sticking with it!

Ancient Chinese Flying "Birds"

Ancient Chinese books describe how a Chinese craftsman named Lu Ban created some flying machines between 770–475 BC. In *Hongshu* Lu Ban makes a passenger plane! According to *Youyang Zazu* (a collection of essays from Youyang) of the Tang Dynasty, Lu Ban once worked in a place very far away from his hometown, possibly Egypt. He missed his wife very much, so he made a wooden bird. After being redesigned several times, the wooden bird was converted into a kite that could fly long distances very quickly using the earth's jet stream. Lu Ban went home on the kite to be with his wife and returned to work in the faraway land the very next day!

In 1898, French archeologist Lauret found a wooden bird in an ancient Egyptian tomb in Saqqara. It was dated at around 200 BC. The wooden bird is now in the Egyptian Museum in Cairo. (See illustration 44.) Because the archaeologists believed that the ancient people had no concept of flying at that time, it was labeled "wooden bird" and had gathered dust for more than seventy years in a museum in Cairo. In 1969, Khalil Messiha, an Egyptian doctor who likes making models, happened to see it. This "wooden bird" reminded Messiha of his earlier experiences with making model airplanes. He thought it was not just a bird, since it had no claws, no feathers, and *no horizontal tail feathers*. Surprisingly, its tail was *vertical*, and it had an *airfoil* for wings, which qualified it to be a model airplane, not a bird. He then made a replica of the model. Although he didn't know how ancient Egyptians flew it, when he threw the model, it glided through the air. Further testing showed it was not only able to glide, but was also on a scale similar to modern gliders.

Aeronautical specialists have found that this model was very similar to modern propelled gliders. With a small engine they can fly at a speed of forty-five to sixty-five miles per hour and can even carry cargo. Since ancient Egyptian artisans used to build models *before* constructing real objects, it is possible that this kind of bird-plane was a model from which a real plane would have been constructed. This could have been the flying "bird kite" that Lu Ban used to fly from Egypt to his home in China and back again the next day!

Alexander the Great Is Attacked by Airships

Around 326 BC Alexander the Great invaded India. To his surprise and the surprise of his men, they were initially repelled by an aerial attack of "flying fiery shields." Is it possible that some Indians still possessed flying vimanas as late as this date? Whatever the case, the Indians were unable to sustain them and were ultimately defeated. Apparently, they also did not possess their ancient bombs or simply did not use them because of the horrible suffering that resulted from their initial use. Alexander was unable to find any of these flying shields once he got into the country.

If the ancients did not have flight, they certainly wrote a lot about it. We have very physical evidence of their knowledge of not only air travel but also underwater travel and even space flight! There are numerous carvings, drawings, models, and an amazing number of manuscripts about flying machines. And the evidence of flight is found in cultures around the planet—in Indian, Chaldean, Babylonian, Egyptian, Mayan, Incan, South American, and Asian. There are literally hundreds of documents in India that date back to ancient times that can only be described as flight manuals for many different aircraft models!

15

THREE CACHES OF PREHISTORIC RECORDS

A most curious piece of information in the Cayce collection of psychic discourses is his claim that there are three hidden chambers on this planet containing stone tablets upon which Atlanteans wrote a prehistoric story of a time when human spirits began to enter material bodies. He said that the stone tablets document millions of years of semi–physical activity in the mythological lands of Mu, Lemuria, Atlantis, Og, Oz, Zu, and others. The stones tell of a time when the life forces of the *godlings* of the Creator were attempting to manifest themselves in this three–dimensional world from multidimensional realms beyond our normal perception. These ancient beings retained their immortality and projected into matter from out of what we would consider to be pure energy or spirit. They were soul–minds and could push their consciousness into matter or withdrawal into higher dimensions at will.

The Mayans, Egyptians, Greeks, and many other major civilizations on this world have tales of these ancient times, but few today give much thought to these having been real events, and few would give any credence to these tales without some *bones* to support the story. But these early beings did not have bodies like ours today. According to Cayce, their bodies were not as dense as ours, and in the earliest periods they were more like ghosts than physical humans.

Chapter 6 in Genesis records that there once were four significant beings on this planet: the sons of God, men, the daughters of men, and the Nephilim, who were the offspring of the daughters of men mating with the sons of God. The Nephilim were giants with great power. In the biblical book of Numbers 13: 32-33, we find this account of the Nephilim: "The people that we saw in that land are men of great stature . . . the Nephilim, the sons of Anak, who come of the Nephilim; and we were in our own sight as grasshoppers, and so we were in their sight." A pre-Inca legend tells of an unexpected landing of a remnant group of Nephilim on the shores of their lands. This legend describes the Nephilim as so gigantic that a good-sized native warrior stood only as tall as the kneecap of a Nephil! The legend says that these Nephilim were struggling to survive. They had no women among them and were hated by everyone. According to this ancient tale, the great Creator God cleansed the pre-Incan lands of these remnant giants from ancient times in one single disastrous flood.

Mayan legends tell how the immortal children of God were tricked by the "Lords of the Underworld" into playing a game in which the penalty for losing was death, and the children lost every game, thus trapping them into a mysterious cycle of birth, death, and rebirth—the so-called wheel of karma. The Egyptians and the Greeks have a complex mythology of the intermingling of gods, superhuman beings, and normal humans. Even the Hopi have legends of a time when the spirits of humans could come and go from this world because the door to heaven was open in those ancient times. All of these legends are conveying the story of an ancient descent of celestial beings from heavenly realms into earthly activities, a descent that eventually trapped the spirits in the cycles and evolution of matter, causing them to consider themselves to be only terrestrial beings. The Aztec Sun Disk depicts three ancient ages ("suns") when the children of God lived in this world, then came a fourth age when they entered simian (monkey) bodies, concluding that the once great "eagles" of God were now little more than "turkeys," no longer able to fly to their once great heights. (See illustration 45.)

According to Cayce, the three record chambers containing these ancient stone recorders are located in three separate locations on the planet. One is under the waters near the Bahamian island of Bimini near the Gulf Stream in a sunken Atlantean temple. Another is underground near the Sphinx in Giza, Egypt. The third is beneath an overhanging temple in the Mayan lands. According to Cayce's readings, each of the record halls will be found and opened. Each cache contains the same story on thirty-two stone tablets—they are three sets of the same story.

Cayce explained that the set in the waters of the Bahamas is in a submerged temple beneath the slime of ages belonging to an Atlantean high priest and governor named Atlan, who mistakenly believed that he could safely keep a set of the tablets in this region of Atlantis, even though the continent was going through serious physical changes resulting from earthquakes, heightened volcanic activity, and even the "fiery rain" of terrible meteor showers. Atlan underestimated the destructive power of the earth changes, and his temple along with this portion of Atlantis sank beneath the sea. Cayce said that this temple "will rise and is rising again."

The set of records hidden in the Mayan lands belonged to another Atlantean, a high priest named Iltar, who sailed from sinking Atlantis and first stored his tablets in a temple he built in the Yucatan Peninsula. However, Iltar's first temple was destroyed when another inundation occurred in nearby portions of Atlantis. Iltar was forced to take his stone tablets and move deeper into the Mayan lands. Cayce's readings indicate that he then stored them at the massive Mayan site at Piedras Negras, Guatemala, called *Y-Okib* by the Mayans, meaning the "entrance" or "cave," located just over the border of Mexico in Guatemala. Iltar likely entered the Usumacinta River and traveled to the Piedras Negras site, which is on a high hill at a bend in the river. Cayce said that Iltar's temple will "rise again." In our times archaeologists have conducted many explorations of the massive Mayan temple complex at Piedras Negras, but it is a very difficult place to explore. (See illustration 46.)

The records stored in Egypt are in a subterranean chamber near the Sphinx. In some discourses Cayce described its location as being off the right front paw of the Sphinx in line with the Great Pyramid. In another discourse he clearly stated that the Egyptian record cache is between the Nile and the Sphinx, off its right front paw in line with the Great Pyramid.

He also said that the base of the sphinx was "laid out in channels," and in the left rear corner of the Sphinx, which is facing the Great Pyramid, one can find the wording of how the Sphinx was "founded, giving the history of the first invading ruler, Arart, and the ascension of Araaraart to pharaoh."

The Hall of Records in Yucatan may also be laid out in underground channels because both Mayan and Aztec complexes are known to have underground tunnels, chambers, and passage ways.

Cayce stated, "as time draws nigh when changes are to come about, there may be the opening of those three places where the records are one, to those that are the initiates in the knowledge of the One God . . . "

According to Cayce, the three record caches contain stone tablets, linens, gold, and artifacts of import to the cultures that stored them. He indicated that mummified bodies are buried with the records. As to the question about what language the records may be in, Cayce did not answer directly, saying only that this was a time when the entire world spoke one language, a time prior to the Tower of Babel legend in the Bible. Therefore, we could assume that each set of the records is in the same language as the others. In one reading he indicated that the Atlanteans had a slightly different dialect or perhaps pronunciation of the worldwide language from the rest of the world. In another reading (EC 2329-3), he actually stated that there are exactly "thirty–two tablets or plates" in the Egyptian hall of records. He said that these tablets would require interpretation, and this interpretation would take some time. Let's hope it does not take as long as the interpretation of the Dead Sea Scrolls of the Qumran caves.

The records are from Atlantis. They recount the times of the beginning when "the Spirit took form" and began to enter bodies. They describe the development of these bodies and these people throughout the ancient era of legendary Lemuria and Atlantis and the new peoples' subsequent migrations to new lands, including early Egypt. The records also describe the final destruction of Atlantis and the new construction in Egypt. Cayce said they contain the *who, what, where,* and *when* of these ancient times and the rediscovery that is to come in our times. (EC 378-16)

With his eyes closed and breathing rhythmically—his longtime stenographer, Gladys Davis, quietly recording the spoken words in shorthand—Cayce explained how the ancient ones were actually "rebuilding" already aged monuments on the "plains" of Giza as well as building new ones. Among the rebuilding projects was the Sphinx, which is, according to Cayce, older than the Great Pyramid. He directed our attention to the buildings that connect to the Sphinx—the Sphinx Temple and the Valley Temple.

He described how a Temple of Isis was lost during the ancient deluge "centuries before" the Sphinx existed. Cayce dates this great flood to 22,006 BC, so his dates are long before any archaeologist's dates for early Egypt. Cayce's predynastic period begins with builders who were invaders of Egypt, coming from the area of Mt. Ararat—connecting them to the supposed resting place of Noah's ark. These invaders were the demigods of ancient Egyptian lore and carved the amazing Sphinx (ca. 10,700 BC) prior to the building of the Great Pyramid (EC 195-14), which occurred between 10,490 and 10,390 BC. (EC 5748-6) Many archaeologists have found and published evidence of a significant influence in Egypt from peoples along the Euphrates and Tigris Rivers, Lake Van, and Mt. Ararat.

Around this time a surviving band of Atlanteans arrived on the Egyptian shores with their precious prehistoric tablets in tow. The Egyptians and Atlanteans agreed to build what Cayce called variously a "pyramid of records" (EC 2390-7), a "hall of records" (EC 519-1), and a "tomb of records" (EC 2329-2) in front of the Sphinx.

When asked exactly where this record cache was, Cayce said it was between the Sphinx and the Nile. (EC 378-16 and 5748-5) He also said that the "storehouse" was "facing the Sphinx" (EC 5748-5) and in "a pyramid of its own." (EC 2329-3)

In illustration 47, you can see how the Sphinx complex is laid out with its two temples. The pyramid of records may be under the Sphinx Temple, off the Sphinx's right front paw, as Cayce directed.

Cayce said that there were underground "connecting chambers from the Sphinx's right paw" to the records. The Dream Stela of Thutmose IV that sits between the front legs of the Sphinx reveals an underground chamber with a door (see illustration 48). Ground-penetrating radar conducted in the 1990s revealed an anomaly beneath the Sphinx that may well be this chamber. I have been all over this sight more than thirty times and can assure you that we are going to need the miraculous, magical help of the Spirit to find these records. As Cayce said, it cannot be entered until "the time has been fulfilled," and it "may not be entered without an understanding, for those that were left as guards may *not* be passed until after a period of their regeneration in the Mount, or the fifth root race begins." (EC 5748-6) The fifth root race is an evolving people with new, enlightened bodies that are coming during the shift to the new era. The regeneration in the Mount refers to our crown chakras. Cayce's insights into these most mystical concepts are very ethereal and otherworldly. He sees the climax of evolution as the return to our spirit-nature from whence we originally descended into matter.

When people would ask Edgar Cayce if they could be a part of the discovery and interpretation of these records, he would answer yes, but not necessarily the *physical* records. As strange as this may seem, according to Cayce, the records are also recorded in consciousness, in the deeper collective mind of humanity, and therefore, one could open and study the records anytime by entering deep meditation. Here is an excerpt from one of these strange readings:

"Q: How may I now find those records, or should I wait—or must I wait?

"A: You will find the records by that channel as indicated, as these may be obtained *mentally*. As for the physical records— it will be necessary to wait until the full time has come for the breaking up of much that has been in the nature of selfish motives in the world. For, remember, these records were made from the angle of *world* movements. So must thy activities be in the present of the universal approach, but as applied to the individual. Keep the faith. Know that the ability lies within self."

From the perspective that Cayce gained in his deep, hypnotic "sleep," all time is one. There is no space, no time. These are only characteristics of the limited dimension of physical, terrestrial life. Within us is a gateway to oneness, timelessness. The records may be reached by journeying within consciousness and through dimensions of consciousness, as Cayce did. He himself never physically went to Egypt, Bimini, Yucatan, or Piedras Negras. But he so completely set aside his terrestrial, outer self that he could journey through dimensions of consciousness to the Akasha, the mental hall of records, and from there he could read the records and explain them to us.

The great landmasses of Mu, or Lemuria, in the Pacific Ocean and Atlantis in the Atlantic Ocean were in their final stages of destruction; remnant islands were all that was left of their original greatness. Poseidia was the last island of the Atlantean continent. Iltar and Atlan were priests in the worship of the One God. In other readings Cayce called these worshipers the "children of the Law of One." The Yucatan peninsula appeared to be a good land to migrate to and establish a new community. Iltar and his ten cohorts did just that. They traveled to these new lands and there built temples and altars. According to Cayce's reading, on their altars they did not sacrifice humans; they sacrificed their weaknesses, attempting to make themselves spiritually stronger and purer and their minds more cosmically aware. They did this by altering their consciousnesses using circular magnetic stones and evoking the spiritual influences from the One Source. Even so, more earth changes occurred, and Iltar's initial temples and altars were destroyed, as were Atlan's. Iltar journeyed further inland and built new temples. In other readings Cayce recounts that Atlan lost his temples and altars when the island he was on finally sank.

Yucatan, Central Mexico, Southern California, Arizona, and New Mexico were fast becoming lands of mixed peoples from around the world.

The cause behind much of this destruction was that the high level of spiritual attunement and worship had slipped into self-gratification and glorification, leading to the worship of Baal, which was a self-gratifying approach to life rather than a cooperative oneness with nature and the cosmic forces. Cayce explained that using the same powers and methods, one could create a god or a Frankenstein—it all depended upon the ideals and purposes motivating the effort. Apparently, all the best of intentions slipped into darkness and selfishness, and the higher attunement was lost; even human sacrifice crept into the once pure rituals. Cayce asked, "Who may the true seekers be? Those who put and hold trust in the fact that they, as individuals, are children of the universal consciousness of God!" (EC 5377-1)

The records of the ancient world and its activities remain in Yucatan in one of Iltar's covered temples, in Atlan's cache under the waters of Bahamas, and under the ground near the Sphinx in Egypt.

An interesting bit of news that adds to this great story comes from a little-known discovery in China in 1900 by a Taoist monk named Wang Tao-Shih. The monk found a hidden ancient library in a series of caves. The texts in this library speak of an ancient time and place in "Motherland Mu." Mu is the original name for the great Pacific Ocean continent of Lemuria, which actually began before Atlantis. Chinese legends tell of the semimythical "Five Monarchs" who ruled China during a golden age of wealth and wisdom. This period is considered to have paralleled the early age of the Egyptian Pharaohs: 2852–2206 BC.

There have been many attempts to discover the halls of records in Mayan lands, the Bahamas, and Giza, Egypt. There have also been discoveries that indicate that the dating of the Great Pyramid and the Sphinx may be older than currently believed.

In 1992 U.S. Geologist Dr. Robert Schoch and amateur Egyptologist John Anthony West (author of *Serpent in the Sky*, Harper & Row, 1979) announced to the world press that the age of the Sphinx was much older than originally thought. This revelation sent a shockwave through the international community of professional Egyptologists. In the spring of 1996 in a letter to the Egyptology journal *KMT* (pronounced *k-met*; it is the ancient name for Egypt and means, "The Black Land," owing to the rich, black silt left by the Nile after flooding season). In this letter John Anthony West outlined his and Dr. Schoch's points:

"1. The Sphinx is not wind-weathered as most Egyptologists think, but water weathered, and by rain;

"2. No rain capable of producing such weathering has fallen since dynastic times;

"3. If it had, other undeniably Old Kingdom tombs on the Giza Plateau cut of the same rock would show similar weathering patterns; they do not;

"Ergo, 4. The Sphinx predates the other Old Kingdom tombs at Giza. Simple as that."

Dr. Schoch estimated the Sphinx had to have been constructed from

between 7000 to 5000 BC "and that the current head of the figure—
which everyone agrees is a dynastic head—is almost surely the result of
recarving." (*KMT*, Summer 1992, p. 53)

Another date-changing piece of evidence comes from the work of
Adrian Gilbert and Robert Bauval, published in their best-selling book
The Orion Mystery (Crown, 1994). Actually, the initial ideas about Giza star
alignments came from Edgar Cayce who stated from his trance state in
the 1920s that Giza was laid out according to the stars above it. In 1964
Egyptologist Alexander Badawy and astronomer Virginia Trimble published their findings on how the airshafts and passageways in the Great
Pyramid aligned with important stars in both the northern and southern heavens. In Gilbert's and Bauval's book they identified many correlations between the stars and structures on the Plateau:

1. The three great pyramids of Giza—Menkaure, Khafre, and Khufu—
    match the stars Mintaka, Al Nilam, and Al Nitak (*delta, epsilon,* and
    zeta Orionis) located in the Belt of Orion, noting that the third pyra-
    mid (Menkaure) is set off from the other two pyramids just as the
    third star in the belt (*delta Orionis*) is set off from the other two
    stars;

2. The alignment is most exact in the year 10,500 BC, the date Edgar
    Cayce gave for the construction of the Great Pyramid;

3. The star Saiph is over the pyramid of Djedefre, to the north of
    Abu Rawash, and the star Bellatrix is over the "Unfinished Pyra-
    mid" at Zawyat Al Aryan to the south. When Orion is on the
    meridian, the star cluster *lambda Orionis* representing the Head of
    Orion is over the Dashur pyramids;

4. When Taurus is on the morning horizon, the two pyramids of
    Dashur, known as the "Red" and the "Bent" pyramids, match the
    stars Aldebaran and *epsilon Tauri,* the two "eyes" of the bull in the
    constellation Taurus;

5. The hieroglyphic texts inscribed in the pyramids of Unas (2356–
    2323 BC) and Pepi II (2246–2152 BC) refer to the deceased king
    ascending into the southern skies in the region of the constella-
    tion of *Sahu,* which Gilbert and Bauval identify with the constel-
    lation Orion. The authors believe that these texts support the idea

that there had been some kind of spiritual relationship intended between the Great Pyramid and the Orion constellation.

Another discovery by Gilbert and Bauval was the time period when the sun rose on the eastern horizon in front of the lion-body Sphinx in the constellation of the lion, Leo. It was Cayce's date of 10,500 BC!

Andrew Collins—explorer and author of *From the Ashes of Angels: The Forbidden Legacy of a Fallen Race* and *Gods of Eden: Egypt's Lost Legacy and the Genesis of Civilization*—discovered that the constellation Cygnus (also known as the Swan or Northern Cross) overlays the Giza Plateau more perfectly than Orion, revealing some key underground passages. He published his finding in a book titled, *The Cygnus Mystery*; later he published more findings in his book, *Beneath the Pyramids: Egypt's Greatest Secret Uncovered*. This led to further investigations into underground caves and passageways that may lead to hidden chambers.

The ancient Egyptians were amazing tunnelers into bedrock. In the summer of 1999, Dr. Zahi Hawass and his team explored a water-filled shaft going some thirty-one meters into the bedrock of the Giza Plateau. Here's how he described their exploration: "We found that the first segment of the shaft, almost ten meters deep, leads to a single chamber about 8.6 by 3.6 meters in size. When we entered this chamber, it was empty. A second vertical shaft in the northern part of the chamber leads down for another 13.25 meters, ending in a 6.8 by 3.5 meter chamber, surrounded by six smaller side-chambers and a recess from which yet another shaft descended. Three of the side-chambers contained stone sarcophagi in the style of the Twenty-Sixth Dynasty, and two of the sarcophagi contained human bones. We also found shabtis [funerary figurines] and fragments of Late Period pottery in this level. In addition to the side-chambers, there is a recess in the southeastern corner of the main chamber, from which a third vertical shaft descends. After about eight meters, this last shaft ends in a chamber about nine meters square. The final chamber is the most interesting of all. Much of it is taken up by a rectangular emplacement in the center, carved from the living rock with the remains of a square pillar at each corner. The space left between the walls of the chamber and the emplacement in the center forms a kind of channel. The channel is broken at the entrance to the chamber, where the floor has been left at a higher level to connect it with the emplacement. This gives the channel the shape of the hieroglyphic sign *pr*, meaning 'house.' In the center of the emplacement, there is a large sarcophagus made of black basalt. The sarcophagus contained the remains of a skeleton, along with several amulets dating to the Late Period. We were surprised to find that there was also some red polished pottery with traces of white paint, which probably dates to the Sixth Dynasty [2325–2150 BC]."

All of this is vertically carved deep into the bedrock between the Valley Temple and the second pyramid—amazing workmanship, revealing just how capable the ancient Egyptians were of tunnel through bedrock and carving chambers.

As you might expect, many have gone searching for these record caches, or for *any* records that may shed light upon the great stone builders of the ancient world. Egyptologists have often stated that much of ancient Egypt is yet uncovered. Excavations are turning up new artifacts all the time. But there is no indication of a highly evolved civilization dating back to 10,500 BC. Even the texts in the China caves tell only of an ancient motherland Mu; there are no actual records from Mu in the caves. And, unless we are misinterpreting the hieroglyphic records that have already been discovered in Egypt, there is no report of a sophisticated ancient civilization predating the Pharaonic period, of which we have so much evidence. However, the hieroglyphic records do tell that the great Egyptian god Thoth (Hermes) hid *his* records in Egypt. This is an important message and has driven many to search for the hidden records of Hermes-Thoth. Since he was a god from the original creation time, his records could well tell of predynastic ages. His cache may even have artifacts from pre–Pharaonic times. In Edgar Cayce's discourses, Hermes is identified as one of the architects of the Great Pyramid and a key influence in the development of the impressive Egyptian civilization.

Throughout the 1990s and early 2000s in connection with Florida State University and with his partner Joe Jahoda, Dr. Joseph Schor, of the Schor Foundation and a Life Member of the A.R.E., led research on the Giza Plateau using ground–penetrating radar to locate underground passageways, halls, and chambers. His efforts resulted in some successes and some failures, as this type of investigation often does. One of his most interesting discoveries, yet to be fully investigated, is a supposed chamber under the Sphinx. The possible chamber or large room is possibly 26' wide, 40' long, with approximately a 30' floor-to-ceiling depth. Cayce identified this as an antechamber to the Hall of Records, with a passageway leading to the records. In 2009 Dr. Zahi Hawass, the then Secretary General of Egypt's Supreme Council of Antiquities, and Dr. Mark Lehner, long-time archaeologist on the Giza Plateau and especially knowledgable about the Sphinx, drilled holes into the limestone bedrock in order to check how high the ground water was rising since he was concerned that it would have a detrimental impact on the great monument. But this would also allow them to drop a camera down into any cavity that was found and view its contents. Their first drilling was only ten meters (32' 10"). They found no cavity, but plenty of evidence of ground water damage. The Dream Stela shows that the opening to a chamber beneath the Sphinx is some thirty-seven meters beneath the base of the monument. Considering this, Dr. Hawass drilled again; this time his crew drilled fifty meters into the bedrock (see illustration 49). And again he and his team found no opening in the bedrock.

Since the 1960s people have been searching for ancient records off the coast of Bimini. In 1998 researchers, funded through the A.R.E. by Don Dickinson, another Life Member and President of the Law of One Foundation, used submarines in an attempt to find submerged ancient structures off the coast of Bimini. Promising formations were found under millennia of sand and a hardened, coral-like crust. Dr. Joan Hanley of the Gaia Institute, Dr. Douglas Richards of the Meridian Institute, and others had been searching for decades. Drs. Gregory and Lora Little have conducted explorations in the Bahamas. They produced two DVDs of their findings, both available from Amazon.com.

The Littles also conducted archaeological research in Guatemala at a site Cayce implicated as the one where Iltar may have hidden his set of the Atlantean tablets. On this exciting and dangerous trip through the jungle and on the Usumacinta River, the Littles journeyed to the ancient Mayan site in Piedras Negras, Guatemala. Their findings indicate that cave entrances J-9 and O-13 appear to fit Cayce's description of the records being beneath an overhanging temple. (See illustration 46 for an idea of how the record chamber may appear.)

Each year new explorations are made in the continuing hunt for these ancient Atlantean tablets. A.R.E. reports on the progress of these explorations in their membership newsletter *Ancient Mysteries* and their magazine *Venture Inward* and on their web site, EdgarCayce.org. The records of all of these investigations are in the library at the headquarters of the A.R.E. in Virginia Beach, Virginia.

For now we are going to have to read these ancient records via the mental dimensions through deep meditation, as Cayce suggested. Eventually, we will have the stone versions to view—if not in this incarnation, then the next.

16

AMAZING PYRAMIDS

I magine the rays of the rising sun striking polished white limestone and a golden capstone on a massive structure sitting atop a high plateau. Imagine how the reflected light would move across your land as the sun made its path through the sky. Imagine the full moon shining on this edifice on a starry night and how its reflected light moved across your darkened land. This would have been the daily experience of those who lived near the Great Pyramid of Giza in those very ancient times.

The Great Pyramid

Dating these edifices of antiquity has been a challenge, especially with the recent discoveries of flaws in carbon–dating methods. Radiocarbon dating works by comparing the amount of normal carbon that is found in a sample with the amount of radioactive carbon. Both carbon and radioactive carbon are found in organic matter. While carbon is quite prevalent in organisms, radioactive carbon is present only in tiny amounts. Most scientists believe that the relative ratios of carbon and radioactive carbon that are found on the earth have remained constant over time, and using known rates of decay, they can estimate age on the basis of changes in this ratio in a particular artifact. Although the practice of radiocarbon dating is well established, there are several inherent problems with the process. The first of these problems is the fact that the original ratio of carbon and radioactive carbon is unknown. A second one is that factors as diverse as changes in the earth's magnetic field and changes in the amount of carbon available to organisms in times past could translate into perceivable differences in the carbon ratios in artifacts from ancient times. A third problem deals with changes in the atmosphere that could impact this carbon ratio. We know that atmospheric changes have occurred over time and are still occurring today. The fourth problem is the fact that carbon and radioactive carbon are independently formed so it means that their ratios to one another could have changed substantially from ancient times to today. Finally, the biggest problem is that the possibility of contamination of the sample over time is quite high—in fact, the older the sample, the higher the probability of contamination. Using carbon dating to date very old samples is chancy.

For example, the majority of the archaeological community believes that the Step Pyramid of Pharaoh Djoser at Saqqara (also spelled Sakkara, see illustration 51) is the oldest pyramid on the planet. It was constructed about 2620 BC. Surprisingly, some archaeologists have evidence that the pyramids in Greece are even older! The Hellenikon pyramid (see illustration 52) has been dated to 2720 BC, making it 100 years older than Djoser's and about 170 years older than the dating archaeologists give to the Great Pyramid, believed to have been built around 2550 BC. Of course, Edgar Cayce's reading of the Akashic record dates the building of the Great Pyramid at 10,500 BC. Early in Dr. Mark Lehner's career on the Giza Plateau, he carbon dated the mortar between the massive building blocks that compose the Great Pyramid. In order to get the most objective results, he sent his samples to two different labs. To his amazement and the amazement and distress of many others, both labs dated the mortar from the bottom blocks of the pyramid to 1400 BC, and the mortar between the top blocks of the pyramid to 3000 BC. The pyramid had been built upside down—its top before its bottom! A more likely explanation is that the carbon dating was actually dating mortar *exposed* to contaminating elements dating to the time of the *removal* of the original covering stones. Very few of the original covering stones remain today. But if this is the explanation for the odd dating, then the top of the pyramid was exposed in 3000 BC! That is 450 years before it was supposedly built!

Since the covering stones would have protected mortar between the building blocks, and it is not likely that the covering stones were removed shortly after they were put on, this carbon dating indicates that the Great Pyramid was built much earlier than archaeologists had imaged. They believe and continue to teach that Pharaoh Khufu built it around 2550 BC. But Khufu may have been the repairer of the Great Pyramid, which by Khufu's time had lost some of its covering stones, exposing the building block mortar to contamination, giving us a carbon date prior to Khufu. Also, a stone tablet called the "Inventory Stela" contains glyphs stating that Khufu built the temple of Isis beside *the already existing* Great Pyramid and Sphinx. The text reads:

Live Horus Mesdau; (to) King (of) Upper and Lower Egypt, Khufu, is given Life!
He founded the House of Isis, Mistress of the Pyramid,
beside the House of the Sphinx.

It certainly appears from this text that the Khufu built the House of Isis when the Pyramid and the Sphinx were already standing on the Giza Plateau.

Add to this that the only existing statue of Khufu (Cheops), the supposed builder of the greatest monument in Egypt and one of the Seven Wonders of the Ancient World, is a three-inch tall, poorly carved piece of ivory. He, whose men could carve granite, could not carve a statue of their pharaoh in some significant size and in stone? This is not likely. If Khufu were the builder of this edifice, wouldn't there be statues and stelae everywhere proclaiming his greatness? But there is only this little piece of ivory.

Edgar Cayce's readings of Akashic records say that the Great Pyramid was built by Hermes (Thoth) and the high priest Ra-Ta over a hundred-year period between 10,490 and 10,390 BC. And as we learned in an earlier chapter, it was completely sealed by Hept-supht, until Caliph Al Mamoun and his men broke into it in the year AD 832.

Let's move on to the features in these amazing structures. The complexity of some of these edifices is truly mind-boggling. Let's look at two: the Great Pyramid and the Chichen Itza pyramid.

I don't have space to cite all the amazing features of the Great Pyramid, but here are the most striking. It is aligned true north to within three minutes of a degree, despite centuries of settling and earthquakes. Modern man's best efforts were at the Paris Observatory and came only to within six minutes of a degree. The Great Pyramid is 485 feet high and covers thirteen acres (see illustrations 53 and 54). The pyramid rests on a platform that is perfectly square and level to within 8/10th of an inch. It has been estimated that over 2.3 million stones compose it. If the pyramid was built in twenty years, as some ancient sources state, it would mean setting over 13 stones per hour, 24 hours a day, for the entire 20 years, no days off. If Edgar Cayce was correct in saying that it took one hundred years to build, that is still over 2.6 stones per hour, 24 hours a day, for 100 years, no days off.

The surface of the Great Pyramid is 5.25 acres per side. Amazingly, each side is actually two sides, as the sides slope in to a center line (see illustration 54). The surface casing stones were straight to within 1/100th of an inch. The joints between the stones average only 1/50th of an inch in width, and yet there is an extraordinarily thin film of white cement between them that bonds the blocks together (this is the material Dr. Lehner carbon dated). The average weight of these casing stones is sixteen tons.

The slope of the Great Pyramid is 51° 51', making the height of the Great Pyramid in proportion to its perimeter at the base exactly the same as the radius of a circle in proportion to its perimeter. This is the well-known value of pi, or 3.14. In fact, it has been found that the perimeter of the Great Pyramid is exactly equal to a half minute of latitude at the earth's equator. The "sacred cubit" seen on the boss mark in the antechamber to the King's Chamber is exactly 1/10,000,000th of the radius from the center of the earth to the North Pole. Can this be mere coincidence when we know that the French meter was taken as 1/10,000,000th of the distance of a line drawn from the North Pole to the equator along a meridian that passes through Dunkirk?

The walls of the King's Chamber are formed by five courses of stone containing exactly one hundred blocks. The ceiling is made of nine massive granite beams each twenty-seven feet long and weighing between fifty and seventy tons each! As if this isn't amazing enough, four more layers of such beams and intervening spaces lie above the chamber ceiling, finishing in a gabled roof of limestones.

The sarcophagus in the King's Chamber is too large to fit through the door, thus requiring the room to be built around it. This coffer has the precise interior volume of the Ark of the Covenant. Could it have been used in a manner similar to the Ark—to contact God?

In 1986, a French team discovered an anomaly along the right wall of the passageway to the Queen's Chamber. To orient you, see illustrations 55 and 56. Illustration 55 shows the entrance to the Queen's passageway. Above it is the Grand Gallery, leading to the King's Chamber. Illustration 56 shows the end of the passageway with a step that allows the traveler to stand up a bit more, though not fully. The dark area at the end is the Queen's Chamber. On the wall opposite the modern light is the area of the passageway where the anomaly was discovered. Basically, the anomaly indicated that there was not solid rock behind that part of the wall. This may possibly be a chamber with no apparent entrance. The French team, consisting of Gilles Dormion and Jean–Yves Verd'hurt, received permission from the Egyptian authorities to drill through the stone wall into the open chamber on the other side. When they did, sand came out in volume. They stopped, concerned that this sand chamber had something to do with the ballast of the Great Pyramid and the estimated 2.3 million stones. However, when the sand was analyzed, it was found not to be indigenous to Giza or, for that matter, to Egypt! Where had this sand come? Why would the builders of the pyramid store sand from some other region of earth, if indeed it is from earth? Is there a message in this that we are to discover? Initially, there were also rumors that the sand was radioactive! But I've been unable to confirm this. Some sources say it was not; others that it indeed was. Years later, a British theorist, Peter Renton, came to the A.R.E. and shared his ideas about this sand chamber. But his ideas did not occur to him until after the discovery of the next mystery. So let's visit that first; then we'll review Mr. Renton's fascinating theory.

The Egyptian authorities hired a German team to explore the airshafts in the Queen's Chamber. The German team built a little robot that could traverse the airshafts while transmitting a video image back to the team and its monitors and recording devices. Amazingly, the robot came to what appeared to be a door with copper handles. These handles (if that is what they are) are curious, since 4300–3200 BC was the Copper Age (or *Chalcolithic* period) and the pyramid was supposedly built during the Bronze Age, 3300–1200 BC. Could the Great Pyramid be older than we think?

Copper could have been used purposefully to conduct an electrical current. We use copper wire for just such a purpose today. But we're unlikely to use copper for door handles. Here's where Peter Renton's theory comes into play. He believes that the handles are actually contact points for connecting an electrical current that will open the orifice beneath the sand chamber, allowing the sand to drain into a chamber below it, so one can pass through to another secret chamber on the other side. Interestingly, a Japanese team determined that there was indeed an empty chamber beneath the sand chamber and an additional chamber on the other side of the sand chamber. Of course, no one wants to take a chance on this, just in case the sand does have some important ballast role in keeping the pyramid's 2.3 million stones in place. However, the Egyptians, still believing it to be a door, drilled a hole to see what was on the other side. To their disappointment, there was another block. The Great Pyramid continues to hold many mysteries yet to be revealed. But we are living in a time of revelation, and news of new discoveries comes out of Egypt almost weekly.

The Kukulcan Pyramid

The pyramid of Kukulcan at Chichen Itza is equally impressive (See illustration 57). Each face of the four-sided structure has a stairway with ninety-one steps. Together the steps and the platform of the rooftop altar total 365—the number of days in a year. Each day shadows fall upon a different step, as if the pyramid was counting the days of the sun's passage. These stairways also divide the nine terraces of each side of the pyramid into the eighteen months of the Mayan calendar. The axes that run through the northwest and southwest corners of the pyramid are oriented toward the rising point of the sun at the summer solstice and the setting point at the winter solstice. At sunset on the vernal and autumnal equinoxes, an interplay between the sun's light and the edges of the stepped terraces creates a fascinating shadow display upon the sides of the northern stairway: a serrated line of seven interlocking triangles gives the impression of a long serpent undulating downward to the stone head of Kukulkan at the base of the stairway. It is truly a masterpiece of astronomical wisdom and metaphysical symbolism.

The ancient people had an affinity for pyramids and were masters at constructing them in alignment with the planet's key features and the movements of heavenly objects. Currently, over five hundred ancient pyramidal structures have been discovered around the planet. Clearly, "ancient" does not necessarily mean "primitive," as these pyramids so clearly attest.

When asked, "By what power or powers were these early pyramids and temples constructed?" Cayce answered, "By the lifting forces of those gases that are being used gradually in the present civilization, and by the fine work or activities of those versed in that pertaining to the source from which all power comes." The ancients were using natural forces of gases that are lighter than air in combination with unexplained methods using the source of all power.

How were the ancients able to cut and fit stones so perfectly that when they are stacked on top of one another, as in the Great Pyramid, a razor blade cannot be pushed between each stone? We know from Cayce's other readings that the Atlanteans were experts at harnessing power from solar and stellar radiation using giant crystals. We know that crystals have the power to channel waves, as our crystal radios capture wave frequencies emitted from distant towers. Could these be the physical "source from which all power comes"? Could these sources harness powers that would allow these ancient masons to make perfect granite blocks and fit them precisely one to another? The Great Pyramid is composed of roughly 2.3 million stone blocks; such a number would require a very rapid process in order to build the edifice in any reasonable time frame. There is a legend that the massive and marvelous Magician's Pyramid in Uxmal, Mexico was built in a single night!

The Coral Castle

Edward Leedskalnin, possibly a reincarnated Atlantean, build the Coral Castle in southern Florida with numerous megalithic stones (mostly limestone formed from coral), each weighing several tons (see illustration 58). Leedskalnin never allowed anyone to view him while he worked, but a few teenagers claimed to have witnessed his work, reporting that he had caused the massive blocks of coral to move like hydrogen balloons. Perhaps Leedskalnin used something like Cayce's "lifting forces of gases." The only tool that Leedskalnin spoke of using was a "perpetual motion holder." The single-rock gate entrance weighs nine tons but swings open easily. Leedskalnin never told anyone who asked him how he made the castle. He would simply answer, "It's not difficult if you know how." This was one man; imagine how much could have been done with several experts in these ancient arts.

The Pyramid of Records

As we covered in the previous chapter, Cayce also comments that some pyramids contain hidden records. He was asked, "In which pyramid or temple are the records mentioned in the readings given through this channel on Atlantis?" He answered, "That temple was destroyed at the time there was the last destruction in Atlantis." He explained that this was the temple in Poseidia, Atlantis, in what is now the Bahamas. These records sank with the temple and, according to Cayce, are located somewhere along the Gulf Stream near the Bahamian island of Bimini. He also mentions two other temples/pyramids containing records, one in Yucatan or Guatemala, built by an Atlantean named Iltar, and another in Egypt near the Sphinx. Cayce continues with this reading, "Yet, as time draws nigh when changes are to come about, there may be the opening of those three places where the records are one, to those that are the initiates in the knowledge of the One God: The temple by Iltar will then rise again." According to Cayce, Iltar sailed from Poseidia to the Yucatan Peninsula with a set of these Atlantean stone records: they were tablets written in a pre–hieroglyphic language. Cayce continues, "Also there will be the opening of the temple or hall of records in Egypt, and those records that were put into the heart of the Atlantean land may also be found there—that have been kept, for those that are of that group. The *records* are *one*."

According to Cayce, Hept-supht sealed the Egyptian cache of records as the capstone of the Great Pyramid was being lowered onto the pyramid. Hept-supht struck the metallic capstone, causing it to ring, and as it came down upon the pyramid, its vibrations rang out down the pyramid to the bedrock and across the entire Giza plateau. The ringing vibration reverberated throughout the bedrock—moving various gates, doors, and blocks in all the monuments, temples, and pyramids, thereby sealing them and numerous chambers within them until a future time. Historical records reveal that the Great Pyramid remained sealed until AD 832.

When Cayce was asked, "Did I have any constructive part in either the building of the Great Pyramid or the records therein?" he answered, "They are in the records of the Pyramid of Records, not the Great Pyramid. The Great Pyramid was the initiating building. The records of the entity are in the Temple or Pyramid of Records." This reading was given to a woman, and other readings indicate that women were more in power in ancient times than we realize. For example, one woman asked him, "Was I a man among those that put up the first of the pyramids?" Cayce replied, "Rather that as a woman, the entity was the ruler over those of man—and had many men as husbands, then."

Interestingly, in this same reading Cayce stated, "The later pyramids, those yet not uncovered, are between the Sphinx and the Nile." The problem with this statement is that the limestone bedrock on which the pyramids of the Giza Plateau are built ends in front of the Sphinx Temple, directly in front of the Sphinx itself. This area has been excavated and found to have been a harbor. Ancient boats came up to the Sphinx and Valley Temples to moor. As best anyone has been able to determine, the land in front of the Sphinx, Sphinx Temple, and Valley Temple is riverbed that runs to another limestone bedrock plateau nearer to Cairo than Giza. That area of land is on the other side of the river Nile and therefore could not be *between* the Sphinx and the river.

Could there be an underground pyramid of records beneath the Sphinx Temple or the Valley Temple? The most likely place would be under the Sphinx Temple in its southwest corner, which is directly off the right front paw of the Sphinx. Fortunately, Cayce says that the chamber directly under the Sphinx has a hallway that leads to the undiscovered Pyramid of Records and the Hall of Records it houses. Searching for the chamber beneath the Sphinx is the first stage to finding the record cache.

A pyramid of records could be small, like the pyramids that contain the pyramid texts—Unas, Teti, and Pepi I and II.

Cayce said that Hermes and Ra directed the building of the Great Pyramid. He also said, "the Temple of Records and the Temple Beautiful were built" by them and by the White Brotherhood, which was a metaphysical group of souls that attempted to keep the light shining in the earth. This Brotherhood, Sisterhood contains both discarnate and incarnate souls. In this reading he stated that the Great Pyramid was built for the initiates, ceremonies, and celebrations, and as a chronological prophecy of events related to the spiritual passage of humanity through the ages of earth sojourns. This chronology was published in the 1910s, and in the 1930s Cayce confirmed the work as being "in the whole correct." We will go into detail of the prophecy in a later chapter.

The Sun and Moon Pyramids and Others

Egyptian pyramids were not the only pyramids that Cayce's readings addressed. When Cayce was asked "Have the most important temples and pyramids been discovered?" he responded, "Those of the first civilization have been discovered, and have not all been opened; but their associations, their connections, are being rebuilt." Archaeologists were indeed rebuilding the Sun and Moon pyramids at the time of this reading. Cayce goes on, "Many of the pyramids of the second and third civilization may never be discovered, for these would destroy the present civilization in Mexico to uncover same!"

Let's not overlook his quick, casual statement that among the pyramids discovered in Mexico, "not all have been opened!" Recently, archaeologists have indeed found chambers in the Moon pyramid at

Teotihuacan containing Mayan artifacts. The once hidden chamber is located on one of the upper terraces of the giant pyramid. Cayce's readings of the Akashic record indicate that in ancient times the people of the planet all spoke one language and traveled extensively. The readings state that the high priest Ra-Ta was frequently in contact with spiritual leaders in other countries, sharing information and methods. Since pyramids are found around the world, we could assume that these structures were commonly considered to be the best structure (as the readings indicate) for initiation, sacred ceremonies, and tracking the passage of heavenly bodies. They also tracked the seasons on earth.

Opening Hidden Chambers by Song

Back to Egypt: When elaborating on the ringing capstone story, Cayce notes that "the pyramids, the House of Records as well as the chamber in which the records are built in stone were put together by song." By *song?* He explains to the person getting this reading that his soul was there at the site, doing "chants upon the river." (EC 2462-2) If vocal vibration combined with higher consciousness (chanting?) was the method used to build the record pyramid and the chamber, then voice vibration with higher consciousness may be the way to open it.

Pyramids and Megaliths around the World

As we continue to discover ancient structures, it is amazing to learn how many of the ancient peoples built pyramids. They are found around the entire planet: in China, Turkey, Greece, and England; North, Central, and South America; and, of course, Africa. Many are marvels of architecture and astronomy. Some of the granite stones used in the Great Pyramid of Giza, for example, would be nearly impossible for us to move today, weighing seventy tons. The astronomical arrangement of the Kukulcan Pyramid at Chichen Itza, with a serpent shadow moving down its steps as the Earth rotates before the sun, is astounding. Isn't everything ancient supposed to be primitive? Aren't we the apex of

218 Edgar Cayce's Tales of Ancient Egypt

civilization? According to evolutionary theories, ancient peoples should not have been able to build structures that would be extremely difficult to build today. Yet they exist around the globe. And if we include obelisks, the "unfinished" obelisk in Aswan, Egypt has been estimated to weigh twelve hundred tons! How were these ancient Egyptians going to moving this? The obelisk at Baalbek, Lebanon, has been estimated to weigh 1,158 tons and is miles from where it was going to be placed. The standing obelisk of Hatshepsut in the Karnak Temple is made of granite, is 96 feet high, and weighs 323 tons. How did they lift it and place it so perfectly? The two statues known as the Colossi of Memnon, located on the west bank of the Nile across from Luxor, are estimated to weigh 720 tons each and are 420 miles from where their stones were quarried.

Everything ancient is not primitive.

17

THE PYRAMID PROPHECY

The Great Pyramid is not only a magnificent structure used for worship and initiations. Contained within this only survivor of the original Seven Wonders of the Ancient World is a prophecy-in-stone—a prophecy that chronicles the descent of souls into matter, their long journey through ages of evolution, and their ultimate resurrection out of here, back to the infinite cosmos and the universal, collective consciousness.

When this prophecy was first discovered, the detailed findings of several researchers were so exact that today, long after their measurements were published, we see that the prophecy foresaw the beginning and the end of WWI, the Great Depression, and the beginning and end of WWII!

How can this be? How could ancient Egyptians see our present destiny from such a long time ago? It shakes our sense of free will and choice. It reminds me of Jesus' comment, "Every hair on your head is numbered." How could such wisdom be in an ancient edifice? And from where were these researchers getting their crazy ideas? How did an ancient Egyptian icon end up in the Great Seal of the United States? Take a look at a U.S. dollar bill. The pyramid and the all-seeing eye are on the Great Seal of this young, modern country. Cayce answers these questions by explaining that prior to the evolution that we are so familiar with, there was an "involution" into matter—souls, energy beings, descended *into* form, into matter. In the earlier stages of this descent they retained their cosmic wisdom—a wisdom we are only now regaining. These billions of souls have been reincarnating in cycles of physical life and nonphysical life, and deep within their (our) consciousness they retain knowledge of the origin and destiny of the journey of souls.

These esoteric researchers of the 1800s and early 1900s were reincarnated souls—former Egyptians. And whether they were aware or unaware of this fact, they were driven from within themselves to reveal the mysteries of Egypt. Physically they stimulated their memories from chapters and verses in *The Egyptian Book of the Dead* (illustration 83), which spoke about something called "The Light" (*Ta Khut*). Because the hieroglyph over the original entrance to the Great Pyramid is the Horizon of Heaven, upon which the light of heaven rises, the researchers reasoned that The Light was in fact the Great Pyramid. Therefore, the chapters and verses in *The Egyptian Book of Dead* that speak about The Light are giving careful readers insights into the ancient Egyptian teachings about each of the passageways and chambers in the magnificent structure. If you add to this physical information their soul intuition, you have many hundred souls searching and publishing their findings during the heydays of Egyptology.

In 1932 a question about correlating passageways and chambers in the Great Pyramid with a mysterious timeline of humanity's destined journey was put to Edgar Cayce. Cayce confirmed that indeed the builders of the Great Pyramid had hidden a timeline prophecy in the monument. The specific question put to Cayce was concerning the findings of David Davidson and H. Aldersmith published in 1924 in a large book titled *The Great Pyramid: Its Divine Message*. In this book the prophecy timeline was detailed and correlated to ancient Egyptian papyruses. Davidson first got his idea of a time line from Marsham Adams (1838–?), a British Egyptologist, fellow of Oxford's New College, and author of *The House of the Hidden Places: A Clue to the Creed of the Egyptians* (1895) and *The Book of the Master* (1898). Adams wrote that the unique system of passages and chambers in the Great Pyramid have little meaning as a tomb but have an allegorical significance explained only by referring to *The Egyptian Book of the Dead*. He wrote that *The Egyptian Book of the Dead* calls attention to an "ideal structure and to the passages and chambers therein, and that these passages and chambers followed precisely the order and description of those of the Great Pyramid." The ancient name for the Great Pyramid was *Khut*, which means "Light." The literal title of *The Egyptian Book of the Dead* is *Book of Coming Forth by Light* (commonly translated, *by Day*). The hieroglyphs in the manuscript give this literal title, but E.A. Wallis Budge, the first interpreter of the manuscript, was influenced by the recent discovery of *The Tibetan Book of the Dead*, and he decided to arbitrarily title the Egyptian text after the Tibetan one—despite the actual hieroglyphs.

Sir Gaston Maspero (1846–1919)—a French Egyptologist, professor of archaeology, and developer of the Egyptian Museum in Cairo—explained, "The pyramid and *The Egyptian Book of the Dead* reproduce the same original, the one in words, the other in stone."

The pyramid timeline covers a period beginning with the descent of human souls as the "Morning Stars" in the book of Job 38:7 to the "fifth root race" and the New Age, according to Cayce. The last date in the pyramid chronograph is 2038.

Pyramidologists David Davidson and H. Aldersmith used a measurement they called the "pyramid inch." The length of a pyramid inch is the space on the underside of the "boss mark" in the antechamber to the King's Chamber (see illustration 59). The boss mark is in the shape of a solar disk that has not fully risen above the horizon; therefore the bottom portion of its circle is the horizon line, and leaves a depth of one pyramid "inch" between the base slab and the outer surface of the projected solar disk.

There are critics of this measurement, such as the famous Sir Flinders Petrie, an English archaeologist known as the "father of modern Egyptology" who wrote in 1883, "This boss on the leaf is very ill-defined, being anything between 4.7 and 5.2 [in inches] wide, and between 3.3 and 3.5 high on its outer face." Petrie felt that "this boss, of which so much has been made by theorists, is merely a rough projection, like innumerable others that may be seen; left originally for the purpose of lifting the blocks."

Despite Petrie's opinion, the slab and the boss relief are more than a lifting mechanism shaped as a rising solar disk with a measurable space on its bottom.

From passages in *The Egyptian Book of the Dead*, researchers concluded that the pyramid inch not only correlates to a measure of space in the stone structure but also to a measure of *prophetic time*. The measurement equals one year in time, from the original entrance to the pyramid through the descending and ascending passages until reaching the great step at the top of the Grand Gallery. From that point on, the inch equals one month. At this point, time is condensed—the same amount of activities happen in one-twelfth of the time they used to take.

In 1932 Edgar Cayce was asked if the deductions and conclusions made in 1910 by David Davidson and H. Aldersmith were correct. From his deep-trance attunement, Cayce said that for the most part, "they were correct, though in some, far overdrawn." This was an interesting choice of words when we consider that most of Davidson and Aldersmith's materials were drawings, some containing broken lines extending beyond the halls and chambers in the Great Pyramid (see illustration 60). These broken-line areas are likely those that Cayce is calling "far overdrawn." But when we stick to the timeline that uses the actual halls and chambers in the pyramid, we then have a fascinating prophecy that can give us some insights into our soul's journey and our present and future times.

In Cayce's reading on this, he actually said, "There are periods when even the hour, day, year, place, country, nation, town, and individuals are pointed out. That's how correct are many of those prophecies as made."

Cayce's readings on Davidson and Aldersmith's thesis explain that the variations in the character of the stones and the twists and turns of the passageways as one moves through the Great Pyramid signify shifting conditions in the world through the ages (past and present) as related "to the spiritual experiences of man." For Cayce, these prophecies are not so much about world affairs as they are about religious, spiritual thought and perspective: "All changes that came in the religious thought in the world are shown there [in the pyramid chronograph], in the variations in which the passage through same is reached, from the base to the top—or to the open tomb and the top." This is significant because Davidson and Aldersmith stopped their calculations at the wall in the King's Chamber, believing that the chronograph ended at the far wall of the chamber (see illustrations 61 and 62). Cayce, however, is directing us to measure up the wall to the top. Cayce continues this reading by explaining that we need to be cognizant of the nature and color of the stone: "These [changes are] signified by both the layer and the color in what direction the turn is made [as one moves and measures one's way through the pyramid]."

Cayce identifies the chronological span covered by the Great Pyramid as beginning with "the journey to the Pyrenees"—which is a reference to the end of the old lands of Atlantis, Mu, Oz, Og, Zu, and others by a series of great floods, earthquakes, and volcanic eruptions (an age the Mayans and Aztecs called the "Age of Fiery Rain", see illustration 45). These terrible earth changes forced the migration of a remnant of old-world peoples to new, higher ground, such as the Pyrenees Mountains between Spain and France. From this migration Cayce said that the chronology continues to Egypt and the building of that great culture and then from Giza's era to Jesus' times, which Cayce described as the "death of the Son of Man as a man." Cayce goes on to say that the chronograph continues "to the year 1998," the date Cayce sets as the *beginning* of the changes to a new age.

Cayce's readings say that the timeline ends at the apex of the King's Chamber (see illustration 62). The apex date marks the shift to a new era and a new body-type: what he called the age of the "fifth-root race," indicating that there had been four previous body types used by human souls incarnating in this world. The body change is to evolve or mutate into a more accommodating body for our soulful consciousness to use during future incarnations.

My son James and I carefully calculated the measurements in the illustration, but the final measurements near the very top chamber (Campbell's Chamber) are difficult to determine with certainty. From my study of Cayce's readings, I'm inclined to believe that the fifth-root race and new era year is 2038 rather than 2039, simply because Cayce gave such a clear pattern for century divisions and events: each century takes forty years to make a transition to a new level of awareness (from '98 of the previous century to '38 of the new century); it then takes twenty years to express and establish the new beliefs and ideals ('38 to '58); then a forty-year period of testing occurs to see if the generations really, truly believe what they claim and hold as their ideals, despite

224 ^ Edgar Cayce's Tales of Ancient Egypt

severe challenges (the period from '58 to '98 in each century). Then the souls make a transition toward a newer, higher level of comprehension and perception, and the century cycle begins anew ('98 to '38), spiraling upward until the whole journey is completed.

Since astrological effects begin to assert their influence long before they actually engage and continue to influence long after they have passed, this new body and era have already begun. The so-called Indigo Children may be the forerunners of the new body and new mind of the new era.

David Davidson and H. Aldersmith thought the pyramid timeline ended in August of 1953, when they reached the far wall in the King's Chamber. But twenty years later Cayce corrected them, stating that they were supposed to go up the wall through the ceiling stones and so-called relieving chambers about the King's Chamber to the apex of limestones creating a gabled chamber and ceiling.

Since we are most interested in prophecies concerning our times, let's concentrate on the King's Chamber and, as Cayce instructed, "from the open tomb to the top," which are the years 1958 through 2038 or 2039.

Look at illustration 62, and you'll see that from the floor of the King's Chamber, where Davidson and Aldersmith ceased their measurements, to the top, to the very apex of the chamber, there are six distinct "ceilings," creating five chambers. The first five crossing stones you see in this illustration are actually *rows* of huge granite beams, each beam weighing between fifty and eighty tons, and there are nine beams in each row—a total weight between 2,250 and 3,600 tons! At the very apex are two rows of slabs of limestone that create a gable roof. But what is important to us, according to Cayce, are the stones' colors as well as their layers. The first five ceilings are made with red granite. The top gable ceiling is made with white limestone.

It is well known that Egypt considered the color red to be that of the ruler of Lower Egypt, symbolic of our lower self, and white to be the color of the ruler of Upper Egypt, symbolic of our higher self. Therefore, the first five layers of red stones may symbolize stages in the ongoing development of our human nature (our lower self), and the top white stones may symbolize the development of our divine nature (our higher self). We might then conclude that from June of 1980 to June of 2030 we will be concentrating on modifying our lower nature and conscious- ness, and from June 2030 to November 2038 or '39 manifesting our higher nature and consciousness. This leads us into a new age of en- lightenment when, according to the biblical Revelation, "Satan is bound for a thousand years," indicating that the new age is one without evil, temptation, and the dark forces, but an era of light, love, and soul growth. Then, as recorded in the Revelation, "Satan is loose a little while," indicating that there is another test period and a period for those souls who did not make it the first time to have a second chance—but the rest of us will have to endure their dark tendencies while they strive to illuminate their hearts and minds to higher truth, the higher purpose for life and free will.

The Whole Prophecy Timeline

Before we leave this pyramid prophecy, let's look at it more closely— with the advantage of hindsight.

Using illustration 60 we can trace our soul journey from the entrance of the Great Pyramid to the Chamber of Upside-Downness, then back up to the Hall of Truth while still in Darkness, to the Chamber of the Second Birth, then up the Grand Galley of the Hall of Truth while in the Light. This leads us to take "the Great Step" and move into the Chamber of the Triple Veil, in which we awaken again to higher levels of con- sciousness. Then, after more tests, we enter the Chamber of the Open Tomb, and through several initiations, we learn that there is no death. We are immortal beings who have been lost in an illusion of physicality and cyclical life patterns. Then we begin to imbue ourselves with these truths by going through the seven stages of descent into matter and selfishness and the ascent up through illumination and transformation (indicated by the seven stones above the King's Chamber.) This is the metamorphosis of earthy, terrestrial being to heavenly, celestial godling.

Using illustration 61 we can see the Great Step, which changes the pyramid inch measurement from one inch equaling one year to one inch equaling one month—everything speeds up, happening in 1/12th the time it used to take!

A most fascinating detail of this prophecy is found at the exit of the Hall of Truth in Darkness. Davidson's measurements showed that the last step occurred at 4 BC and the head cleared at AD 30¼. Despite Davidson's knowledge of the accepted dates for the birth and crucifixion of Jesus Christ, he went ahead and published these measurements as revealing the correct dates of Jesus' birth and dead as a man. Little did he know that many years later researchers would calculate that the edict issued by King Herod to kill all male children two years of age and younger, in an effort to kill the newborn Jesus, had to have been dated between 6 and 4 BC, because Herod died between 4 and 2 BC.

18

MYSTERIOUS PYRAMID TEXTS AND MAGICAL HYMNS

The Pyramid Texts are among the oldest known writings in the world, dating back more than five thousand years. In Pakistan's Harappa region pottery fragments with markings are 5500 years old. In Neolithic graves in central China etchings on 8600-year-old tortoise shells were found. However, the pyramid texts are true writings, not simply marks or etchings. Many researchers believe that these pyramid texts are the basis of all later religious theology and literature in ancient Egypt! There is evidence that these texts eventually became *The Egyptian Book of the Dead*, originally titled, *Book of Coming Forth by Light* (commonly translated, *by Day*); this text consists of a number of magic spells intended to assist a dead person's journey through the underworld and into the afterlife.

The main text is found in the Unas Pyramid (Fifth Dynasty, also written Unis), located near the Step Pyramid of Djoser (pronounced *zo-ser*), dating to the Third Dynasty 2630 BC. The Unas texts form the oldest extant body of religious texts written in "Old Egyptian." These writings *predate* the dynastic period. Add to this that the inscriptions are without any precedent in the archaeological record elsewhere in Egypt, and this mystery puts into question the standard Egyptological timeline. And if we add to this that they were called "utterances," indicating that they were never meant to be written, only spoken as part of an invocation, we then have an even bigger mystery. In fact, some scholars believe that the texts belong to a much earlier group that lived long before the dynastic people who later inscribed them on the walls and that this earlier group was a "cult" of metaphysical seekers who were traveling through dimensions of consciousness! This is exactly as Cayce described Ra-Ta and his community.

If we include coffin lid texts with the wall texts, there are over seven hundred "utterances," so called because each begins with the expression *djed medu*, "words to be said." They were likely spoken by attending priests and priestesses in the course of a death–like initiation or practice that assisted incarnate souls in making passage through the realms of the underworld (the unconscious) up into the planes of the heavens (higher realms of consciousness) and then return again to this world— much wiser for the journey.

Among the many utterances are numbers 273 and 274, called by the archaeologists the "Cannibal Hymns," because they deal with the ingestion of the powers of the gods into one's own being. This is not true cannibalism. It is a common concept in many of the world's mystical practices, including the ancient Kabbalists, in which the Emanations of God are assimilated into one's being to gain direct conscious access to one's Creator. Even Jesus made a mystical directive to eat his flesh and drink his blood: "Truly I say to you, if you do not take the flesh of the Son of man for food, and if you do not take his blood for drink, you have no life in you. He who takes my flesh for food and my blood for drink has eternal life; and I will take him up from the dead at the last day. My flesh is true food and my blood is true drink. He who takes my flesh for food and my blood for drink is in me and I in him. As the living Father has sent me, and I have life because of the Father, even so he who takes me for his food will have life because of me. This is the bread that has come down from heaven. It is not like the food which your fathers had, that they took of the manna, and are dead; but he who takes this bread for food will have life forever." (John 6:53–58 WEB) Any archaeologist who thinks Jesus and the ancient ones were talking about cannibalism does not understand mysticism and its metaphors.

Interestingly, these utterances appear to be a process that was no longer practiced during the dynastic times. The scribes were copying these utterances or "hymns" to preserve them, but they were not using them or had lost awareness of how to use them. The original and oldest texts appear only in the Pyramids of Unas and Teti at Saqqara, all the others are believed to have been copied from these two pyramids' walls, even the coffin lid texts of subsequent dynasties.

Let's look at some of these utterances:

Note: The names of the gods are replaced with the qualities they personify in order to convey what an ancient Egyptian would have known. For example, the goddess Nut is "the celestial cycle," because she personifies such. If you look closely at the picture of her, you'll see how her body is overarching our realms of existence and is filled with the stars and the red sun, which she swallows in the evening, thus bringing darkness, and then gives birth to each morning, bringing sunlight. This whole scene symbolizes the celestial cycle (see illustration 63).

Here are some lines from the hymns that give us a sense of the celestial passage and mind expansion that Unas is to achieve as he moves through the dimensions of life, especially life beyond the body. Let's read them as if they were meant for our soul; imagine ourselves bathed, hair scented with oil, dressed in white linen and a gold belt, as these words are spoken by a priest and priestess:

"O Unas, you have not gone dead, you have gone alive to sit on the throne of Resurrection and Judgment (Osiris, representing our conscience). Your scepter is in your hand that you may give orders to the living, the handle of your lotus–shaped scepter in your hand (the shaft of the scepter symbolizing the flowing of the kundalini to the crown chakra lotus). Give orders to those of the Mysterious Sites! (Cayce's readings would say that this is the need for us to use our God–given gift of free will to make choices and give direction to our soul and subdue distracting influences.)

"Your arm is that of the father of gods (Atum), your shoulders are those of the progenitor of gods (Atum) . . . your two legs are those of the god of gods (Atum), your face is that of the guide to the dead that live (Anubis). The sites of the Savior (Horus) serve you, the sites of the Redeemed One (Set, our wayward self) serve you.

"*To say four times:*

"The messengers of your spirit (ka) have come to you, the messengers of your father have come to you, the messengers of the Source of Light and Life (Ra) have come to you."

"Go after your Source of Light and Life! You are to purify yourself. Your bones are those of the female hawks (light enough to fly high, and conceive new views, new understandings), and of the goddesses who are in heaven, so that you may be by the side of the God and leave your house (body) . . .

"You are to purify yourself with the cool water of the stars, and you will climb down upon ropes of brass, on the arms of the Savior (Horus), in his name *He-of-the-boat-of-the-gods*. (We were originally created in the image of God and are the godlings. Psalms 82:6: "You are gods, sons [and daughters] of the Most High"; and John 10:34 where Jesus refers to this psalm and our godly nature.)

"The glorified humanity bewails you after the Imperishable Stars have carried you. Enter then into the place where your father is, where the god of the Earth (Geb) is! He gives you that which was on the brow (third eye, also raised cobra symbolizing the kundalini) of the Savior (Horus), so that you become powerful and full of glory through it, so that you become the *One-at-the-Head-of-the-Endings*.

"O Unas! Your messengers go; your heralds hurry to your father, to the father of gods. 'Father, let him rise to you, fold him in your arms!' There is no god who has become a star without a companion. Shall I be your companion? Look at me! You have seen the forms of the children of their fathers, who know their spell, who are now Imperishable Stars (the hearts of all the souls are the stars, and the souls are immortal). May you see the two inhabitants of the Palace: these are the Savior (Horus) and the Redeemed One (Set)!

"May you put your divine spittle on the face of the Wounded Savior (Horus contaminated by Set's poisonous ways and thoughts) and re–move his wound! May you catch the testicles of the Deceiver who has been redeemed (stop Set's conceiving of distractive thoughts and urges) and remove his mutilation! That one is born for you; this one is con–ceived for you.

"You are born, O redeemed one (now Unas is the redeemed one, as are we), as the one whose name is *He-before-whom-the-earth-quakes; He be-fore-whom-the-sky-shakes*. You have no wound; you have no mutilation!

(Because he perceived the wound and mutilation and healed them.)
"You are born for resurrection, O redeemed one!
"You have become more glorious . . .
"You have become more powerful . . .
"There is no seed of a god which has perished, neither who belongs to him. You will not perish, who belong to him. The Primordial Creative Force (Ra–Atum) does not give you to the Judge (Osiris), he does not reckon your heart, he has no power over your breast. The Primordial Creative Force (Ra–Atum) does not give you to the Judge, he has no power over your breast.

"Judge (Osiris), you cannot have power over him, your son cannot have power over him. Slayer of Evil (Horus), you cannot have power over him, your father cannot have power over him.

"You belong, O this one, to this god, as the Twins of Creation and Preservation (breath and order) said: 'Lift yourself up,' so said they, 'in your name God,' and so you become Father or every god. [This is just as Cayce's reading said: "Not only God is God, but self is a portion of that Oneness."]

"Your head is that of the Savior (Horus) of the Unconscious Realms (Duat), O Imperishable One, your brow is the One-with-the-Two-Eyes, O Imperishable One, your ears are (those of) the Twins of Creation and Preservation (hearing life (breath) and order (truth)), O Imperishable One, your eyes are (those of) the Twins of Creation and Preservation (seeing life (breath) and order (truth)), O Imperishable One, your nose is (that of) a jackal (capable of picking up the trail taken as we originally journeyed from heaven and are now on our journey back to heaven— (as Jesus taught: "No one has ascended into heaven but he who first came down from heaven, even the son of Man."—John 3:13).

"O Imperishable One, your teeth are (those of) the scorching heat of the summer (Sopdu), O Imperishable One, your arms are (those of) embracing his Father and adoring of his Mother (Hapi and Duamutef), which you need to ascend to heaven—*and you ascend*. Your legs are (those that) lift others up and liberate his siblings (Imseti and Qebehsenuf), which you need to descend to the lower heaven, and you descend. All your members are (those of) the Twins of Creation and Preservation (life and truth or breath and order), o Imperishable One! You did not pass away; your spirit does not pass away.

"You are a spirit!" (as Jesus taught: "God is a spirit, and those who worship Him must worship in spirit and in truth." John 4:24.)

What a wonderfully guiding and affirming voice to have directing us through our resurrection and redemption into the arms of God and all of God's emanations.

Now let's take a brief look at the first utterance or hymn in the Unas Pyramid, and we need to keep in mind that the Cayce readings stated that Hermes (Thoth) was an incarnation of Christ or the Word, the Logos, and that Ra-Ta met Hermes in the mountains of "Upper Egypt" which is the mountainous area of southern Egypt, known today as Aswan, Nubia, and Sudan. Why do we need to keep this in mind? Because you are going see an amazing similarity between the words of this ancient hymn about the Word, the Logos, and those found in the Gospel of Matthew.

"I say by the celestial cycle—the brilliant, the great—this is my son, my first born, opener of my womb; this is my beloved, with whom I am well pleased."

Now compare this with Matthew 3:17: "And lo, a voice from heaven, saying, 'This is my beloved Son, with whom I am well pleased.'"

The texts include these: "The Great Virgin who dwells in the City of the Sun has placed her hands on you, because there is no mother among men who could bear you, because there is no father among men who could beget you. Oho! Oho! I will shout this acclaim, 'O my father, because you have no human father and you have no human mother; your father is the Powerful One, your mother is the Virgin."

Many researchers have expressed amazement at the similarities between Christian stories and ancient Egyptian ones. It is a mystifying correlate.

As for these pyramid texts, they are a marvel of spirituality and soul growth, reflecting human mystical pursuits of nonphysical realms beyond this world and this body.

Interestingly, these hymn writers and star travelers may have been the same people who built the "Egyptian Stonehenge" in Nabta Playa, located about sixty-two miles west of Abu Simbel near the Egyptian-

Sudanese border. It is estimated to have been an active ceremonial site at least 6500 years ago, possibly as many as 11,000 years ago! These dates fit right into Cayce's dating of ancient Egyptian times.

19

THE SEVEN STAGES OF HUMAN ENLIGHTENMENT

S ince he was the reincarnation of one of the high priests of Egypt, it is not surprising that Edgar Cayce had much to say about ancient Egypt and the initiations our souls experienced in those ancient times. These initiations were intended to embed deep within our psyche the truth about our origin, the purpose for existence, the unique gifts we were given at the time of our spiritual conception, and the special service we were trained to do. Our subtle bodies were also *marked* in a way that would bring to our minds (even if only to our deeper minds) the understanding of who we really are and what our life is truly about.

In one of his discourses on the Temples of Sacrifice and Beauty, Cayce stated that there were seven stages to human soul growth in this world. The implication being that we would not be in the realms or on the surface of the earth forever, only as long as it takes us to complete the "seven stages." In fact, he actually gave some fifteen individuals the message that this was their last incarnation—their souls were done with earth lives; they were moving on to activities in other realms of soul life.

Each of these stages, ages, or cycles has specific lessons to teach us before we move on to enjoy the entire universe that our Creator has made for us! Throughout Cayce's fourteen thousand readings, he gives the clear vision of us as celestial beings who are only temporarily sojourning in terrestrially, because our souls got caught up in the dynamics and lessons of this world.

Our first age began (as recorded in the biblical book of Job) "when the morning stars sang together." This passage is when God came to Job and asked him a very unusual question: "Where were you when I laid the foundations of the earth? When the morning stars sang together, and all the sons of God shouted for joy?" (Job 38:7) At the time of the question Job was about sixty years of age; he had to wonder why God would ask him such a question. The answer was because, like us, Job's soul had been among the morning stars and the sons of God. (For the women reading this, know that the "sons" of God actually refers to you too, for the "sons" were godlings in which the yin and yang, the feminine and masculine, had not yet been divided into separate bodies as they are today. The Bible records this separation occurring later in the creation process, in Genesis 2:21.) Your soul was created in God's image in Genesis 1:27. The term "sons of God" refers to androgynous, celestial beings living more in spirit than in flesh. The Egyptians saw that, long before we became men and women, we were rays from the great Ray (Ra) and that all of us were stars in the heavens, the "morning stars" of Job, and the feminine-masculine sons of God. Even the Mayans, Toltecs, and Aztecs taught this: *Quetzalcoatl* (Aztec and Toltec), *Kukulcan* (Yucatan Mayan), and *Gucumatz* (K'iche Mayan) were the Mesoamerican names for the winged serpent god who guided the "children of God" to put their hearts into a sacred fire, which caused the black, infinite space to be filled with shining stars, representing each soul's heart. Our deeper selves were the morning stars spoken of in Job.

After his casual statement about the seven stages, he was later asked during one of his amazing trance-state attunements to the universal consciousness, "What were the symbols of the seven stages of man's development?" He answered: "The world as the beetle; birth as the cockerel; the mind as the serpent; wisdom as the hawk. The varied activities in the cross, the crown, the gate, the door, the way." (EC 281-25) As we read the following, we can refer to illustrations 64 through 69.

Before we read these, it would be helpful if we understood Cayce's teaching about cycles. Soul life is not linear, occurring in sequence, but it is cyclical in the sense that we experience every aspect of the whole journey over and over and over. However, Cayce explained that the cycles were spiral; they ascended in a manner that reflected our growth with each stage of development. Though the ages were associated with time frames (ancient, classical, present, and future), our souls holistically know them as a whole. This means that even today we may have some issues in our present life that deal with each of the various stages/ages of soul growth.

Stage/Age 1: "The World as the Beetle"

In Egyptian mysticism, the world is indeed seen as a beetle—a *dung* beetle. Yet the ancient Egyptians taught that from the dung of human life one can, as the dung beetle does, roll one's mess toward the light and warmth of the rising sun, plant a seed in this mess, and at high noon, when the sun is at its highest and hottest, that seed will bring forth resurrection. Out of the hardships, turmoils, and challenges of our life, out of our weaknesses and vices will come breakthroughs to a new life, a new awareness. (See illustration 64.)

Stage/Age 2: "Birth as the Cockerel"

The cockerel, or rooster, is the symbol for birth, the birth of our physical, lower selves. As the rooster, we were once cocksure of our beauty and virility, ready to fully incarnate in matter and to find mates, so reminiscent of the passage in Genesis 6:1–3: "And it came to pass, when men [our earthy, physical aspects] began to multiply on the face of the ground, and daughters were born unto them, and the sons of God [our divine, angelic aspects] saw the daughters of men that they were fair, they took them wives of all that they chose [just like a rooster]. And the Lord said, 'My spirit shall not strive with man forever, for now he also is flesh.'" Yet the rooster, for all his physical lust, is irresistibly moved from deep within to crow when light penetrates the darkness as the sun rises on a new day, a new opportunity. The most famous cockerel in mystical lore is Abraxas from the Egyptian Gnostics. The seven letters of his name were believed to be symbols of the seven rays of power—corresponding to the chakras. In the accompanying illustration 65 of Abraxas, we see imagery from Hinduism related to the kundalini and the reins for controlling the stallions of our earthly senses and desires. This was an early stage/age in our souls' experiences in this world.

Stage/Age 3: "Mind as the Serpent"

Mind as the serpent is revealed in the Garden of Eden, when we listened to our mind's reasoning that we could disobey God and "not *surely* die," as God had warned. But, once eaten, the death we experienced was much worse than we had reasoned. Egyptian mysticism presents two serpents. One called *Apep*, who bites at the feet of our Ra-consciousness (God-consciousness), poisoning us with its distractions and temptations, as indicated in the biblical story of the Garden; the other is a winged serpent and lifting off the ground, symbolizing our ability to raise our consciousness and energy sufficiently to know higher awareness and vibrations again. (See illustration 66.)

Stage/Age 4: "Wisdom as the Hawk"

The hawk as wisdom is a symbol of our ability to see from higher perspectives, as the hawk does from a mile above the ground, floating on the winds and wings of the spirit. This is the symbol for the awakened higher mind. In ancient Egypt, the messiah was Horus, immaculately conceived by Isis; his icon is the hawk or falcon. The higher mind is our redeemer. It lifts us to a higher, truer vision. (See illustration 67.)

Stage/Age 5: "The Cross and the Crown"

The cross is symbolic of a key stage in our development (see illustration 68, A cross with a circle). As Cayce stated in reading 2475-1 (and others), the crucifixion of our self-centered desires is required in order for us to awaken to our true, eternal nature and the real abilities of helpfulness that lie within our grasp as sons and daughters of God, as godlings in the image of God.

Cayce: "This is found to be experienced by all: that there was the necessity, for man's understanding, for the entering in of the Son of man, and that the Cross becomes the emblem of Him who offered himself, of himself. For that cause, for that purpose came He into the world, that He himself—in overcoming the world—might gain the Crown. So, each in their respective lives, their own experiences, find their cross overcoming the world, overcoming those things, those conditions, those experiences, that would not only enable them to meet the issues of life but to become heirs with Him of the Crown of Glory." (EC 262–36) This age may correlate to the Piscean Age that we have been living in and is rapidly coming to a close.

Stage/Age 6: "The Gate, the Door"

The gate or door is in our mind, heart, and body (as a chakra), and we control it with our free will. As the Spirit of God informed us through the disciple John in the Revelation: "As many as I love, I reprove and chasten; be zealous therefore, and repent. Behold, I stand at the door [of your heart, mind, and body] and knock; if any one hears my voice and opens the door, I will come in to him/her, and will sup with him/her, and he/she with me." (Revelation 3:19–20) Several Cayce readings indicate that the time we are entering is the time of opening the door to higher consciousness, greater love, and even higher chakras (there being a total of twelve chakras rather than the seven we know of now, according to Cayce). (See illustration 69.)

Stage/Age 7: "The Way"

The Way is expressed in the *living* of the two greatest commandments: 1. Love God with all our being, and 2. Love others as we would be loved. Love is the way. The essence of God is that vibration, that spirit we know as *love*. It is the single most powerful cleanser of all that hinders us—as the disciple Peter wrote: "Love covers a multitude of sins." (1 Peter 4:8) When we live lovingly, we know the glory that was ours before the world was, when we were conscious of being sons and daughters of God, when we were the morning stars.

"So attune yourselves that you may harken, not as to an experience only; but rather *live* and *be* the experience in the hearts of those that are seeking to find their way; whether in the troubles of the body, of the mind, or whether they are lost among those turmoils."

"Be the experience to someone to light their lives, their bodies, their minds to your *living* Lord, your brother, the Christ! For He has promised in His words in your own heart, that keeps the hope, that keeps the fires of your own heart aflame, 'You finding me may know the *joy* of the Lord.'"

If we look at these stages/ages as indicators of where we are in soul growth and resurrection, we can see that, on the macrocosmic scale, we are finishing fifth stage/age, the Cross and the Crown. As we leave the Piscean Age and enter the Aquarian Age, we move into the stage/age of the Gate, the Door, opening to a new consciousness. Interestingly, this correlates to a prophecy secretly hidden in the Great Pyramid and *The Egyptian Book of the Dead*, indicating that we are indeed in the latter stages of soul growth and resurrection from this world and these experiences. (See the chapter on the pyramid prophecy.)

20

SEVEN GATES TO THE
BEAUTIFUL HIDDEN PLACE

The following is a selected text from the *Book of Coming Forth by Light* (commonly translated, *by Day*), popularly called *The Egyptian Book of the Dead* (illustration 83). It is an initiation text. Try using it in a ceremonial manner as you prepare for a period of meditation. Use incense and candles, perhaps some bells or music. Special clothing may also add to the ceremonial nature of the initiation process. Each Gate is associated with a specific chakra or spiritual center. The words and thoughts are quite powerful. Wherever you see [Your Name], speak your name.

GATE 1: Root Center

Here begins the Entrance on Light, and of coming forth from and going into the Territory of the Holy Dead, in the beautiful Hidden Place.

Homage to thee, O Guardian of the Hidden Place. O you who make perfected souls to enter into the Temple of Reunion.

May you cause the perfected soul of the Reunited One, the seeker [Your Name], to be victorious with you in the Temple of Reunion. May he/she hear as you hear; may he/she see as you see.

O you who open the way and lay open the paths to perfected souls in the Temple of Reunion, open you the way and lay open the paths to the soul of Reunited [Your Name].

Homage to thee, O thou who art at the head of the Hidden Place. Grant that I may arrive in peace in the Hidden Place and that the lords of the Ascent may receive me.

GATE 2: Navel Center

Here makes the Spirit Body to enter into the Upper Gate of the Ascent.

Homage to thee, O thou that dwellest in the Holy Mountain of the Hidden Place. Grant that I may arrive in peace in the Hidden Place and that the lords of the Ascent may receive me.

Here begins the Entering on Light and living after death.

Hail, One shining from the Moon! Hail, One shining from the Moon! Grant that the Reunited [Your Name] may come forth from among those multitudes which are outside; and let him/her be established as a dweller among the citizens of Heaven; and let the Hidden Places be opened unto him/her. And behold, Reunited One, Reunited [Your Name], shall enter on Light.

GATE 3: Solar Plexus Center

Here begins the Passing over the Celestial Road of the Upper Gate of the Tomb.

The Resurrected Infinite One, triumphant says: I open out a way over the Watery Abyss which forms a path between the two Combatants: Darkness and Light, Evil and Good, Death and Life, Law and Love, Self-ish self and Reunited Self.

May a path be made for me whereby I may enter in peace into the beautiful Hidden Place. And may a path be made for me whereby I may enter in and adore the Reunited One, the Lord of Life.

Praise to The Attuned One when he rises upon the Horizon.

GATE 4: Heart Center

Here begin the praises and glorifyings of coming out from and of going into the glorious Inner World which is in the beautiful Hidden Place.

I am Yesterday, the Timeless One; I know Today.

What then is this? It is the Hidden Place wherein were created the souls of the gods when the Father was leader in the Mountain of the Hidden Place.

I know the God who dwells therein. Who then is this? It is the Reunited One.

What then is this? It is the horizon of his Father, the Unmanifested One.

What then is this? It is the cutting off of the corruptible in the body of the Reunited One, the earthly [Your Name]. It is the purification of Reunited [Your Name] on the day of his/her birth.

I pass over the way, I know the head [Crown Center] of the Pool [Navel Center] of the Well of Life.

What then is this? It is the gate, the door; and it is the northern door of the tomb [Crown Center].

Now as concerning the Pool [Navel Center] of the Well of Life, it is Abtu; it is the way by which his father, the Unseen One, travelleth when he goes forth to the Realms of Initiation.

Now the southern gate [second chakra] of the Ascent is the gate of the Pillars of He who rises. It is the gate where the god who rises lifts the disc of Heaven. The gate of the north [pineal center, beginning at the base of the brain and continuing through the brain to the third eye center] is the Gate of the Great God. The northern gate of the Ascent is the two leaves [the two hemispheres of the brain] of the door through which the Unmanifested god passeth when he goeth forth to the Eastern Horizon of Heaven [from the back of the head, over the crown of the head and on toward the forehead].

GATE 5: Throat Center

Here begins the Entering on Light in the Inner World.

I am Yesterday, Today, and Tomorrow, the Dweller in Eternity, and I have the power to be born a second time. I am the divine hidden Soul who gives meals unto the citizens of the Inner World, the Beautiful Hidden Place and Heaven.

I am the Lord of seekers who are raised up; the Lord who comes forth from out of the unconscious.

Hail, Lord of the Shrine which stands in the middle of the Earth. He is I, and I am He. Make thou thy roads glad for me. Send forth thy light upon me, O Soul unknown, for I am one of those who are about to enter in.

Come thou who dwells above the divine Abyss of water.

The god who is the Conductor of Souls transports me to the Chamber of rebirth, and my nurse is the divine, double Lion–God himself, Yesterday and Tomorrow. I am made strong and I come forth like he that forceth a way through the gate. "I know the depths" is thy name.

I am he who Enters on Light. The doors of Heaven are opened for me; the doors of earth are opened for me. Hail, thou soul who rises in Heaven. Strengthen thou me according as thou hast strengthened thyself, and show thyself upon earth, O thou that returns and withdraws thyself.

Messiah, Redeemer, son of the Mother of all, avenger of the Father! Strengthen thou me, according as thou has strengthened thyself, and show thyself upon earth, O thou that returns and withdraws thyself.

GATE 6: Crown Center
Here begins the way of Causing the soul to be united to its body in the Inner World.

The Reunited [Your Name], triumphant, says:

Hail, thou god "the bringer"! Hail, thou god "the runner," who dwells in thy hall! Great God! Grant thou that my soul may come unto me from wheresoever it may be—NOW. [Pause here to receive the permission.]

Hail, ye gods . . . who make souls to enter into their spiritual bodies. Grant ye that the soul of Reunited [Your Name], triumphant, may come forth before the gods and that it may have peace in the Hidden Place. May it look upon its body and neither perish nor suffer corruption forever.

The paths which are above me lead to the gateway.

Open unto me!

GATE 7: Forehead/Third Eye Center
Here begins the Entering into the Hall of Double Truth.

And they say unto me, who art thou then? And they say unto me, what is thy name?

Come, then, they say, and enter in through the door of this Hall of Double Truth.

We will not let thee enter in through us, stay the bolts of this door, unless thou tell us our names.

"Tongue of the Balance" of the place of right and truth is your name. [Pause to allow the doors to open.]

The heavens are opened, the earth is opened, the West is opened, the East is opened, the southern half of Heaven is opened, and the northern half of Heaven is opened.

Now, here begins the Entering into Heaven.

The Attuned One lives, the Earth Bound One dies. Sound is he/she who is the chest, Reunion triumphant.

May those who build up grant that the Reunited [Your Name] shall arrive happily in the Hall of Double Truth. May He Who Makes Reunion to-be-Secret grant that the Reunited [Your Name] may be a lord of strides in the habitation of the Ascent. And there shall be made an offering by the Reunited [Your Name] when he/she enters through the hidden pylons.

May the company of the gods who rule over the Hidden Place grant that Reunited [Your Name] shall go in through the secret door of the House of Reunion. And there shall be made an offering by Reunited [Your Name] when he/she shall walk up the Great Staircase.

The Lady of the Hidden Place, mighty dweller in the funeral mountain, lady of the Holy Place, receive the Reunited [Your Name]. The Attuned One lives, the Earth Bound One dies. Sound is he who is reunited triumphantly. —Amen.

We used this text in a ceremony at one of the A.R.E.'s annual Ancient Mysteries conferences with wonderful results. We've also used the ceremony prior to meditation in the King's Chamber of the Great Pyramid. Almost everyone had an extraordinary experience. It does help when done with others, but on your own it can also be profound.

21

EGYPTIAN IMAGERY: A THOUSAND WORDS IN ONE PICTURE

E gyptian imagery is filled with mystical, metaphysical messages meant to convey deep truths about life, death, rebirth, and our truer nature and ultimate destiny.

Consider the famous Egyptian eye (see illustration 71). It is drawn with mathematical precision. When it is drawn as a left eye, it is the eye of Horus, the messiah god in Egyptian mythology. When it is drawn as a right eye, it is the eye of Ra, the sun god, first among the Egyptian gods. The message is that Ra's eye was the original eye that saw clear and ideally, but evil, darkness, and temptation came, and a new eye was created—one that had seen good *and* evil, light and dark, oneness and multiplicity and had subdued all negative influences to regain some semblance of what had been lost. The eye of Horus is an enlightened eye, a wiser eye. It discerns what is before it and chooses wisely.

Another fascinating glyph is Ra, symbol for the sun, with rays projecting downward. (See illustration 72.) In simple usage it means "to shine," but its deeper message is intended to remind all who grasp even the slightest hint of our distant origins that we were and will be again "Beings of Light," having descended from heaven and destined to return. As Jesus explained to Nicodemus, "No one ascends to heaven but he or she who first descended from it." When I look deeply into this glyph with a meditative mind, I see a centered place of stillness in the dot; I see the white circle of radiance around it, and the pouring out of its life essence as its rays move downward and away from the original oneness.

Another telling image that conveys a deeply important message is the Ra glyph surrounded by the cobra with his head raised. (See illustrations 73a and 73b.) Here is the teaching of the kundalini, that energy that lies within us at the base of our spinal column, waiting to be raised by higher consciousness to its original place of dignity and illumination. Ra consciousness, or God consciousness, draws the energy upward to its original vibration levels. Again, Jesus explained to Nicodemus that, "as Moses raised the serpent in the desert so must the sons and daughters of God be raised up to eternal life." Higher consciousness attracts the kundalini life force from its lowly place in the body. When this energy is retained in the higher chakras and consciousness, it revives what has died, what had lapsed into unconsciousness during the descent into matter and carnal life.

The glyph depicting goddess Mut holding a staff and an ankh further reveals the value of God consciousness and raised vibrations. (See illustration 80c.) The staff has the head of Anubis on top and the prongs to pin down and subdue the low but powerful serpent, or crocodile urges. To an initiate of these ancient messages, this was an important bit of information, vitally necessary for the journey to resurrection. Anubis symbolizes the guide through the underworld, or the unconscious, to the heavens above. (See illustration 74.) The jackal was chosen for this role because of its innate ability to detect even the faintest scent left on a trail. If one went on a long journey away from home and became lost, the jackal could pick up the scent of the trail and lead one back home, through even the darkest darkness. Thus, though the unconscious mind seems black and unnavigable, yet one's deep, intuitive self can detect any remnant scent left by our souls' descent from heavenly consciousness and find our way through the darkness to the lost light. But it requires that we pin down the lower, earthly influences, symbolized by serpents on the ground or crocodiles. In some beautiful and profound Egyptian drawings, the scent that we are searching for is depicted as a lotus blossom. The way home smells like the fragrance of the lotus blossom. Of course, the lotus has been a symbol of enlightenment since very ancient times. In the Egyptian images, the lotus is opened by the inflowing of the Water of Life. The Water of Life pours forth when consciousness and the vibrations are raised sufficiently to open the upper gate, sometimes called the Jade Gate. Cayce identifies this gate with the pineal gland and the crown chakra. Hinduism concurs, depicting the crown chakra as a blossoming lotus.

Another fascinating icon is the one for the goddess Hathor. (See illustrations 79a, 79b, and 79c.) She is the goddess of love and beauty. She is the consort to Horus, the messiah god, who represents the higher mind in the form of a falcon. Hathor's hieroglyph is the symbol for "the place." Inside this symbol is the symbol for Horus. Therefore, initiates would know that the place of the higher mind is with the heart. Higher knowledge and wisdom is best when combined with the heart, with a loving disposition. In Far Eastern teachings it is said that the right knowledge and understanding is only one wing of the bird of heaven; the other is the right heart. The bird of heaven does not fly with only one wing. The Egyptians also knew the importance of love in balancing wisdom and knowledge.

Another insightful image in the Egyptian teachings is the winged scarab. (See illustration 77.) Ancient Egyptians looked around their environment to find outer representations of inner, often unseen truths important to soul growth and enlightenment. In the beetle they found the human struggle and human potential. The lowly beetle rolls his dung toward the rising sun in the morning. In his dung ball he plants the seed of rebirth. By high noon the seed is hot enough to awaken. By the setting sun it is a new life with wings to lift up into the air again—reborn, resurrected.

Egyptians understood that in this life, this world, dung happens. But in the dung of our life lies the potential for resurrection. Hardships, disappointments, and tragedies may come, but within them is the opportunity to plant a seed for a new life, a new opportunity—an opportunity to resurrect as a new, wiser, more loving, more patient person. The winged scarab is a wonderful message for all.

For those of us who seek to know and apply the deeper secrets in our lives, Egyptian imagery can be a source of inspiration and guidance.

When we consider the whole of Edgar Cayce's readings, it becomes apparent that the souls most attracted to this work are often reincarnated Egyptians, having had a most important sojourn or sojourns during the thousands of years that this great culture thrived. This being the case, Egyptian imagery should have significant, if subliminal, meaning to us. Therefore, let's view some of the images that grace Egyptian papyruses, temple walls, and stelae.

In illustration 78, we have a woman holding up two lotus stems with blossoms, two cobras wearing little hats, and two ribbons. On the top of her head is a vulture wearing a little hat and two more cobras with Ra sun disks on their heads. Directly on her head is a vulture headdress with wings extending behind her ears. This image reveals important spiritual concepts.

Raised serpents, especially cobras, are a common spiritual symbol in ancient times. In Hinduism they represent the kundalini life force within the human body. The life force is "coiled" in the lower torso, but as one awakens spiritually, the force rises along the spinal column to the base of the brain, then to the center of the brain and the top of the head, and finally over to the forehead and the legendary third eye (according to Cayce's readings 281-29, -30, -54). Therefore, raised serpents symbolize the life force rising to higher vibrations. Of course, the lotuses also symbolize spiritual awakening. In fact, in Hinduism, especially ancient yogic teachings, the spiritual centers of the body, the chakras, are also called padmas, Sanskrit for "lotuses." This woman's cobras symbolize the power and pathway of the life force, and the lotuses represent the spiritual centers that gradually bloom.

The ribbons are unique to Egyptian mysticism. They are associated with the god Anubis, the jackal-headed god who is the guide through the underworld to heaven. In one of the most beautiful Egyptian tombs (Sennedjem's) the blue jackals, with their ribbon collars, can pick up the scent of the trail to heaven by smelling lotuses. (See illustrations 75a, 75b, and 75c.) The woman's ribbons signify our inner ability to catch that scent and find our way to heavenly consciousness. As Jesus taught Nicodemus, "No one ascends to heaven but he or she who first descended from it." And as Jesus said at the last supper, "Where I am going you know, and the way you know." Now we may cry out like Thomas, "We do not know where you are going. How can we know the way?" Yet deep within us, this knowing lies still waiting for us to awaken it, to pick up the scent again, and as our padmas open, the scent returns.

Let's turn our attention to the woman's vulture, a symbol of death today. The word *mother* in Egyptian is made with the hieroglyph of a vulture. The vulture, especially in the New Kingdom, is the symbol for the mother of all godlings and all creation. Her name is Mut. She is wife to the hidden, unseen god, Amun Ra, and mother of the moon god, Khonsu (see illustrations 80a, 80b, and 80c). Myth has it that she conceived all creation with the wind, not with a male. All life therefore comes from the wind. Again we find a comment by Jesus that seems to help with this idea: "The wind blows where it will, and no one knows from where it comes or to where it goes, even so are all those who are born of the spirit." In ancient mystery schools the wind represented the spirit, while the breath represented the soul (personal wind), and a bird gliding on the wind symbolized our higher mind gliding on the currents of the spirit! It's all so wonderfully mystical, isn't it? For the ancient Egyptian, the vulture may be associated with physical death, but it is a symbol for spiritual life.

The two serpents on her head, each with sun disks on their heads, symbolize the *ida* and *pingala* in yoga, which are the deeper pathways of the life force, which Cayce correlated to the autonomic nervous system. The outer pathway is the spinal column, corresponding to the *sushumna* in yoga. Ra's sun disks on the serpents' heads reveal that the influence that is raising the life force is God–consciousness, or "God on your mind."

It is amazing what is conveyed in this one image.

In illustration 80c we see a strange staff. At its top is the head of a jackal and at its bottom is a two–pronged device used to pin and hold fast the head and neck of a serpent. In front of this staff is a woman holding in one hand a smaller version of this staff and in the other an ankh, the Egyptian symbol for life. She is wearing the vulture headdress (mother of spiritual life) and the twin crowns of the rulers of Upper and Lower Egypt, representing our higher and lower self. The jackal on the head of the staff, as we've learned, represents our inner, intuitive sense of the way to heaven. In Egypt, the serpent that crawls on the ground is called Apep; it represents our lower, self–centered urges that nip at the heels of our higher consciousness, attempting to poison us as we try to live an enlightened life. The ankh is a fascinating symbol too, conveying more than might first be seen. Notice that it is a cross symbolizing sacrifice and has a loop at the top symbolizing higher consciousness. Therefore, this illustration teaches us to subdue our lower urges and gain the strength that comes from our lower and higher aspects cooperating in the pursuit of an enlightened, happy life.

In illustration 17, we have a two-headed being. The head on the left is ancient Egypt's Satan, called Set, Seth, or Seti. The head on the right is that of the immaculately conceived savior of ancient Egypt, Horus. This image of the two opposites coming out of the same body represents the double-mindedness that we can develop if we attempt to enjoy both earthliness and godliness, or as Jesus put it: mammon and God. There is a wrestling match that goes on between our human nature and our divine nature. Cayce identified the two-horned beast in the Revelation with this same weakness: double-mindedness. The mind, like the eye, must be single in purpose and intent. This is perhaps why Cayce viewed the setting of an ideal to live by as so important. Without an ideal, one is pulled in both directions. Jesus noted, in his discussion with Nicodemus, that we are born of flesh but must be born a second time of spirit, for we are ultimately spiritual beings temporarily living in a physical world. Double-mindedness divides, but balance between the human and the divine unites and integrates us for better purposes and a happier, more eternal life.

In illustration 77, we see the winged scarab with two raised cobras and the sun disk in the center. The scarab and the dung beetle are Egyptian images of our earthly self. The human body is seen as a hard, beetle-like encasement for the normally free-flying soul. And from the soul's perspective, life in the body is comparable to the life in a beetle. Yet, like the beetle, we can roll the dung of our life toward the sun, plant the seed of hope and higher purposes in it, and by the sun's noon-day heat that seed will open and our soul will resurrect again, taking wing and flying high above it all! The wings, the sun, the raised serpents all symbolize the power to resurrect our sometimes disgusting and little self to its higher, more eternal nature and happiness.

In illustration 76, we see two of the greatest gods of ancient Egypt, Horus (on the left, as the Higher Mind) and Hermes-Thoth (on the right, as mindful of inner and outer realities), pouring the Water of Life over the body and into the hand and heart of pharaoh. What is the Water of Life? The image gives the viewer the exact ingredients: the pouring water is composed of little staffs and little ankhs. The ankhs symbolize life, especially life that comes from the Source and is held onto (as seen in his left hand). The staffs symbolize guidance from the Source and the strength that results from receiving such. Our hearts and minds need this.

The Egyptians were mystics. Their images are packed with fascinating messages that we can use in our soul growth today, especially if our soul had an incarnation in those grand times.

22

A Light Heart: Egyptian Key to Heaven

One of many wonderful scenes in ancient Egyptian art is "The Judgment," sometimes called "The Weighing of the Heart." (See illustration 26.) It appears in the papyrus scrolls of *The Egyptian Book of the Dead*. The scene shows a deceased Egyptian named Ani being led to the chamber of his judgment. He is led by the god Anubis, the underworld guide, who brings Ani before a huge scale. On one side of the scale, Ani's heart is placed in a jar. On the other side of the scale is the feather of the goddess of Truth and Justice, Ma'at. Observing the weighing of the heart are various other gods. Thoth (Hermes, to the Greeks) stands nearby with Ani's Book of Life in his hands, ready to inscribe the outcome of this weighing. Horus, the god who was immaculately conceived by Isis to save the world from Egypt's Satan, waits to see if Ani's heart is light enough for him to lead Ani out of the underworld through Osiris' chamber and on up into the heavens. Isis and Nephthys stand behind Osiris, who is seated on his throne. All await the outcome.

If one's heart were heavy with regret, unfinished earth business, or the pull of physical desires, then the ancient Egyptian—in this case, Ani—could not enter the heavens. Therefore, his heart would be eaten by a beastly creature, and he would have to return to earth to get a new heart, one light enough to rise into heaven (presumably by reincarnating and living a better life in which he or she lightened the heavy heart).

Do we have light hearts? Or are we carrying around a lot of unresolved issues, unfulfilled desires, regrets, the weight of broken dreams and promises, or other heavy feelings and mental concerns that weigh on us? The Cayce readings tell the story of an Egyptian high priest named Ra-Ta who, at a very old age and in decrepit condition, was able to rejuvenate himself and live another one hundred years in order to work on the building of the Great Pyramid of Giza. When Cayce was asked how this priest rejuvenated his aged body, he answered: "through the casting aside of the years of toil and strife through which the body of Ra-Ta itself had passed." In other words, by letting go of the things that had aged him. We tend to hold on to our disappointments, pain, sacrifices, and regrets—all of which age us and weigh down our hearts. Forgive and forget is a much healthier prescription.

Such rejuvenation was not done in one day or in one thought; it took Ra-Ta seven years to fully rejuvenate himself.

When in deep-trance attunement to the universal consciousness, Cayce was asked to give some light on the word *heart*. He replied in this fashion: "As in the physical body the heart is considered the source that impels life to all portions of the body. In that sense, then, one seeks God's help in creating a pure heart, a pure soul, a pure purpose in body and mind, that one may bring life, light, understanding, to those contacted—as does the heart to the body. The heart is used to signify that purpose, that intent, that life. It represents an entity, a body, a mind, an imaginative being that through the conscious and subconscious or soul forces brings life to all contacted. As in: 'Create within me a pure heart, O God, and *renew* a right, righteous, holy spirit within me.'"

In his teachings about actions and reactions, he encourages us to achieve a light heart by helping others' hearts be lighter: "Keep thy smile of encouragement to others; for it lightens the heart of many."

In a reading for a member of his study groups, Cayce gave this insight and encouragement about keeping our light shining: "Thy light has shone out before the darkness in the lives of many. Keep that light burning in thy own heart. Grow not weary in well doing. Let thy heart open to those things that bespeak the closeness of His walks, His talks with thee. Thy light of love and faith and hope and thought will not lose its reward in Him. For whom He loves He comforts, every one."

A light heart, both in weight and luminescence, is an important part of our personal spirituality. How do we achieve such? Through being often in prayer, meditation, and doing good for others.

In his parable of the seeds of the word of God sown along the road-side of life, Jesus says that the seeds that fall "in the good ground, these are such as in an honest and good heart, having heard the word, hold it fast, and bring forth fruit with patience." A good heart in patience is the important point here. Letting go of what weighs our hearts down is achieved with patience. We cannot jump straight out of our present condition into our hoped-for goal. We grow from where we are to that goal, step by step, little by little, day by day, one situation at a time. Whether we have a week to live or many years, today is the time to begin to lighten and enlighten our hearts and the hearts of those around us. Cayce commented, "some grow old gracefully, some tolerantly, some fussily, and some very meanly." The key factor may well be *patience*.

In the Egyptian scene, Ani's heart is indeed lighter than Ma'at's feather, and Ani is allowed to enter the higher heavens. Let's lighten our hearts and the hearts of those we contact, because it is a healthy spiritual practice—coming to us from ancient Egypt.

23

CAYCE AND THE GREAT INITIATE

Here is a most amazing tale from Cayce's collection. It began with Cayce's story of the "lost years" of Jesus, those years from his childhood to the beginning of his ministry. These are not recorded in the Gospels. In the telling of the lost years, Cayce begins using the strange title "The Great Initiate" when referring to Jesus. Later in his readings we learn that this is because the young John the Baptist and Jesus were both initiated while living in Egypt prior to beginning their ministries. According to Cayce, John reached the higher levels of initiation but could not pass the final test. Jesus successfully completed the entire initiation process—a feat that John knew was exceptional. This could be why John later says, "He that comes after me is mightier than I." (Matthew 3:11)

According to Edgar Cayce's reading of the Akashic record, the Magi returned several times to Galilee to visit the Holy Family and keep up with the progress of the boy's growth. They returned at least five times and not always the same Magi. Cayce said, "They came from Persia, India, Egypt, and also from Chaldea, Gobi, and what is now the Indo or Tao land." According to these readings, at the fifth visit, when Jesus had become "of age" (which in those days would have been twelve years old), the Magi took him from Jerusalem to their temples for training and testing. These temples were in Persia (modern day Iran), India, and Egypt.

Cayce explained that the three Wise Men and their gifts "represent in the metaphysical sense the three phases of man's experience in materiality: gold, the material; frankincense, the ether or ethereal; myrrh, the healing force as brought with same; or body, mind, soul." In these readings, Egypt was the source for the gold. Cayce gives the source of the

frankincense as a Persian Wise Man named *Achlar* and in another reading as an India Wise Man named *Ashtueil*. Perhaps, in one of the many
visits, the Wise Man from Persia brought the frankincense, while on
another visit, the one from India brought it. In those days, myrrh came
from East India. Myrrh was used in the holy oil of the Jews and the
religious and medicinal incense in ancient Egypt called *Kyphi*. In the
initial visitation by the Magi, it is likely that the myrrh came from India,
the frankincense from Persia, and the gold from Egypt. Therefore, using
Cayce's correlations, we could conclude that ancient Egypt represented
the material phase, ancient Persia the ethereal phase, and ancient India
the healing phase of human experience.

As for the young Jesus' training and testing, the readings say that he
first went to Persia. There he would have been trained and tested according to the ways of Zoroastrianism, from the sacred books *Avesta* and
the *Gathas* ("Older Hymns"). This faith is at the same time monotheistic
and dualistic: teaching that there is only one God but two distinct forces
battling for the hearts and minds of God's children: good and evil. Each
soul must choose which of these forces it will adhere to, using its free
will to do so. Those following the path of evil are called "The Followers
of the Lie." Despite this battle, there is an underlying optimism in Zoroastrianism because it is understood that God and Good are destined
from the start to win the battle.

After Persia, the Cayce readings say young Jesus went to India and
was there for three years, studying under a teacher named *Arcahia*. Jesus
attended many schools in India, including the large ones in Jagannath
and Benares.

In India he would have been trained and tested according to ancient
Hinduism, which would be found in the sacred texts of the *Vedas*,
Upanishads, and the *Bhagavad-Gita* ("The Lord's Song," ca. 200 BC). He
would have learned about Brahman and Atman. Brahman is an
uncreated, eternal, infinite, transcendent, and all-embracing *essence*,
which includes both being and nonbeing. It is the only true reality.
Atman is the Self, the Logos, and the central consciousness of Beingness.
In Western terms, it is the great "I AM" and is reflected in all the little "I
ams." Atman gives self-consciousness to all beings. Atman is personal.

Yet Atman exists within Brahman, which is impersonal. Brahman is the One, the Whole, within which and through which everything exists. Brahman is also expressed in a Trinity: Brahma (the Creator, a personification of Brahman), Vishnu (the Preserver), and Shiva (the Destroyer of Illusions). Jesus' teachings about the Trinity have some degree of harmony with ancient Hindu concepts: The Father (Creator), the Son (Savior, and emulator of the Father's spirit), and the Holy Spirit (the inner spirit of truth, inner comforter, and bringer of all things to our remembrance).

For those readers who may be uncomfortable with trinity concepts of God, know that Cayce, and many others, see this as *one* God with three aspects, phases, or dimensions—but only one, omnipresent, omniscient God.

Like Zoroastrianism, ancient Hinduism teaches that there is a battle raging between the good gods (*devas*) and the demoniac anti-gods (*asuras*). The cosmos (*sat*) is naturally governed by order and truth but is always in danger of being damaged or even destroyed by the powers of chaos (*asat*). These correlate well with Egypt's Ma'at (order and truth) and Set (chaos). During his time in India young Jesus would have also learned about reincarnation and karma.

The Cayce readings indicate that Jesus did as much teaching as he did learning, because much of what he experienced were tests rather than initiations. However, once he arrived in Egypt, initiation was the primary experience. This is why Cayce gave him the title of The Great Initiate.

Since Cayce identifies one of the Wise Men as coming from "Tao Land," young Jesus would have also learned about Taoism (pronounced dow-ism). Along with Confucianism, Taoism was one of the chief religions of ancient China. Taoism conveys a positive, active attitude toward the occult and metaphysical, in contrast to the agnostic, pragmatic Confucian traditions of social duty and austerity. The sacred texts of Taoism are *Tao-te Ching* written by Lao-tzu, the *Chuang-tzu*, and the *Lieh-tzu*. Tao (dow) means "Way," referring to the way to fulfillment and immortality. According to Lao-tzu, there is a Tao that is named and can be studied and practiced, but then there is a Tao that is unnamed and can be experienced only through an ecstasy that transcends normal reality. Taoism teaches that all *multiplicity* is returning to a former *oneness* that it enjoyed before the creation. This can be mystically achieved in a moment of deep stillness, when all beingness returns to nonbeing, all action to nonaction. In Taoism there are again two forces in the world: those that disperse and those that unite. The force that disperses sees only the manyness, while the force that unites sees the oneness.

Certainly in India and under the influence of those from Tao Land, young Jesus would have learned to meditate, transcending normal consciousness to experience the peace, oneness, and ecstasy of reunion with the Source of Life.

After Persia, India, and the Tao Land, young Jesus, according to Cayce, spent the rest of his time in Egypt, being trained and tested in Heliopolis (modern-day East Cairo) but taking his most significant initiation in Giza, *inside* the Great Pyramid. The readings say that John the Baptist was also there but in a different class. Cayce says that the "unifying of the teachings of many lands was brought together in Egypt; for that was the center from which there was to be the radial activity of influence in the Earth . . . until the new cycle begins." This "new cycle" began in 1998, according to Cayce, and will lead to the much-anticipated New Age.

In Egypt Jesus would have again found several Trinity themes; an example would be: Ra, the creator; Osiris, the preserver; and Horus, the subduer of chaos. He would have again learned of the struggle between Good and Evil. He would have learned about the feminine and masculine forces that appear separate but actually compose a united whole in the higher state of consciousness. He would have learned about powerful feminine goddesses that helped save humanity from evil: Isis, Nephthys, Ma'at, Hathor, and others.

Cayce says that young Jesus reached the training level of a priest in Egypt. The readings indicate that it was he who broke the corner of the sarcophagus in the King's Chamber of the Great Pyramid. This occurred during his final initiation, when he overcame death. This prepared him for his victory later at the crucifixion and resurrection: "For, read ye, 'He was crucified also in Egypt.'" (EC 315-4) This is a comment on his initiation in Egypt as being like a crucifixion, a dying to self in order to resurrect as a result of making oneself in harmony and oneness with the Source of Life. Another reading states: "There should be the reminding that, though He bowed under the burden of the Cross, though His blood was shed, though He entered into the tomb—through that power, that ability, that love as manifested in Himself among His fellow men He broke the bonds of death, proclaiming in that act that *there is no death* when the individual, the soul, has and does put its trust in Him." (EC 5749-13)

But the Cayce tale of The Great Initiate is even bigger than Jesus. Edgar Cayce channeled the astonishing ideas that, "there never was a time when there was not a Christ"; "Christ in all ages, Jesus in one"; and "Christ is the Spirit, Jesus is the man." Over time Cayce's readings developed these ideas by explaining that the central, indivisible essence of all expression, all life was in the beginning with God, was God, and yet came into the earth to enlighten any who received the light. The disciple John wrote this concept in the first paragraphs of his gospel. Here are those passages, but with a few changes that better reflect the original Greek that it was written in. The now famous term "the Word" has been translated "the Logos," because the original text used *logos*, not *word*. In Greek, *logos* means much more than the English term *word*. Also, there is no masculine pronoun in the original first sentences of the text; rather it uses "this One." With this in mind, here is the opening of the Gospel of John:

In the beginning was the Logos, and the Logos was with God, and the Logos was God. This One was in the beginning with God; all things were made through this One, and without this One was not anything made that was made. In this One was life, and the life was the light of men [humanity]. The light shines in the darkness, and the darkness has not overcome it. The true light that enlightens every person was coming into the world. This One was in the world, and the world was made through him, yet the world knew him not. He came to his own home, and his own people received him not. But to all who received him, who believed in his name, he gave power to become children of God; who were born, not of blood nor of the will of the flesh, nor of the will of man, but of God. And the Logos became flesh and dwelt among us, full of grace and truth. (John 1:1-5 and 1:10-14)

For those who have studied ancient Hindu and Egyptian spiritual texts, the concept of a singular Light that is of God but can manifest in and through humans is a fundamental teaching. In the Western world this idea is only recently taking hold. When Cayce was asked if Christ influenced any other religions, he answered that wherever the concept of the one God and the brotherhood, sisterhood of all humankind was taught, the Christ Spirit.

In one instance, Cayce explained that the Christ consciousness is *God* consciousness. When any soul touches that Divine contact point deep within itself, the Spirit of God imbues the soul with the truth that comes from direct connection with the Creative Forces and the Universal Consciousness (as Cayce called them).

Cayce explained that destructive forces came later, when free-willed souls began to rebel against the natural ways of the Creator, and the dark forces of hate, contention, spitefulness, meanness, self-seeking, and self-glorification began to take hold in the hearts and minds of many. These rebellious souls descended out of heaven into the realm of earth, of physical life, bringing their darkness with them. To counter this, many of the souls of Light entered this world to avoid complete darkness ruling this world. Egyptian legends tell of how Isis, after seeing how evil was flourishing on earth, called up to heaven to ask if the godlings of heaven were simply going to abandon the lost souls or help her in overcoming this darkness and resurrecting the lost ones. The story continues with Isis receiving the help she needs, and a savior is born that overthrows the dark forces.

Eventually, according to many ancient legends, even the Logos, the central essence of the Light, incarnates among humanity in order to save as many as would be saved or resurrected to their former glory with the creative forces, with the Creator and the community of celestial, heavenly beings.

Cayce's readings indicate that the first incarnation of the Logos was in Atlantis, in the name of Amilius, around 106,000 BC. Fascinatingly, Cayce's channeled wisdom states that the Logos was and is both masculine and feminine—Amilius was only the male half, the legendary Lilith was the female half of the Logos. This yang and yin incarnating has continued through many incarnations. Cayce explains that Mary, the mother of Jesus, was in fact the return of the feminine Logos, the feminine Christ, just as Jesus was the return of the masculine.

Cayce stated that there were thirty key incarnations of the Logos or Christ Spirit and Consciousness, and he intimated that there were more. The few that Cayce actually gave were: "Jesus came to the earth plane as Amilius, Adam, Melchizedeck, Zend, Asapha, Joshua, Joseph, and Jesus; and He manifested through many other great leaders and teachers of other ages. For the Spirit of the Christ has walked with the priests of France, the lowly monks in England, the warriors in America. Those labored until their own personalities were laid aside in individuals." (EC 364-13)

Additionally, Cayce's longtime assistant, stenographer, and indexer of his readings, Gladys Turner wrote: "Because of the inferences in the text of reading 281-10 and others from time to time, it would seem to be implied that Jesus [or the Logos] had an incarnation in Egypt at the time of Ra-Ta under the name of Hermes [Thoth]." (EC Report 281-10)

Here's a reading that reveals how young Jesus experienced his initiation in the Great Pyramid.

"Q: Please describe Jesus' initiations in Egypt, telling if the Gospel reference to 'three days and nights in the grave or tomb,' possibly in the shape of a cross, indicate a special initiation.

"A: The record of the earth through the passage through the tomb, or the pyramid, is that through which each entity, each soul, as an initiate must pass for the attaining to the releasing of same—as indicated by the empty tomb, which has *never* been filled, see? Only Jesus was able to break same, as it became that which indicated His fulfillment. And there, as the initiate, He went out—for the passing through the initiation, by fulfilling—as indicated in the baptism in the Jordan; not standing in it and being poured or sprinkled either! [full submersion] He passed from that activity [the baptism] into the wilderness to meet that which had been His undoing in the beginning. [the three temptations by Satan]"

Cayce's reference to the baptism in the Jordan was recorded in the Scriptures thusly:

"I [John the Baptist] indeed baptize you with water unto repentance, but he that comes after me is mightier than I, whose shoes I am not worthy to bear. He shall baptize you with the Holy Spirit, and with fire; whose fan is in his hand, and he will thoroughly purge his floor [separating the chaff from the grain], and gather his wheat into the garner; but he will burn up the chaff with unquenchable fire.

"Then comes Jesus from Galilee to Jordan unto John, to be baptized of him. But John forbad him, saying, 'I have need to be baptized by you, and you come to me?' And Jesus answering said unto him, 'Suffer it to be so now, for thus it becomes us to fulfill all righteousness.' Then he suffered him. And Jesus, when he was baptized, went up straightway out of the water, and, lo, the heavens were opened unto him, and he saw the Spirit of God descending like a dove, and lighting upon him; and lo a voice from heaven, saying, 'This is my beloved Son, in whom I am well pleased.'" (Matthew 3:11–17)

The descent of the Holy Spirit upon him was followed by three temptations from the Devil:

"Then Jesus was led up by the Spirit into the wilderness to be tempted of the Devil. And when he had fasted forty days and forty nights, he was afterward hungry. And the tempter came to him, saying, 'If thou be the Son of God, command that these stones be made bread.' But he answered and said, 'It is written, Man shall not live by bread alone, but by every word that proceeds out of the mouth of God.' Then the devil took him up into the holy city, and sat him on a pinnacle of the temple, and said unto him, 'If thou be the Son of God, cast yourself down, for it is written, "He shall give his angels charge concerning thee, and in *their* hands they shall bear thee up, lest at any time thou dash thy foot against a stone."' Jesus said unto him, 'It is written again, "Thou shalt not tempt the Lord thy God."' Again, the devil took him up into an exceeding high mountain, and showed him all the kingdoms of the world, and the glory of them; and said unto him, 'All these things will I give thee, if thou wilt fall down and worship me.' Then said Jesus unto him, 'Get thee hence, Satan, for it is written, "Thou shalt worship the Lord thy God, and him only shalt thou serve."' Then the devil left him, and, behold, angels came and ministered unto him." (Matthew 4:1–11)

Cayce's readings explain that these temptations were intended "to meet that which had been His undoing in the beginning." Here we step into the mysterious again. Cayce is correlating Jesus' experiences with soul challenges experienced way back in the beginning. Cayce explains this as the early incarnations of the Logos in which the goal was to understand what the temptations were that possessed the children of God. Thus, the Logos incarnated first as Amilius, who led souls into the earth as "thought forms." Then He came as Adam, the first physical man, who fell in the flesh by eating the "forbidden fruit," and thus it became necessary for him to eventually become the "last Adam" (as Paul calls him in I Corinthians 15:45) to show us the way. Next, He came as Enoch, who walked with God and was not because God took him (Genesis 5:22). Then He came as Melchizedek, the King of Salem and priest of the God Most High (Genesis 14), without father, without mother, without days; he was not born and he did not die. Melchizedek broke bread and served wine to Abram to celebrate his rescue of lost brother Lot. Many parallels can be found here with the life of Jesus. According to the readings, Melchizedek had attained a state of mastership found in Eastern masters. In order to save the souls who had become involved in the earth, he realized he would have to go through all the trials and tribulations that faced every incarnate soul. He came then as Joseph. We see many parallels between the story of Joseph and that of Jesus, including their time in Egypt. Then He came as Joshua, who, according to Cayce, was the medium through which Moses obtained the laws on the mount. Next He came as Jeshua, who compiled and rewrote much of the Biblical record as we have it. Then He came into the earth as Zend (San or Zan), father of the first Zoroaster, who, the readings say, wrote the *Zend Avesta*, the sacred writings of the Zoroastrianism. Finally He came as Jesus, the "last Adam" in whom we all may be made one with the Creator.

Until he became Joseph, he had not actually taken on the trials and tribulations of human beings. He chose, as Melchizedek, to come down into the depths of materiality, and from there He returned to the heavens. Having chosen to do this, it was not possible then for him to get out of the flesh without perfecting himself *in* the flesh. Gradually, life after life, here a little, there a little, the soul liberated itself from the temptations that had been humanity's undoing in the beginning. According to the Cayce readings, each of us is on a journey to accomplish the same, and the Logos is a pattern we can emulate.

When asked, "In which pyramid are the records of the Christ?" Cayce replied, "That yet to be uncovered." When asked, "Are there any written records which have not been found of the teachings?" he replied, "More, rather, of those of the close associates, and those records that are yet to be found of the preparation of the man, of the Christ, in those of the tomb, or those yet to be uncovered in the pyramid." Asked, "He said He would come again. What about His second coming?" Cayce replied, "The time no one knows. Even as He gave, not even the Son Himself. *Only* the Father. Not until His enemies—and the earth—are wholly in subjection to His will, His powers." Asked, "Any message to the group gathered here?" he replied, "You seek to know the manner of *His* preparation, seek also to prepare *yourselves* to be His subjects with that same diligence."

I cannot think of any modern source of inspirational insight into Jesus Christ and his role in our lives today that is as exciting and meaningful as Edgar Cayce's channeled visions and wisdom. Mr. Cayce loved Jesus and all that He means to those of us seeking to find enduring happiness, eternal fulfillment, and lasting contentment.

Let's take a closer walk with Him, using Cayce as our guide. I have selected three of his profound readings: 5749–4, 262–29, and 2072–11. We begin with a reading in which the soul of John, the apostle and writer of the Revelation, is speaking through Cayce to us in this world today. It all begins with a question.

"Q: Please explain: While meditating I had the realization of the forces within and the forces without being the one and the same force. Then as if someone said: 'Why not look to the within?' When I turned to the within, I received a realization of the Christ which seemed to take form in body.

"A: In this the body-consciousness [you] experienced much that I, even John, experienced when I looked behind me from the cave and saw that the without and within are *one*, when the desires of the heart make each atom of the physical body vibrate with the consciousness of, the belief and the faith and the presence of, the Christ life, the Christ Consciousness."

The apostle refers to his own experience in "seeing" the revelation, as he wrote so long ago: "I was in the Spirit on the Lord's Day and I saw and was told to write. I *turned* to see the voice that was speaking to me, and on turning I saw seven golden lampstands, and in the midst of the lampstands one like a son of man, clothed with a long robe and with a golden girdle round his breast; his head and his hair were white as white wool, white as snow; his eyes were like a flame of fire, his feet were like burnished bronze, refined as in a furnace, and his voice was like the sound of many waters; in his right hand he held seven stars, from his mouth issued a sharp two-edged sword, and his face was like the sun shining in full strength." (Revelation 1:10-16) In this reading, a woman asked (through Cayce) about her "turning" and "seeing" Christ take form in body. John tells her that she experienced what he experienced during his revelation on the Isle of Patmos.

The soul of John, through Cayce, continues:

"Life is an essence of the Father. The Christ, taking up the life of the man Jesus, becomes life in glory; and may be glorified in each atom of a physical body that attunes self to the consciousness and the *will* of the Christ Spirit."

The spark we call *life* is an attribute of our Creator. As we take up the life of incarnate, physical humans, we can have this attribute in fundamental levels, but if we attune ourselves and our wills to the Christ Spirit, we can enliven our bodies and earthly minds to levels of glorification that fill us—each atom of our earthly being—with glory!

We continue with another question, one that attempts to locate the celestial realm.

"Q: Is the Celestial Sphere a definite place in the Universe or is it a state of mind?

"A: When an entity, a soul, passes into any sphere, with that it has builded in its celestial body, it must occupy—to a finite mind—space, place, time. Hence, to a finite mind, a body can only be in a place, a position. [But also] an attitude, sure—for that of a onement with, or attunement with, the Whole."

The wording here is difficult, but the gist is that we think in a manner that requires a spatial answer. However, John shifts us to thinking of the Celestial Sphere as an *attitude* of at-onement with or attunement with the Whole. This causes our three-dimensional minds to expand into the Infinite—conceiving that within it (the Whole) all of celestial life exists. We are forced to move out of individualness into universalness, out of finite boundaries to endlessly inclusive infinity. An attitude is not confined to a body. In another reading, Cayce taught us to feel ourselves expand as we rise out of our bodies into the mental dimensions of the Universal Consciousness of our Creator, within whom all exist and have their being.

Now John touches on a topic he first wrote about in his epistles: God is Love.

"For, God is love; hence occupies a space, place, condition, and [also] *is* the Force that permeates *all* activity. So, Christ is the ruling force in the world that man, in his finite mind [and] the material body, must draw to self of that sphere of which the entity, the soul, is a part, of whatever period of experience, to be conscious of an existence in that particular sphere or plane."

"Drawing" to ourselves that consciousness, that attitude that is universal, infinite, and celestial, we need to use the "ruling force," which is Christ—Christ Consciousness and Christ Spirit.

Now the questioner attempts to locate Jesus Christ.

"Q: Is Jesus the Christ on any particular sphere or is He manifesting on the earth plane in another body?

"A: As just given, all power in heaven, in earth, is given to Him who overcame. Hence He is of Himself in space, in the force that impels through faith, through belief, in the individual entity—as a Spirit Entity. Hence not in a body in the earth, but may come at will to him who *wills* to be one with, and acts in love to make same possible. For, He shall come as you have seen Him go, in the *body* He occupied in Galilee. The body that He formed, that was crucified on the cross, that rose from the tomb, that walked by the sea, that appeared to Simon, that appeared to Philip, that appeared to 'I, even John.'"

Jesus Christ is a Spirit Entity in the impelling forces that make for faith and belief. If we wish to contact Him, to have His direct help and counsel, we must *will* ourselves to be one with Him *through* our *actions* of love. This reading states that He will come. He may also manifest his body, the body God glorified and resurrected in Galilee. In another reading, Cayce taught that Jesus Christ would first come to us in our hearts and minds, and then eventually, as we prepared ourselves, in the same body He took with Him.

The next person didn't quite catch the guidance and asks more pointedly.

"Q: Wherever He is, how may I contact Him so that I may see Him and hear Him speak?

"A: The making of the will of self one with His will makes a whole attunement with Him. He *will*, with the making of self in accord and desiring same, speak with you. 'Be not afraid, it is I.'"

Here Gladys, Mr. Cayce's stenographer, places quote marks around these final words because she believed that Jesus Christ spoke through Cayce at that moment.

The next question reveals that there are transitions and phases to our spiritual growth and conscious awareness of the resurrected Jesus Christ.

"Q: Was the vision I saw early one morning several months ago a vision of the Master?

"A: A passing shadow, yes. Pray rather to the Son, [to] the Father through the Son, that He walks with you—and He *will* walk and talk with you. Be *not* satisfied with *any* other. He may oft give His angels charge concerning you, yet know the Master's touch, the Master's voice; for He may walk and talk with you. *He* is the Way; there is no other. He in body suffered; for himself, yes – for you also. Will you turn, then, to any other?"

Truly one of the most revealing attitudes in the entire body of the Cayce readings is the one that every soul is worthy of experiencing direct contact with God the Father and Jesus Christ—directly and personally. For Cayce, even the least among us possesses a birthright to know his or her Creator directly—no one between them—not Cayce, not angels, not guides, not even priests and ministers. God wants to speak directly to each of His children, His companions.

Cayce, or John through Cayce, calls for us not to accept anything less than direct communion with our Father, and our elder brother, Jesus Christ. Cayce even takes a step further. He wants us to willfully seek to know the companionship of the Master. We are often hesitant because our lives and our minds and our bodies are not as pure as they should be. Jesus Christ knows that. He became completely human—as human as you and I—and therefore knows all of the trials, bad habits, weaknesses, and temptations we face. He knows our vices and our virtues. And, as one of his greatest disciples wrote, "love covers a multitude of sins." (I Peter 4:8) With a little love in our hearts, we can become a comfortable house in which the Master may visit and commune with us.

"Q: When Jesus the Christ comes the second time, will He set up His kingdom on earth and will it be an everlasting kingdom?

"A: Read His promises in that you have written of His words, even as 'I gave' [John in the Revelation]. He shall rule for a thousand years. Then shall Satan be loosed again for a season. (Revelation 20:2)

Now John, still speaking through Cayce, quotes from the prophecy in the Revelation about a thousand years of a golden age on earth that is followed by a brief period of tests and challenges. Personally, I believe this last period is to give all those who did not make it another chance to come into harmony with their Creator and unite for eternity.

"Q: How may I raise my vibrations so as to contact the Christ?

"A: Making the will, the desire of the heart, one with His, believing in faith, in patience, all becomes possible in Him, through Him to the Father; for He gave it as it is. Do you believe? Then, 'according to your faith be it done in you.'"

Here Cayce and John once again reveal the importance of our will! We must use our wills to willfully choose to cooperate with God's will. We must *desire* this in our hearts. We must also believe it is true and will eventually become a reality for us. We must have sufficient patience to endure long enough to realize oneness with our Father.

In this next reading, we study the nature of the Christ Consciousness and the Christ Spirit.

"Q: Please explain clearly the difference between the Christ Consciousness, the Christ Spirit.

"A: As the difference might be given in that which makes for the birth in the flower, and the flower. The consciousness of the Spirit and the abilities to apply same are the differences in the Christ Consciousness, the Christ Spirit."

Such a wonderful insight: the Spirit is that which is the life impulse, the spark, while the Consciousness is that which is the manifested condition. One quickens, the other sentiently existent.

For readers who may be uncomfortable with so many Christian terms, know that Edgar Cayce's content was universal, crediting all religions and faiths with key contributions to soul growth. In one reading he correlated Christ Consciousness with God Consciousness.

In this next paragraph, Cayce states that even devils know the truth, are conscious of the truth, but do not manifest it.

"As has been given, the devils believe, the devils know, individuals that may be conscious of an activity [are not] those with the abilities to call upon, to be so unselfish as to allow the Spirit to operate in self's stead, [yet] are aware of the Spirit's activity. Those that may be conscious or aware of a truth may not wholly make it their own without that which has been given, 'He that would have life must give life;' for *He* thought it not robbery to be equal with the Father, yet of Himself did nothing, 'but the Father that works in me, through me.'"

In this next paragraph, Jesus Christ speaks to us through the attuned Cayce.

"Do you likewise, that you may know the consciousness of the Christ Spirit, and experience the operation of that witness, that 'My Spirit bears witness with your spirit, that the Father may be glorified in you, even as I am glorified in the Father through you. If you love me, keep my commandments and I will abide with you. I will *not* leave you comfortless; I will make you aware of that glory I possessed with the Father before the world was.'"

The phrase about the "glory I possessed with the Father *before* the world was" refers to the ever-existing Christ. Cayce states: "there never was a time when there wasn't a Christ and Christ-mass." It is important to our spiritual growth to realize that Christ, the Logos, is always available to us, to all of us. In this same paragraph, Jesus reveals the manner by which we become aware of the Christ Consciousness and become one with the Christ Spirit: "Keep my commandments, and I will abide with you. I will *not* leave you comfortless; I will make you aware . . . "

In this next paragraph, Cayce picks up on this process and prophesies the return of Jesus Christ and the Christ Spirit.

"In such a manner may individuals become aware of the Christ Consciousness and become one with the operative forces of the Christ Spirit abroad in the earth; for He shall come again, even as you have seen Him go. *Then* shall the Christ Spirit be manifest in the world, even as the Christ Consciousness may make you aware of that promised as the Comforter in this material world. Then, the Christ Consciousness is the Holy Spirit, or that as the promise of His presence made aware of His activity in the earth. The Spirit is as the Christ in action with the Spirit of the Father."

Here Cayce correlates the Christ Consciousness with the Holy Spirit, explaining that the Spirit is the Christ in *action* with the Spirit of the Father. This is why Cayce's "Search for God" material contains daily disciplines and application of the truths taught. Only through action—applying a truth or principle in our daily thoughts, words, and actions—does the Spirit *flow* to and through us. As we give out, more comes. The Spirit's presence in us naturally imbues us with a comfort that cannot be found in this world. Through daily application of what we know is right, we are spiritualized. We become a temple of the Holy Spirit.

The Body Is the New Temple

When Moses left Egypt to go out into the desert to find who he really was and to find God, one of the first things God taught him was how to build a *portable* temple of poles and curtains that traveled with him and the people. This was the first step toward the greater understanding that the temple of God is within us.

Paul asked in I Corinthians, "Don't you know that you are a temple of God, and that the Spirit of God dwells in you?" and "Don't you know that your body is a temple of the Holy Spirit which is in you, which you have from God?" In II Corinthians he comes right out and says it plainly, "We are a temple of the living God; even as God said, 'I will dwell in them, and walk in them; and I will be their God, and they shall be my people.'"

The disciple John hints at this in his gospel as he recounts an event when Jesus was in the great temple in Jerusalem and was asked to show the people a sign. "Jesus answered them, 'Destroy this temple, and in three days I will raise it up.' The people at the temple said, 'Forty-six years was this temple in building, and will you raise it up in three days?' But he spoke of the temple of his body."

Jesus said, "The kingdom of God is within you." (Luke 17:21)

From Edgar Cayce's attunement to the universal consciousness, he, too, saw and taught that our bodies are more than physical vehicles for living in this world. Here are five brief excerpts:

"Know that your body is the temple of the living God; there you may seek communion. There you may seek counsel as to the choices to be made, the directions to be taken."

"He has promised, 'If you will but open the door of your conscious-ness, of your heart, I will enter and abide with you.' This is not a fancy; this is not hearsay. You may experience such. For it is the law, it is the way, it is *life* itself!"

"Seek and you shall find. Not without but from within. For in your own temple He has promised to meet you."

"All that you may learn of the Father God is already within self. For your body is indeed the temple of the living God, and as you meet Him there, you may gain in your own consciousness the satisfaction of walk-ing and talking with Him. When these consciousnesses are yours and you are one with Him, then indeed may you see that the kingdom of heaven dwells within."

"This is a promise to you, to each soul; yet each soul must of itself find that answer within self. For indeed the body is the temple of the living God. There He has promised to meet you; there He does. And as your body, your mind, your soul is attuned to that divine that answers within, so may you indeed be quickened to know His purpose; and you may fill that purpose for which you entered this experience."

When I first read these teachings many years ago, I would sit quietly and go within my temple. With my physical eyes closed, I would scan inside my head with my mind's eye, looking for God. I would begin conversations and then sit silently, listening for a response. In those early days it was like sitting in a dark, empty room by myself. There was nothing in there but me. If I began to perceive a response, I would not know if it was truly God speaking or some aspect of me. Now, forty-some years later, I cannot close my eyes without feeling the nearness of a vast inner universe of life, information, creativity, and God. In preparing to write this section, I spent some time recalling how I went from sitting by myself to awakening to the heavens within. It is true that if one seeks, one will find; it's a matter of seeking long enough. And it was a long journey, with some side trips that led nowhere. But, through it all, there was a thread that I can now see in hindsight. There were spontaneous moments of enlightenment, of direct contact with God, and of knowing the truth. Sustaining those proved more difficult than expected because outer life affected inner growth. If I stopped living the fruits of the spirit in the outer life, the inner life dried up. But the inner life is the ultimate, eternal life, and it is only lived by going within the temple of the body and awakening to it.

There are two safe ways to enter the temple within: deep sleep and deep meditation. A good biblical example of deep sleep producing a vision of the life within would be Jacob's dream of the ladder to and from heaven and his wrestling with the angel. (Genesis 28:12 and 32:30) You'll recall that upon waking from deep sleep, he said, "This is none other than the house of God, and this is the gate to heaven." (Revelation 1:10) The place of deep sleep and illuminating dreams is indeed the house of God and the gate to heaven. A good biblical example of deep meditation producing a vision of the life within would be John's description of how The Revelation began. John tells us: "I was in the spirit [in deep meditation, caught up in the spirit] on the Lord's Day and I heard and saw and was told to write."

The Way

In this next section, Cayce is asked to explain fully how the Christ Spirit is "the way." He takes five paragraphs to answer fully. Notice that

Cayce refers to us as individual Jesuses who can and should become as aware and in accord with our Father as He was. By doing so, we become the way—not only for ourselves but for those around us who enjoy the Holy Spirit flowing through us.

"Q: Explain and expand fully the thought that the Christ Spirit, not the man, should be the door, the truth, the way.

"A: That which has been given may be used to illustrate the difference that may be felt by a soul that has become aware of itself, as the Christ, or as Jesus the man became aware of the Spirit of the Father through those experiences of the man as he 'went about doing good,' and at those periods when there was received those acknowledgements of the Father that he *was* the one who could, *would*, through those activities, become the Savior of man. First, as 'in whom I am well pleased,' then as 'This is my son; hear ye him!'

"In the overcoming, then, He *is* the way, the manner in which individuals may become aware of their souls that are in accord with that as may be one with the spirit of truth; for corruption inherits not eternal life. The Spirit is the true life. Then, as individuals become aware of that ability *in Him* to be the way, so they become the door, as representatives, as agents, as those that present the way; and the door is thus opened; and not to the man but the spirit of self that bears witness with the spirit of truth through Him that overcame the world, thus putting the world under His feet.

"So we, as heirs of the kingdom, as brothers one with Him, may enjoy that privilege as He has given to those that hear His voice and put on the whole armor; that we may run the race that is set before us, looking to Him, the author, the giver of light; for in Him you live and move and *have* your being. Do you become rebels? Do you find fault one with another, that are as self heirs to that kingdom? Rather be in that humbleness of spirit, that His will 'be done in earth as it is in heaven.' Thus do we become the children of the Father, the door to the way, and joint heirs with Him in glory.

"Let your yeas be yea, your nays be nay. 'Let others do as they may, but for me I will serve a *living* God,' who has shown in man—*all* men, everywhere—that image of the Creator, in that the soul may grow in grace, in knowledge, in peace, in harmony, in understanding.

"Be you doers of the word; not hearers only. Thus you become the door that the *Way*, the Christ, the Savior, may enter in; for *He is* the way, the truth, and the light."

In this last reading, we learn how the life force within our bodies can be raised to help us become better temples and channels of the Spirit.

"Q: Please give advice that would help in those times when there is the beginning of Kundalini to rise or there is the circulation of Kundalini through the body. What should be the next step?

"A: Surround self with that consciousness of the Christ Spirit; this by the affirmation of 'Let self be surrounded with the Christ-Consciousness, and the *directions* be through those activities in the body-force itself.'

"Do not seek the lower influences, but seek the Christ-Consciousness."

CLOSING THOUGHTS

A ncient Egypt is with us today. All of the souls that experienced ancient Egypt have reincarnated over the recent centuries, and this soul group has awakened the world to those enchanting times. Today the Egyptian images fascinate us; they whisper a sweet, faint remembrance. And now, here again, we reincarnated Egyptians are scattered across the planet in new places with new faces. Some are wondering why ancient Egypt so captivates our minds and hearts. Others feel the influence of ancient Egypt upon us and know we were there.

My forty years of studying Edgar Cayce's readings on Egypt, my thirty-three tours of Egypt, as well as my inner revelations of my soul's time in Egypt have convinced me that Egypt was a very special time for incarnating souls—a time of enlightenment, creativity, beauty, nature, and, of course, godliness. It was an incarnation that marked us deeply and remains with us today. Our souls carry the vibrations and consciousness of that ancient time forward to our lives today—and for good reason. We knew we were immersing our spiritual selves into matter, slipping out of celestial spirit and purer energy into physicality and flesh, and we wanted to remember from whence we came and whither we go.

The tales, the teachings and images, and the icons of ancient Egypt were designed to softly remind to us of who we really are and where we ultimately belong. Now, even our astronomers and physicists tell us that we are made from stardust and are actually quantum fluctuations that only appear to be solid and mortal, the stuff of stone and earth. But we are the godlings of the infinite, eternal forces of life and consciousness—formless and forever.

Cayce's amazing readings taught: "As the entity moves from sphere to sphere, it seeks its way to the home, to the face of the Creator, the Father, the first cause." (136-8) Cayce identifies the first cause as this: "That the created would be the companion for the Creator." This is the reason we were created, and as a result, the created (our soul) is given opportunities to "show itself to be not only worthy of, but companionable to, the Creator." (5753-1) Since we are talking about the Creator of the entire Cosmos and everything in it, we are celestial star travelers, even though we feel so earthly and terrestrial in our daily lives.

Cayce said that our taking many forms in many different dimensions and spheres helps us to experience the whole of our being and of our Creator's consciousness. He said that "self is lost in that of attaining for itself the nearer and nearer approach that builds in manifested form, whether in the Pleiades, Arcturus, Gemini, or in Earth, in ... Vulcan or in Neptune." (136-83) Yet, despite our taking on many "forms" as we manifest ourselves, our true nature is "as light, a ray that does not end, lives on and on, until it becomes one in essence with the source of light." (136-83)

We are Ra and the children of Ra, light rays from the source of light. And with the subtlest shifts in vibration and consciousness we may move into that light and radiate out from it. "Not only God is god ...for the self is a portion of that Oneness."—Edgar Cayce (900-181)

APPENDIX

EDGAR CAYCE READING NUMBERS USED IN THIS BOOK

The readings of Edgar Cayce were filed according to a system: personal names, groups, or topics were replaced with numbers, and then each reading for that person, group, or topic was given a dash number beginning with 1 for their first reading and then continued sequentially as they received more readings. Therefore, Edgar Cayce was given the number 294, and each reading he received for himself was given a sequenced dash number, for example: 294-150, 294-151, and so on. Topics were also given reading numbers; for example the Atlantis Readings Series is 364, thus 364-13, 364-14, and so on. Groups were also given numbers; for example the Search for God Study Group was given 262, the Prayer Group 281, and so on. Numbers were also given to readings that were not associated with any specific person, topic, or group; such as the readings series 5748, which is often referred to in this book. 5748 and others were used as general files for miscellaneous content related to Egypt and other metaphysically related topics.

The following is a list of the key readings used in each chapter—but not all of them because the list would be too long. Remember, the content on Egypt is spread out over many hundreds of readings for individuals, with little tidbits here and there that must be gathered together, studied, and then compiled to capture the overall story. The entire Cayce archive is on CD-ROM and available from his organization. For contact information, go to EdgarCayce.org.

Chapters:

1–A Ray of Sunlight on Earth. Og: 364–6, 442–1, 993–1. Zu: 774–5. King
Raai: 1734–3. Ra–Ta: 294–147, –148, –149, –151, –152, –153, –183, –198;
282–7; 288–1; 1100–26; 2072–8, –10, 254–106, and more. Temple of
Sacrifice and Temple Beautiful: 281–25; 264–50; 294–149; 949–12;
1472–10, and more. Is–ris: 294–152; 341–9, –10; 538–9, –30; and 2329–3.
Mt. Ararat: 294–147. Scribe/Aarat: 341–9; 900–38, 900–275; and others.

2–A Great Atlantean Becomes a Greater Egyptian. Hept–supht: 378–
13, –14.

3–The Mission of the Second Creation. Pushing spirit into matter:
262–114, 900–105, 1448–2, 2462–2, and many more. Atlantean rejuvenation of their bodies: 823–1 and 5037–2. Keeper of seals: 281–25.
Sex queen: 2131–1.

4–The Ancient Earth: 364–13. Five Races: 364–13. Fifth Root Race: 5748–
6; the entire 5748 series on Egypt; and 470–35.

5–The Temples. Temple of Sacrifice and Temple Beautiful: 281–25, 281–
43; 264–50; 294–149, 2067–6, 5118–1, and more. Isris or Is–ris: 294–
152; 341–9, –10; 538–9, –30; and 2329–3. Isi–so and Iso–Isis: 294–151
and 2602–3. Apex–l: 315–4. Seven Spiritual Centers: 281–29, –30, –
54; 993–6, and 5746–1.

6–An Old Soul Returns. Oual, Uzld, and Iskxe or Is–kxe: 993–1, –5; and
294–153.

7–Hermes: A God among Humans. Hermes: 294–151; 1224–1; 5748–5,
–6; 364–4; 790–1; 966–1; 2462–2, 5749–5, and more.

8–A Pharaoh in 11,000 BC? Arart: 294–147, –148; 2420–1; 5748–5.
Araaraart: 195–14; 341–9, –45; 5748–5, –6. Arsrha: 195–14 294–153.
Rhaha: 228–2; 294–153; 341–9, –10. Ex–der–enemus: 2533–1, –4; Tar-
Ello: 2390–1, –7; Cosmic Rays: 262–39; 364–11; Bloodless surgery:
470–33; Chariots driven by gas: 275–38. Male and female in one
body: 288–6, 364–7, 364–5, 2121–2, and others.

9–Six–Hundred–Year–Old Scribe! Aidol and Isis–a–o: 1100–1, –26; 294–
153, 341–9.

10–A Woman God–Child. It–El–Sut: 808–18, 808–19. Ax–Tell: 470–33;
808–18; 3184–1; 487–17; and more.

11–The Ups and Downs of One Egyptian's Life. Ra–La–Ral: 282-7; 275-38; 282-2, –3. Isibio: 275-38; 294-153; 301-5. Del–lli: 282-3; 299-1.

12–The Regeneration of the High Priest. Regeneration of the Priest: 294-150, –151; 275-38; 1223-6; 2390-7; 2329-3; 630-2; and more. Oum–Teck–Pt: 949-12.

13–A Most Important Female Pharaoh. Hatshepsut: 355-1; 444-1. *Ancient Egyptian Legends*, by M. A. Murray, [1920], via sacred-texts.com.

14–Ancient Flight. Atlantean psychic flight: 364-10; Ezekiel airships: 1859-1; Atlantean flying boats: 3184-1; Gas filled pachyderm skins (blimps) and Atlantean electrical impelling ships: 364-6.

15–Three Caches of Prehistoric Records. Hall of Records: 2012-1; 5750-1; 2329-3; 519-1; 195-14; 1436-3; 649-2, and others.

16–Amazing Pyramids. 5748-6; 5750-1; 2390-7.

17–The Pyramid Prophecy. 5748-5, –6.

18–Mysterious Pyramid Texts and Magical Hymns. No readings.

19–The Seven Stages of Human Enlightenment: 281-25, –26.

20–Seven Gates to the Beautiful Hidden Place. No readings.

21–Egyptian Imagery: A Thousand Words in One Picture. 281-29, –30, –54; 262-20.

22–A Light Heart: Egyptian Key to Heaven. No readings.

23–Cayce and the Great Initiate. 5748-5; 5749-2, –4, –13; 2067-1, –7; 1158-5, –9; 364-11; 315-4; 2072-11; 262-29; and more.

Closing Thoughts. 136-8; 5753-1; 136-83; 900-181.

A.R.E. PRESS

EDGAR CAYCE'S A.R.E.

What Is A.R.E.?

The Association for Research and Enlightenment, Inc., (A.R.E.®) was founded in 1931 to research and make available information on psychic development, dreams, holistic health, meditation, and life after death. As an open–membership research organization, the A.R.E. continues to study and publish such information, to initiate research, and to promote conferences, distance learning, and regional events. Edgar Cayce, the most documented psychic of our time, was the moving force in the establishment of A.R.E.

Who Was Edgar Cayce?

Edgar Cayce (1877–1945) was born on a farm near Hopkinsville, Ky. He was an average individual in most respects. Yet, throughout his life, he manifested one of the most remarkable psychic talents of all time. As a young man, he found that he was able to enter into a self–induced trance state, which enabled him to place his mind in contact with an unlimited source of information. While asleep, he could answer questions or give accurate discourses on any topic. These discourses, more than 14,000 in number, were transcribed as he spoke and are called "readings."

Given the name and location of an individual anywhere in the world, he could correctly describe a person's condition and outline a regimen of treatment. The consistent accuracy of his diagnoses and the effectiveness of the treatments he prescribed made him a medical phenomenon, and he came to be called the "father of holistic medicine."

Eventually, the scope of Cayce's readings expanded to include such subjects as world religions, philosophy, psychology, parapsychology, dreams, history, the missing years of Jesus, ancient civilizations, soul growth, psychic development, prophecy, and reincarnation.

A.R.E. Membership

People from all walks of life have discovered meaningful and life–transforming insights through membership in A.R.E. To learn more about Edgar Cayce's A.R.E. and how membership in the A.R.E. can enhance your life, visit our Web site at EdgarCayce.org, or call us toll-free at 800-333-4499.

Edgar Cayce's A.R.E.
215 67th Street
Virginia Beach, VA 23451–2061

EDGARCAYCE.ORG